The Sargasso Bridge

(America Speaks, Africa Answers)

3rd Edition

By Kofi J. Roberts

Copyright © 2024 Kofi J. Roberts
All rights reserved.
No part of this book may be used or reproduced, distributed, or transmitted in any form or by any means, including photocopying, recording, or other electronic or mechanical methods, without the proper written permission of the publisher, except in the case of brief quotations apart, embodied in critical reviews and certain other non-commercial uses permitted by copyright law. Use of this publication is permitted solely for personal use and must include full attribution of the material's source.

Contents

Preface 9
Acknowledgments 12
Introduction 13
Chapter One How It All Began 16
Chapter Two Periods of Interruption 22
    Phase I 22
        Exploitation of Human and Material Resources 22
    Phase II 26
        The Colonial Era 26
    Phase III 30
        Self-Government 30
        African Follies and Shortcomings—Nigeria 33
        Who to Blame for Plan Failures—Congo DR (Belgium Congo) 34
Chapter Three America's Relations with Africa 42
        The Cold-War Era 42
    John F. Kennedy (1960–1963) 42
    L. B. Johnson (1963–1969) 45
    Richard M. Nixon (1969–1974) 46
    Gerald Ford (1974–1977) 48
    James Earl Carter (1977–1981) 48
    Ronald W. Reagan (1981–1988) 54
Chapter Four The New World Order 58

Post-Cold-War Imperatives—Where does Africa fit in? 58
George H. W. Bush (1989–1993) 58
    Africans must first clean house. 60
Chapter Five The Prophesies 67
    Of Condemnation 67
        Misinterpretations (Errors of Omission) 72
Chapter Six African Disunity 77
    A Major Obstacle to True Freedom 77
Chapter Seven Hope for Africa 89
    Is the cup half full or half empty? 89
Chapter Eight The First Overture 104
    In C Major 104
Chapter Nine Is Kinship Significant? 109
Chapter Ten Old Approaches to New Challenges 115
Chapter Eleven Second Overture 119
    In B Flat-Minor 119
Chapter Twelve "The Congo Syndrome" 128
Chapter Thirteen Trade Not Aid, Not AIDS 133
Chapter Fourteen Much Has Changed; Much Remains the Same 141
Chapter Fifteen The Debt Burden 152
    A Sincere Bailout or a Mere Means to Re-Colonize Africa? 152
Chapter Sixteen The Way Out 161
    Good Governance 161

Conflict 166

Corruption 174

Are Africans Ready? 181

Chapter Seventeen Advantage Asia 189

Chapter Eighteen Sankofa 200

What Africans have done before, Africans can do again 200

The Covenant 209

Chapter Nineteen Doing the Right Things 214

The Way Back to Glory 214

The Decline 222

Chapter Twenty Doing the Right Things the Right Way 236

Return to Respect and Favor 236

Chapter Twenty One Where Does the Elephant Sleep? 248

The Leviathan Trap 248

Chapter Twenty Two The Debt Forgiveness 254

Chapter Twenty Three Reparation 266

Chapter Twenty Four Beyond Reparation and Debt Cancellation 273

Chapter Twenty Five A Second Chance 283

The Redemption 285

Chapter Twenty Six Beyond Redemption 293

Chapter Twenty Seven The Need for Midcourse Correction .. 298

(Put on your rally cap.) 298

Chapter Twenty Eight Back to Africa 305

Reconnect with the Motherland. 305

Chapter Twenty Nine Beginning of the African Renaissance.322
Chapter Thirty Back Home at Last..330
Postscript..345
Movies to Entertain You 356
References..359

Dedication

I dedicate this book to all who have made offers and Sacrifices in the belief that a strengthened Africa is Man's contribution to God's grand design.

Preface

By the end of the second millennium, the East/West cold war was over. So too, it seemed, were Africa's chances of catching up with the rest of the world. The visions and sacrifices of legendary Africans that once offered a glimmer of hope suddenly appeared vain, futile, and hopeless.

Crusaders and champions like Dr. W.E.B. and Mrs. Shirley Du Bois; Marcus Garvey; Ghana's first president, Dr. Kwame Nkrumah; the American dentist, Dr. Robert E. Lee, who moved from the Carolinas to settle in Ghana; and the late U.S. congressman from Texas, Mickey Leland, who died chasing away hunger and famine on the continent are all individuals who made ultimate sacrifices. For a while, it seemed they had spent their lives in vain pursuit of unattainable dreams.

The turn of the third millennium ushered in new sets of realities and recognitions— globalization of economies, new and shifting military strategies, and revised political trends. A new light has begun to shine on the continent of Africa, and, with it, new prospects for economic salvation for America, Asia, and Europe have begun to emerge. In addition, new champions who carried, and continue to carry the banner of Africa across the world, have emerged. The list is long, it includes: former UN Secretary-General Kofi Annan; former U.S. President Jimmy Carter; Ambassador Andrew Young; Angelina Jolie and Brad Pitt; Oprah Winfrey; Stevie Wonder; Bono, Reverend Jesse Jackson and Mo Ibrahim— to mention but a few.

Along with many others, they have helped raise the needs and promises of Africa to the rest of the world. Truly Africa promises a lot, and not merely raw materials. In fact, Africa can become the next truly profitable market for American-made durable goods and American exportable services. Some in Western financial circles already refer to parts of Africa as frontier markets, where returns on investments are in double digits. What Africa needs to help America, in particular once again establish itself as a manufacturing and exporting powerhouse is a few more American helping hands.

This is the message that must be conveyed. The idea that Africa, beside raw materials, offers the rest of the world nothing but challenges is an inaccurate characterization. It is true Africa is beset with a wide range of problems, but it is important to also recognize that most of Africa's problems were caused largely, by the depraved nature of relations imposed from outside the continent—occupations, slavery, the slave trade, colonialism, and the prevailing cryptic neocolonialism.

******

For decades, I often wondered what Dr. Martin Luther King would be doing in his later years to help manifest the central force in the vision he expressed in his famous, " I have a dream," speech. What role must Africa play in the manifestations of the vision? Through much of the first half of the 1990s, I served as chairman of the Africa Trade Centre at the De Kalb Chamber of Commerce. Our goal was to help promote trade between the United Stated and Africa and to help raise awareness to Africa's prospects as a consumer market of American-made goods and services, as a potentially important trading partner.

During the latter half of that decade, I often engaged in radio and television discussions on Africa. In the fall of 1998, I was also a speaker at the Summit on Africa held in Atlanta, Georgia, to drum up popular support for the Africa Growth and Opportunity

Act (AGOA) that was still working its way through the U.S. congress. In the summer of 1999, I testified before the U.S. World Trade Commission that was preparing for the World Trade Organization (WTO) summit in Seattle, Washington, later that year.

Through these experiences, I came to the realization that there is a need for the expression of Africa's viewpoint on America–Africa relations. It is a need compelled by the fact that all too often what is presented as expert opinion on Africa is really nothing more than scholarly expressions of projections and personal wishes. This observation, more than any, is what prompted me to start writing. I am not a writer by any measure, but to the extent that Ray Charles and Ludwig Van Beethoven refused to allow perceptual limitations to deter the expression of the music that played in their minds, I am encouraged to help fulfill this need despite the poor level of my writing skills.

One clear advantage I have is the fact that I have read extensively on the subject, and I have been interested in world affairs since my preteens. I am therefore able to write mostly out of memory, without the need for much research, and, by 2003, when I began the second draft, Google was fully established. It provided a most useful source for fact checks. By necessity this is a multi discipline presentation – there is a bit of history, geography, some economics and politics. I make several references to the Bible. Unless otherwise stated, all bible quotes are from the King James version. Join the debate or just enjoy it.

Acknowledgments

I would like to express my sincere thanks to my two daughters, Ama and Dede, and to my son Lance, who provided much-needed technical help for this work.

I would like to thank Jennifer Adjiko Abbey of Accra, Ghana—who thoroughly edited the rough draft of the manuscript—and Stephen Botwe and Seth Martey, both of Prampram, Ghana, who read parts of the manuscript and provided helpful suggestions. I would also like to thank all my well-wishers, especially Madinah Walcott Farakhan and Gayle King, Baji Daniel, Brenda Tillman; all of Atlanta, Georgia, for their encouragement and advice. In addition, I would like to thank my wife, Florence, who gave me inspiration and suggested helpful material sources.

And, finally, to the many Africans and Americans on both sides of the Sargasso Sea, friends and acquaintances who encouraged this work, thanks to you all. Google was simply wonderful for checking facts.

Introduction

"African leaders are much too corrupt." "Africa is too volatile." "Africa is a hopeless case." These are just some of the alarming descriptions of Africa by the Western press we have all grown accustomed to. They have become, largely by default on the part of those about whom they are said and written, factual expressions that need not be challenged. But are they really?

There is some progress in reversing this mind-set, but much hue and cry still remain over prevailing conditions in Africa: poor living conditions, low consumption capacity, poorly managed economies, corruption, and similar references, some of which I must admit are very true, at least on the surface. The most compelling facts are that an estimated 60 percent of Africans live in abject poverty, barely able to subsist on their income. Just imagine a continent with a population of some 1.5 billion people, and more than half, over 750 million, live in poverty. The size of Africa's poor is about the combined populations of all of North America—the United States, Mexico, Canada—and Central America. Imagine further that in this vast population no one is able to meet basic daily consumer needs because they make about $2 a day.

To most Westerners, Africa is nothing but a quagmire of inefficiency, calamities, and human misery. The blame is cast in all directions, from all directions. Africans point to the slave trade, European colonial exploitation, American and European neocolonial manipulations and further exploitation, and the dismal regard of the developed nations of the North. Polite Northerners attribute African difficulties to the harsh environment. Beyond the mundane and polite list of causes, some in the North have, over the past several centuries, boldly put forth theories suggesting that African follies and shortcomings are due to inherent African qualities. Some suggest genetics, and others suggest poor social structures, values, and the lack of reflective history. Then, there are some Northerners who believe Africa's position at the short end of the stick is simply the manifestation of European destiny.

Who is to blame? What is to blame? Everyone agrees on one thing: Africa can and must rise to more appreciable levels in global society and economics. Individuals as well as institutions the world over recognize the potentials of Africa, not only to itself but to the world at large. Indeed, the U.S. government - the administration as well as Congress, recognize the vast potential Africa holds as the next true economic frontier; it is an unavoidable and promising market for American-made consumer goods and services, while it continues to supply most of the raw materials for strategic and consumer manufactured goods.

The more immediate challenge facing most Westerners willing to help is Africa's own projection of itself. Such non-Africans would like to see pragmatic plans drawn by Africans; broad-based, well-managed, aimed at establishing greater capacities that support increases in production. They would like to see African plans to create and to negotiate markets and plans to spend the proceeds prudently for the benefit of all Africans, inclusively. There is really no need to argue the potentials of Africa to itself and to the rest of the world. Everyone who must know is well aware of how much Africa needs and how much it can give in return.

The only arguments still raging at governmental levels in America are arguments on the most applicable and prudent approaches, strategies, and tactics that will yield the most desirable and sustainable results, who will benefit, and by how much. The discussions actually started in the 1950s. They continue, not because "Africa is too difficult to deal with" and certainly not for the total lack of an action plan; to the contrary. Many plans have been proposed over the past half century, indeed over the past century. Invariably, such plans have been designed more for the benefit of their sponsors than for the benefit of Africa and Africans. Nearly to the same degree, Africans have remained a part of their problem, unable to collectively work out a grand design; incapable of looking beyond petty differences and unwilling to cooperate and collaborate to lift themselves up onto the world stage. So the debates and discussions continue, as they must.

Chapter One

How It All Began

I point to some of the facts in the previous paragraph, not to minimize the impact of European intrusions into Africa and the resulting diversions to the course of Africa's development.

Agricultural systems, trade routes, commercial relations, ethics and governance, and, indeed, the general dynamics of ancient African societies were significantly altered or totally destroyed, and, with these problems, the setback or permanent diversion of Africa's logical development trends occurred. Of course, these problems did not all happen in tandem or over a short period of time.

For a cursory view of the history, let us begin with the Greeks, from the time of Alexander of Macedonia and the Ptolemy dynasty he left behind to govern Egypt. They came to Africa not as mere marauders to raid, pillage and return to Europe. They came, settled, and took control and possession of whole societies for material and spiritual gains. Following the Greeks and later the Romans, Turkish and Arab influences also came in through Egypt, up the lower Nile (what is now referred to as "lower" was then "upper"), toward the heart of Africa through the kingdoms of Kush, Nubia, and Abyssinia (then comprising parts of what is now southern Egypt, Sudan, Somalia, Djibouti, Ethiopia, Eritrea, and parts of northern Kenya) from where their influences spread on southward and westward to other parts of the continent.

Before such foreign (European and later Asian) intrusion, the indigenous people of Egypt had developed highly sophisticated systems of building, agriculture, medicine, and other disciplines vital to society. They built the pyramids and other structures and institutions that still perplex modern minds. Other peoples they influenced beyond their borders developed and maintained similarly sophisticated systems for providing the needs of their societies, such as elaborate irrigation schemes and inland navigation networks, trade routes, medicine, and systems of governance. Their profound knowledge of the physical and natural sciences was applied to the many challenges of daily life and for the welfare and progress of societies at large. African societies enjoyed freedom of ownership and expression within a broad communal framework.

When the Turkish and Arab warlords invaded around the seventh century, they occupied much of what was then called "Lower Egypt" (the delta region that surrounds Cairo and Alexandria and is now referred to as "northern Egypt") Perhaps encouraged by the productive character of the people and quality of their surrounding lands, the occupiers steadily replaced the old and freer forms of productive expressions and social order with feudal structures and norms. Before long, Egyptians who once owned land found themselves relegated to menial positions as tenant farmers, farm laborers, commissioned artisans, and employed craftsmen. Their earnings were taxed heavily, and much of it sent abroad for the benefit of the occupiers.

Unlike Egypt, which came under Islamic influence in the very early years of its Turkish and Arab occupation around the seventh century, Nubia—right above it—remained Christian for another seven hundred years, until about the fourteenth century. Through this period, Nubia indeed rivaled Egypt in many respects—in achievements as well as in splendor. The Greek narrator Homer described Nubia as "the favorite of the Gods." From these two splendid, high-achieving kingdoms, disciplines and guilds that included philosophy, architecture, metalwork, agriculture, and others necessary to sustain and advance society spread to other parts of Africa.

Like Egypt and Nubia, Ethiopia—at the source of the (Blue) Nile River (the only major river in the world that flows due north)—enjoyed considerable favor with God at about the same period. Founded by the Sabean dynasty that settled the Abyssinian Mountains in the first century AD, its ruling classes claim lineage from up high: one from the son of King Solomon and the Queen of Sheba (King Malenek) and the other from Moses. Over the centuries, these two lines had alternately ruled the kingdom. Ethiopia is home to the very first Christian sects, The Ethiopian Orthodox Church. To this day it claims to hold custody of the Ark of the Covenant. Along the Nile and the Red Sea, Ethiopia maintained trade and other vital relationships with Nubia and Egypt until the two—weighted down by the forces of layers of occupation and subjugation—could no longer engage in free trade, subjecting all three to diversions in their logical progression of development. Egypt, Nubia, and Ethiopia thus remained basically feudal well into the twentieth century and were never able to transcend rationally into any form or appreciable level of capitalism.

Indeed, so great are the contributions of the northeast quadrant of the continent to Africa's glorious past. However, much of Africa's history, which became connected and relevant to trade with Northern Africa and later with Europe and America, was centered in the west, beginning with the region around the southwestern fringes of the Sahara Desert, The area later referred to as "the Western Sudan." The word "Sudan" derives from the Arabic expression *bilad-as-sudan*. In English, it means lands of the Blackman, and, to the Arabs of North Africa, it refers to the whole of Africa south of the Sahara. Historically, the Western Sudan stretched from present day Senegal and parts of Mauritania eastward into much of present day Mali and southward into the northern fringes of Guinea, Cote d'Ivoire and into Burkina Faso and Niger. Right in the middle of this regions are the legendary cities of Jenne, Gao, and Timbuktu. Look at the center of the map of present-day West Africa. Within this region and the lands below, all the way to the coast between the ninth and fifteenth centuries three great successive empires flourished. There was Ghana, followed by Mali and then Songhai. Common and central to these three empires was the Niger River, which provided water for transport and for various forms of production, especially agriculture. The three empires—Mali in particular and later Songhai—formed and managed wealth and public welfare through massive systems of education, agriculture, mining, trade, taxation, and well- structured systems of governance.

Salt was gold, and both salt and gold were mined and traded. In domestic trade, farm and forest products were also important cash-producing commodities. Livestock, hide, apparel, and similar commodities were bought and sold at weekly markets, along the waterways, and the vast network of land routes that crisscrossed the region. Surpluses were carried across the Sahara to Egypt and Nubia in the east and north to the Maghreb city states of Casablanca, Marrakech, Fez, Tangier, Algiers, and Tunis. Such was the wealth generated in the Western Sudan in that period that one of the kings of the Mali Empire, Kankan Mansa Musa while traveling through Cairo on pilgrimage to Mecca, gave away so much gold as gifts he created instant inflation, upsetting market prices of commodities in and around the city for a considerable length of time. Benevolence or sheer vain extravagance, it remains a subject for debate, but it also demonstrates the level of wealth of the region at the time, which indeed stimulated and encouraged stronger relations with merchants, scholars, and clerics from Egypt who visited Mali so freely and frequently it enabled Malian cities like Timbuktu, Jenne, and Gao to became well-known centers of higher learning of scriptures, literature, alchemy, astronomy, and Hermetic science.

These medieval African kingdoms—those along the Nile in the northeast and those along the Niger, especially in the Western Sudan—along with many others, large and small, across the continent—Zimbabwe, Zulu, Baluba, Sokoto, Kanem-Bornu, Mossi, Dahomy, Fon, Oyo, Abeokuta, Ashanti, Benin, Fulani—all speak to African achievements of high standards of agriculture, trade, mining, and efficient, effective use of the military in governance. They managed vast economic systems. Written accounts of Europeans who reached many of these African kingdoms in the early 1600s attest to this conclusion. In many such accounts, European observers compared what they saw to similar features in Europe.

The following is a quote from, The Growth of African Civilization: A History of West Africa 1000-1800 by Basil Davidson.

An example was of the city of Benin in present-day Nigeria. The town, to this Dutch visitor, seemed to be very great. A quote from page 141-142 of the above text reads like this,

"When you go into it, you enter a great broad street, not paved, and seems to be seven or eight times broader than the Warmees Street in Amsterdam. The street is straight, and does not bend at any point. It is thought to be four miles long. The king's palace is a collection of buildings which occupy as much space as the town of Harlem and which is enclosed with walls. There are numerous apartments for the prince's ministers and fine galleries, most of which are as big as those on The Exchange in Amsterdam. They are supported by wooden pillars encased with copper, where their victories are depicted and which are carefully kept very clean ...."

African history of the fifteenth, sixteenth and seventeenth centuries is replete with similar comments by Arab and European newcomers to the continent. This, unfortunately, was where the comparisons often ended.

Chapter Two

Periods of Interruption

Phase I

Exploitation of Human and Material Resources

In more practical terms, Europe was far more advanced. Europeans had by this time developed institutions for mobilizing and managing capital. Even more importantly, Europeans had developed technologies with commercial, military, and maritime applications. With such advantages, Europeans gained control of the world's waterways and set the stage for an expanded mercantile era, which they charted, dominated, and monopolized to their advantage. Any competition was among them. It can very well be said that global trade began when Portuguese ships first rounded the southern tip of Africa and began to ply the Arab-established routes in the Indian Ocean and parts of southern Asia. Meanwhile, African canoes could only go up and down African rivers, lakes, and streams. By the turn of the seventeenth century, following the papal demarcation that gave the western half of the world to Spain and the eastern half to Portugal, the Spaniards and Portuguese gained a certain moral, perhaps, divine seal and impetus with near-absolute control over world trade without the need for further permission or to apologize to anyonet.

They bought cotton cloths from India to exchange for slaves in Africa. They shipped slaves to South and Central America, to mine gold and silver. Some of the bouillons were taken back to the

Orient to buy spices for sale in Europe for vast profits. The Spaniards and the Portuguese were soon joined by other Europeans, particularly the Dutch and the Danes. In formulating global trade strategies, these European nations that controlled it treated Africa more as a dumping ground than as a true market. European production surpluses, unsold odds and ends, and technologically obsolete tools and devices were what were shipped to Africa for sale. European exports to Africa were certainly not determined by African consumer needs but by European production and consumption capacity. On their return, they sought commodities vital to their material interests.

By the middle of the sixteenth century, as the fervor of capitalism in Europe created even greater demands for gold in all forms, Portuguese and Spanish explorers searched for the precious metal everywhere on earth. They found much of it in African, especially on the Gold Coast (now called Ghana), in the Congo, and in Angola too. In the Americas, especially south and central, they also found silver. Along with silver and gold, the Iberian Europeans also recognized the cash potential of certain crops, especially sugar. What seemed missing was reliable labor with which to realize such potentials. The indigenous Indian populations could not withstand the ravages of diseases such as smallpox and syphilis brought to the Americas by the Europeans. Whole Indian communities had been virtually wiped out by such infections. Secondly, the Europeans were reluctant to tap into their own populations, which had been rendered scanty by similar scourges, for what promised to be harsh, arduous, and rigorous working conditions ahead. Most important of all, they had by that point developed complimentary impressions of African work habits, organization, and capabilities, of the skills and disciplines that built and maintained vast and numerous kingdoms on the African continent. They also noticed that Africans lacked both the will and the means to adequately defend themselves. This, backed by the tacit dispensations of Christendom, gave Europeans the thumbs-up to forage into Africa at will. They did and descended on Africa for gold and for those who mined the gold for them. For the better part of three centuries, the transatlantic slave trade forcibly removed Africans from Africa for the exploitation of their labor in the Americas: south, central, and north. Europeans obtained Africans for slaves, generally by three main methods:

1. Pillaging by European raiders, often aided by Arab middlemen and sometimes with African mercenaries.
2. By trickery and treachery, whereby unsuspecting Africans were ambushed or lured into traps for capture by European merchants. (Watch the movie *Amistad.*)
3. By enticing or coercing one African community to set upon a weaker neighbor for the spoils of slaves. This involved the coercive imposition of quotas by Europeans on stronger African communities.

No one really knows the figures. Some estimates suggest ten million; however, most believe it might be as high as one hundred million. Even if we must accept figures close to the lowest, we can all well imagine and appreciate the extent to which such a process disrupted Africa's own developments in the many and various aspects that depended on its manpower, brainpower, and sheer numbers.

In addition, there were the ripple effects, which were equally disrupting if not more so. Whole farming communities, trade, and learning centers were abandoned by young men and women for the vain material rewards of the capture and sale of slaves or, as was more often the case, to escape the frightening prospect of being captured for sale. As such, even the lucrative trade routes that led east and north to Nubia, Egypt, and to the Maghreb were abandoned for newer, more sinister but lucrative ones to the coastal south of West Africa where European merchant ships came in search of African gold and slaves.

World censuses taken each century during the epoch of the slave trade showed every continent gaining in population except Africa, *(The Growth of African Civilization: A History of West Africa 1000-1800* by Basil Davidson). There is indeed no basis here for an argument; the slave trade had devastating impact on Africa's development trends and potentials—as it would anywhere else—such that, by the time the transatlantic slave trade officially ended in the nineteenth century, even vestiges of past African glories were all but wiped out.

In the American south, slavery was institutionalized and exploited to develop fortunes from agrarian enterprises. In northern cities, profits from the direct sale of slaves financed industrial and commercial ventures. To this extent, it can well be said that even though slavery and the slave trade were initiated by Europeans, America was the trade's foremost beneficiary. It is widely surmised that proceeds from the sale of slaves and from slave productions contributed in large measure to the foundations upon which capitalism was established in America. America's gain was, no doubt, at the expense of Africa's capacity to develop itself.

Phase II

The Colonial Era

While African slaves provided the labor with which the foundation of capitalism was established for Europe and America, the whole of the African motherland and its material endowments also offered the prospect to build upon the foundation. By the mid-nineteenth century, Western Europe was industrialized. A middle class had emerged, driving up both expectations and consumption. Such levels of demand created the need for more raw materials for European factories. Africa was once again recognized for every imaginable supply. When negotiators representing the various European nations met in the German city of Berlin in the summers of 1884 and of 1885, the only topic on the agenda was the apportionment of the continent of Africa among themselves according to their production and market needs (online About.com Guide to Geography since 1997: Matt Rosenberg). This "international share-out", as it was called gave Europeans a systematic approach and the necessary impetus to bring Africa under formal colonial rule.

By the turn of the twentieth century, Africa's precious minerals, forests, and other products were being carted off in earnest to supply European factories. Here again, Africans received relatively little and often times absolutely nothing for parting with their natural endowments. In many cases, the very labor for such exploitation was exacted for pittance if any compensation was given at all. In the Congo, as in many other areas of Africa, forced labor was the method of labor acquisition and management. No wonder European advocacy and efforts for the abolition of the

African slave trade were so vehement and relentless and seemed to have coincided with diligent European planning for colonization and exploitations of Africans.

For the second wave of the European industrial revolution they needed the African in Africa more than elsewhere. Once colonialism formally got under way, its forces remained focused on its goals and purpose. Maximum gain from least expense was the unyielding style of management. "Africa on the cheap" became the guiding principle for windfall profits. For example, hospitals were built mainly to reduce the loss of man-hours of African labor pools serving European needs. Roads and rail lines were laid to facilitate the cartage and export of African raw materials. Even the distribution of utilities was designed to make the lives of European expatriates in Africa bearable and thus retained. If such provisions coincided with indigenous African needs, so be it—'all well and good' (*How Europe Underdeveloped Africa*: By Walter Rodney).

As expectations continued to rise in the face of income disparities in Europe, European manufacturers felt an increasing need to mass produce. First, this was done as the only means to meet rising demands, and, secondly as a way to lower prices such that even those on the lowest end of the income scale could afford much of their cravings: in other words, a way to tap into consumer market at the lower end of the socio-economic pyramid. Such response necessitated wider markets that could absorb surpluses of mass production. Again Africa was the answer. Europe, in fact, had it all as far as its relations with Africa were concerned. Africa supplied every imaginable raw material needed and provided every needed opportunity as a market. Europe had what it took to remain a giant industrial power for much longer if only it had considered and planned for the true welfare of Africa and Africans at least nearly as much as it did for itself and its peoples.

Yes, European colonial powers could well have planned and implemented programs to bolster the consumption capacity of African societies – for instance they could have established protocols whereby all primary products were processed into intermediary products to feed European factories. They could just as well have paid fairer wages and compensations to African laborers. Such measures could have, in the short run, offered European enterprises wider and more prolonged market for European surplus goods. To express it another way, if Europeans had helped Africans to acquire greater capacity to consume European production, Europe would have gained from Africa far more than it actually did and certainly more than what it put into the development of Africa. European producers and merchants would have been the ultimate beneficiaries and European colonial powers could have remained strong much longer. Instead they chose to plough-back such benefits for their own economies. It can well be argued that in the end Europeans did themselves in by thinking they could forever get away with managing their exploits of Africa "on the cheap" and only for their benefit.

It is true, a number of the colonial regimes commissioned plans for development of some parts of Africa. As colonial governor, Gordon Guggisberg commissioned development projects (1920–1928) for the development of the Gold Coast (now Ghana). Governor Guggisberg was remarkably unique in his ideas and his approach. He fervently believed that the African was quite capable of cultivating a standard of living similar to that of the European if only the African was given equal opportunity to develop. Only about half of his plans for the development of the Gold Coast were implemented. They continue to serve Ghana. The dream of Cecil Rhodes to build a trans-African highway from Cape to Cairo is legendary. Any portion of these plans that were successfully implemented offered positive impacts on African society as well as benefits for Europe. Most of the plans and dreams, however, remained just what they were; they never got off the drawing board. The few that were implemented, such as construction and extension of road, rail, and communication lines into outlying and distant areas—as in Governor Guggisberg's plans—were a tiny fraction of what was needed to even constitute a critical mass.

The overriding limitation was simply that the vision for a grand design to develop Africa was conceived rather late and was often considered a lower priority to other demands. For example, the cost of two world wars and the cost of rebuilding Europe were stalwart and stifling. They diverted both funds and efforts. Europe itself was at the mercy of a benefactor—the United States. With the cost of maintaining the colonies mounting, overall European returns on investments in Africa became negligible if not an outright liability.

Phase III

Self-Government

To say that Africans were partners in the conspiracies for their own subjugation and exploitations, is neither reckless nor an overstatement. By the end of World War II, Africa had suffered a fifty-year colonial relation with Europe through which much of its natural and human resources had been exploited with very little in return for Africa. As the hand of colonialism weakened, from the World War II efforts and the challenges of the immediate aftermath, African agitations for self-government became fervent and wide spread.

Sudan was the first of the African nations to gain independence in 1956 followed a year later by the Gold Coast, which immediately changed its name to Ghana. A domino effect ensued, and by the middle of the 1960s, most of the nations in Africa were free of formal European domination. The few remaining were those under Portuguese, Spanish, and Dutch rule as well as the British settler states of East Africa and southern Africa, where Europeans had set themselves up not as intruders in and out with what they needed back in Europe but as settlers, with planted roots.

In such countries, the European settlers controlled politics, the economy, the laws and norms of society. To one degree or other, they excluded indigenous Africans from rights and privileges. Plans for development were carefully directed to the benefit of the European minority. Indigenous Africans were considered mere factors for implementation and as servants for European consumption convenience. These settler states included Kenya, The Rhodesian states (Zambia and its southern neighbor,

Zimbabwe). South Africa, South West Africa (Namibia), Mozambique, Algeria, Equatorial Guinea, Angola, Guinea Bissau, and Cape Verde were the other settler states.

In the non-settler states, self-government had quickly become a problem for a wide range of reasons which included years of colonial exploitations and the rather precipitous and inconsiderate manner of European withdrawal, when they had to. Such was the case in Guinea, where the French left behind vastly depleted treasuries and poorly groomed cadre of African politicians and bureaucrats who were significantly unprepared for the vigorous demands of modern management and governance. The most prevalent challenges for the new order of African governments were the assumption of cost of bureaucracy and of physical infrastructure. Physical structures had been designed to facilitate European trade expeditions. This was most evident where such assets did not coincide with indigenous African priorities.

How Rational are these attributions?

Regardless of the extent and impact of the slave trade and of colonial exploitation, Africa has largely been free for some forty years at the turn of the twenty-first century.

Coincidentally, so too has civil and voting rights in America. Forty years is long enough to show at least some serious cohesion and commitments to strategies that could reverse the effects of bygone distorting periods in African history. In the early years of postcolonial Ghana, its president Kwame Nkrumah commissioned plans that aimed at moving Ghanaian society toward true economic independence. Viewed correctly, independence is after all not a guarantee; it is merely an offer of second chance: a chance to regain control over God-given rights, privileges, security and destiny. It is a chance to pick up from where Africa's path to its destiny was interrupted and diverted and a chance to rebuild Africa into an integrated, self- reliant mixed society capable of holding its own and contributing equitably to world progress, in spite of all its peoples have been through.

Nkrumah's insights and vision were shared by other African leaders, most notably Julius Nyerere of Tanzania, Sekou Toure of Guinea, Modibo Kaita of Mali, and Jomo Kenyatta of Kenya, as also did two of Nigeria's regional prime ministers—Obafemi Awolowo of the West and Namdi Azikiwe of the East. Differences among them were merely of approach, style, and perhaps degree of commitment.

They all realized the dire need to establish a strong foundation upon which stable productive economies may thrive, the need for broad-based education, for well-managed agricultural enterprises, and for markets, both domestic and foreign. By the time Nkrumah was overthrown in 1966, in a military coup instigated and backed by the American Central Intelligence Agency (CIA), only a fraction of his plans had been realized. However, the impact of that tiny fraction has evidently been far reaching, both in scope and in time. It is no mere chance that many nationals of Ghana, Tanzania, and Nigeria occupy notable and responsible positions around the world. It is not by chance that Ghana, Kenya, and Tanzania are high on the list of preferred African destinations for leisure as well as for serious business prospecting.

Progress, sustainable progress, and success demand well-intended, well thought-out planning, and, if well implemented, the results will speak well and loudly for themselves. The rest of African nations showed little if any inclination for similar broad-based development plans. The few that showed interest did not go beyond the drawing board. Africa's core nations, have the potential to radiate much good well beyond their borders. The four I have in mind include: Egypt, Nigeria, Congo DR, and the Republic of

South Africa. For the sake of simplicity, I will dwell on Nigeria and perhaps the Congo DR to make my point.

African Follies and Shortcomings—Nigeria

At the dawn of Nigeria's independence, its leaders, in collaboration with the then British colonial administration, commissioned a seven-year development plan. The plan was unveiled in 1959, which was just months after Ghana had announced its seven-year development plan. By all accounts, the Nigerian plan was impressive. Nigeria's promises were so inspiring that in June 1960, just a few months after its independence was formally proclaimed, the John F. Kennedy administration—itself quite new in office—sent a five-man special economic mission led by MIT professor Arnold Rifkin, to Lagos to review Nigeria's development plans.

The Rifkin mission returned to Washington with raving commentaries on the substance and dynamics of the Nigerian plan, pointing to factors that were crucial to the development of a broad-based, free-market economy that could thrive under Western-style democracy. Even the regional plans that I referred to a bit earlier promised a lot for the ordinary Nigerian. Just for example, the particular plan for the development of Western Nigeria showed remarkable potential to transform much of the region into an enormous breadbasket, not just for Nigerian markets, but for much of West Africa.

Dynamic and promising though they were, the plans were never implemented, because they were undermined by a number of factors—some from outside, but most from within.

These factors included factional differences and petty political squabbles. Then came the civil war followed by the oil boom. Successively, they undermined both the need and the means for embarking on implementation of the development plans. Even worse, the war and the newly found wealth in oil distorted both the vision and the will for any revision of the old plans or the introduction of new ones that could have established the foundations for a sound and strong industrial-based society.

Who to Blame for failures—Congo DR (Belgium Congo)

The old argument that African sufferings are all due to external interventions and manipulation might rage on for a while longer. Before we take sides, let us look at one or two cases in postcolonial Africa. Let us look at the Congo this time. There is no argument against the fact that the Congo DR—if and when developed—will be pivotal in a swirl of prosperity around the midsection of Africa and might even stretch outward beyond the Sudan and the Central African Republic to the north, eastward into the countries of the lakes region, and downward into Southern Africa.

When the Congo gained independence in 1960, its prime minister, Patrice Lumumba, clearly recognized the enormous chasm between his country's level of development and the immense potential represented by immeasurably large deposits of both precious and strategic minerals, a near-infinite supply of forest products, and long stretches of navigable waterways that could be harnessed in various ways for power, irrigation, and transportation. It is a quality of natural resources well matched by the quality of human resources.

The ways and means to realize the recognized potential was the challenge. The Belgians had taken away a lot, and the people of the Congo had been left with nothing to show for parting with their God-endowed assets. Out of a national population of thirty-five million in 1960, there were only three college graduates.

Prime Minister Lumumba accepted the challenge and quickly commissioned a comprehensive plan for national development. Following the examples of Tanzania and Ghana, the Congolese plan was guided by socialist principles in the sense that it was to be implemented and managed centrally and was to serve as a means to establish a foundation upon which a free market economy could thrive later. It was intended to be a process that would necessarily improve the productive and consumptive capacities of individual Congolese and that of the nation as a whole. However, just as what happened in the example of Ghana, interest in the very idea of the plan was killed when Prime Minister Lumumba was assassinated after only a year in office.

Those who blame such abandonment and neglect of African aspirations on outside interventions often pointed to the following:

1. A postcolonial destabilizing agenda by the Western powers led by the United States and that included the United Kingdom, France, Belgium, and Portugal along with South Africa and the State of Israel as regular proxies. This destabilizing agenda, purportedly, is mainly driven by concerns over East/West cold war imperatives (the tension between capitalism and socialism).
2. A collective resolve of the Western powers and their proxies to stifle the efforts, and where possible, eliminate progressive governments that sought to strengthen the minds of their peoples and to create difficulties for American and other Western concerns that sought to negotiate advantageous terms for African resources.
3. That besides the outright change of regimes, methods to control Africa's development efforts had to include
    a) Undermining the country's currency and the general economy

b) Trade barriers that included tariffs, escalating tariffs, or outright sanctions
c) Unsympathetic aid packages made up largely of tie-loans: earmarked for specific projects that were neither productive nor relevant to African priorities. Often, such loan packages were not even sensitive to basic African needs, yet African governments were obligated to pay back the unsolicited and useless loans with meager earnings of the state. Meager earnings much needed for expenditures on health, education, housing, capacity building, and other welfare and dire development demands.

These were widely seen by the African intelligentsia as planned and orchestrated to keep Africa in a neocolonial box. The African intelligentsia holds on to its age-old suspicions that Western intensions for and expectations of Africa and Africans remain unfavorable to Africans and that, to the Western powers, Africa's independence is merely a cyclical downturn in a divine hegemonic relationship in which the Europeans and Americans are free to dominate and exploit all that is African. In other words, as Africans on the streets saw it, Europe and America still believe that "Africans may thrive only at the mercy of Europe and America and must act mainly to satisfy European and American aspirations and needs or at whim by well-disguised and well-finessed ways and means."

To many Africans, such thinking and attitudes provided the impetus for the often clandestine African positions when dealing with Western nations (The Global North). Many incidents occurred in my very early years of high school, and up to this day, I find it both curious and amusing that even back then, with very little background knowledge and as young as my friends and I were, we had these incidents so well sorted and characterized.

Whenever there was a coup or attempted coup in an English-speaking African country or in the Belgian-Congo, we checked it against the American CIA. If the coup happened in a former French colony, we blamed it on Jacque Focart. Jacque Focart was, for decades, director of the African section of the French foreign ministry; he was a man who had been compared, by many Africans, to the founder and director of the Federal Bureau of Investigation (FBI), J. Edgar Hoover, in terms of management style, dedication, and longevity of service. With nearly 60 percent of France's annual domestic budget dependent on its extractive trade and commercial relations with Africa, it is quite easy to understand why a man of such character description was in charge of African affairs for France and why he might indeed have not hesitated to resort to any means he deemed necessary in his dealings with France's former African colonies.

I described my personal awareness as curious and amusing because I cannot quite remember how we got such information in those days. I guess it was from just listening to the news on the radio and or reading the papers and then exchanging views on the streets. I also remember that period for the steady stream of world leaders that came to Accra especially the late 1950s to the mid 1960s: Richard Nixon of the United States; Queen Elizabeth II of England; Golda Maier of Israel; Anastas Mikoyan, who was then deputy prime minister of the Soviet Union; Ernesto Che Guevara of Cuba; Lee Kwan Yew of Singapore (then part of Malaysia Federation); Malcolm X of the United States; and Dr. Subandro, foreign minister of Indonesia—just to list a few. Each time such nobilities came to town, the streets would be abuzz with news and rumors about the goings-on in the world, especially about the part of the world from where such honorable person had come. Much of what we heard, including a few that we dismissed as mere rumor, later turned out to be true. Some have only recently been declassified by the American intelligence services. An example is the plot to overthrow the regime of Ghana's first president, Dr. Kwame Nkrumah(National Security File, Country File, Ghana, Vol. II, Johnson Library). Others have been written about or presented in documentaries and featured films—*Lumumba*, for example.

However, in 1960s Accra, blockbusting news did not circulate only when visiting dignitaries came to town. There were many high-profile citizens of the world domiciled in town. There were embassy staffers who could quite easily be found at one of the many watering holes along a short stretch of the Ring Road—The Arms Hotel, Cobb Lodge, Cozy Inn, The Lido, Tip-Toe, or the Ringway Hotel. These were great places to learn about what was really, really going on in the world. For example, the manager of the Ringway Hotel was a calm, intelligent, and well-informed Irishman by the name of Arthur Dutton. Mr. Dutton was not really much of a talker. Rather, he seemed to like polite, intelligent conversations. Perhaps for that very reason, he seemed to like my friends and me.

Quite often, when the dance hall closed late at night, my friends and I and sometime members of the resident dance band—The Globe-Masters and later the Africana Rythemers—would gather at or near the bar for an hour or more talking domestic and world affairs. Beside the resident band, there was always a guest band as well. Some were local, like the Black Beats, The Ramblers, Gaby Nick Valdo and The Avengers. There were bands from outside Ghana: The Black Santaigos from next-door Lome and the Heart Beats from Freetown, Sierra Leone.

From near or far, the musicians often joined in to make the discussions lively and informative. In such friendly sessions, we sometimes even had the privilege to hear about the views of the more honorable, worldly but secluded personalities domiciled in Accra.

Honorable personalities like: Dr. W.E.B. and Mrs. Shirley Dubois; the renowned poet, Professor Maya Angelou; the American ambassador, Mr. William P. Mahoney, whose son was a student at a local high school founded by Governor Guggisberg - Achimota School, Patrick and Mrs. Sloan; the South African journalist - William Bashner who wrote the newspaper column - *Looking at the World From Accra*; the Irish former Member of the British Parliament, Geoffrey Bing, who was then Ghana's attorney general; and the Irish scholar, Dr. Connor Cruise O'Brien, who was vice chancellor of the University of Ghana. Such sessions always provided material and inspiration to those of us who so passionately combed the "grapevine" looking to bridge the difference between the official news bits and the rest of the story, in the world. This was the period when Patrice Lumumba of the Congo was assassinated and UN Secretary General Dag Hammarskjöld died in a plane crash at Ndola Airport in Zambia (then Northern Rhodesia).

This was a period just after Mr. Hammarskjöld along with the American UN diplomat, Ralph Bunche, and the Irish diplomat, Dr. Connor O'Brien, shuttled between New York and Africa trying to resolve the crisis in the Congo. This was also the period when John F. Kennedy was assassinated.

A lot was going on in the world, and we were always eager to get, not just the story but the whole story. That stretch of the Rind Road seemed to always provide it, and so, when Soviet Premier Nikita Khrushchev was summarily deposed and accused of "revisionism," the word sent us all scrambling to the Ring Road to find out just what the word "revisionism" meant beyond the dictionary's definition. Along the Ring Road, there were many who knew what it meant and knew a whole lot more. As it was explained to us then, Soviet premier Nikita Khrushchev had in fact jumped the gun. By Mr. Khrushchev's reckoning, it was time to dismantle the Soviet Union and to begin to replace communism with a free-market institution as called for in the communist agenda. He was, we were told, too far ahead of the agenda, beyond what the rest of the politburo (the neo-Stalinists) was comfortable with.

That was when we also learned that, after all, communism was never intended as a permanent institution but merely as a mold to establish the foundations upon which a free enterprise, self-reliant and assertive, society could be built. The mold for the foundation was to hold for at least fifty years, which would be until approximately the 1980s. The time table and term of the agenda had been set by Joseph Stalin in 1929. Khrushchev was pro-Lenin, and he hated anything related to Stalin. He insisted that the agenda began in November 1919 when the Bolsheviks began to construct the Soviet Union. He was probably acting out of sheer negativism and spite; perhaps, he wanted to ensure all the credit went to Lenin and not Stalin. It cost him dearly. The neo-Stalinists led by Leonid Brezhnev pounced on Mr. Khrushchev so ruthlessly and ousted him in 1965.

Anyway, we did learn something that not too many people around the world knew, thanks largely to the subculture that fostered the free flow of worldly information and was spurred by small groups of curious Africans like my friends and me and an enlightened cadre of Irishmen domiciled in Accra. There was also Jim Willis. I almost forgot Jim Willis. He was a slim and slick-looking gentleman, always in his Mustang convertible, always accompanied by one or two or more young African women. He was the station manager for Farrell (shipping) Lines. I also nearly forgot to mention William Brennan, who was then head of

National Lotteries. You could very well say the Irish took over Accra when the British left.

Chapter Three

America's Relations with Africa

The Cold-War Era

Until 1960, the United States showed very little interest in sub-Saharan Africa. The only two or rather three notable exceptions were the West African country of Liberia, which America had helped establish, with the resettlement of freed slaves in the early to mid-1800s, the East African country of Abyssinia (Ethiopia) with its historic Christian significance; and South Africa, for economic and strategic reasons. Otherwise, American foreign policy makers showed little, if any interest in the continent, not even the north, where America and its allies had engaged German and Italian forces during World War II. Even then the three exceptions I just mentioned, including South Africa, which was singularly recognized by American policy makers as strategically important and culturally related, were generally treated with marginal interest.

John F. Kennedy (1960–1963)

By 1960, however, a number of African nations including the Sudan, Ghana, and Nigeria, having gained political independence, began to usher in a steady stream of new members into the United Nations with ominous prospects of reshaping, at least significantly shifting, the dynamics of global politics. The Kennedy administration, recognizing the implications of the approaching shift, began to formulate a policy to reflect better relations with the emerging continent.

In fact, such recognition of a more significant Africa was expressed in a 1959 campaign speech when Mr. Kennedy referred to Africa as "the new frontier" and began to advocate friendship and the extension of a Marshall Plan-like aid regimen to strengthen the emerging African nations so as to establish a basis upon which to elicit rational and logical support on the continent for the United States of America and her Western allies against likely Soviet bloc covetous overtures(paraphrased from Journal of American History: December 2008 (vol.95, no.3).

Mr. Kennedy's foresight was indeed based on a liberal international view. In its application, the liberal international doctrine proposed that American interest in Africa should not be limited to narrow strategic and economic pursuits, but must rather be directed at American contributions to eradicate all ills and causes of human sufferings, such as poverty, hunger, disease, civil conflicts, racism, tribalism, and other forms of human rights violations. Above all, it recognized the ill effects of poverty with its ripples and far- reaching, debilitating, and stifling effects. President Kennedy believed that, even if such contributions did not yield obvious and immediate benefits to America, the benefits would accrue in the long run. Thus, the establishment of new thinking, the basis for new attitudes and policy making toward Africa, was delegated to an able bureaucrat and champion: Under Secretary of State Chester Bowles.

Right from the start, Mr. Bowles repeatedly underscored his administration's belief in a strong, prosperous, and self-reliant Africa. He believed it was, at least in the long run, good for America, not just in a few, but in many respects since among others, it would align many of the new African nations with America's global aspirations and provide the rest with no good reasons to be allied with the Soviet bloc.

Mr. Bowles' bold new policy on Africa gained steady popularity. A Gallup Poll at the time showed significant public support for his major proposals, including the establishment of a U.S.-funded and staffed university in Africa in addition to sending young American men and women to offer technical assistance throughout the continent. In more concrete terms, Under Secretary Bowles reaffirmed and proposed Marshall Plan-like offers for Africa by which the developed nations of the Western world would pull together to provide economic assistance to the new African nations until they were able to fend and provide for themselves. Mr. Bowles believed further that if, in fact, such offers were multidimensional—based on politics, education, and economics as well as culture—then it would ensure prosperity to many in Africa and help establish global political stability and ideological cohesion. It sounds ideal; yet, it was a practical and rational approach to the process of globalization, in my personal view.

To express such ideals in concrete terms, the Kennedy administration sought to make country-specific overtures. Impressed and inspired by the Rifkin Report on Nigeria, President Kennedy publicly announced in July 1961 a U.S. financial package of $225 million toward the implementation of Nigeria's development plans. However, even before a mechanism for disbursement of funds could be worked out, suspicions began to rise about the sincerity of the pledge; these were suspicions spurred by growing racial unrest in the United States and what was perceived by Africans as America's covert, at least tacit, support for racist apartheid South Africa and for the overthrow and assassination of Congo's Prime Minister Patrice Lumumba.

Kennedy's novel initiative on Africa, noble though it was, was set on shaky ground on both sides of the Atlantic, but it nonetheless established the foundation and the framework by which successive American governments could build a durable bridge for prosperity between America and Africa. In 1961, the American Peace Corps was born of these ideals and aspirations.

L. B. Johnson (1963–1969)

When Lyndon B. Johnson assumed the presidency in late 1963, he inherited Kennedy's foreign policies, including those on Africa. After all, he had retained the Secretary of State from the Kennedy administration. Before long, President Johnson and his Secretary of State Dean Rusk were beset by more dire issues. First, the war in Southeast Asia was expanding and escalating, and the conspiracy theory of communist expansionist aspirations romantically dubbed "the domino theory" appeared real and rather imminent. Secondly, the arms race with the Soviets was rising to dizzying heights as both racial and labor relations in America continued to deteriorate.

Perhaps due to such preoccupations, the Johnson administration was not able to advance any new policies or to even continue those established by its predecessor. If he had any appreciable interest or vision similar to Kennedy's, it was neither expressed nor implied. What many Africans believe and remember Mr. Johnson for is that the overthrow of Ghana's first president Dr. Kwame Nkrumah, was carried out with his full knowledge and at least his tacit approval. I quite remember, later in Mr. Johnson's full term, when his Under Secretary of State Nicholas Katzenberg visited Africa in late 1966 or was it early 1967. It was shortly after the overthrow of President Nkrumah and the overthrow of other African heads of government, including the Tafawa Balewa regime in Nigeria. Mr. Katzenberg's visit was seen by many Africans as a mission to merely assure the new African regimes of America's support and to further urge those that had socialist inclinations to distance themselves from Soviet bloc overtures and influence. I remember being introduced to Mr. Katzenberg when he came to the office complex in Accra where I worked,icer at the Ministry of Health.

45

Actually, I had run into him walking toward the ministry, where I worked, with an aide from the American Embassy which was right next door. Tall and rather deliberate in his approach, he did indeed appear to be on a mission to win, at least to regain, the hearts and minds of Africans.

As was with the African response to President Kennedy's offers to Nigeria, the visit of Mr. Johnson's Under Secretary of State rather heightened African suspicions.

Much of the suspicion was fueled by word on the street and was centered on the reasons behind the overthrow of the Nkrumah regime. You see, the American ambassador at the time of President Nkrumah's overthrow was an African-America, Franklin Williams. Many Africans suspected that the Johnson administration had ordered the overthrow of President Nkrumah, and the American CIA had exploited the close and confidential relations between President Nkrumah and Ambassador Williams (suspicion that still lingers till this day- Google: Zimupdates by Obi Egbuna 16/06/08) (Wikipedia: CIA activities in Ghana, 1966). The reason, according rumour, was simply to thwart Ghana's and Africa's progressive efforts. The "fear of Soviet influences" was taken by most Africans as mere pretext. Overall, most observers in Africa probably judged President Johnson's dealings with Africa as somewhat neutral if not sinister; it was certainly nothing substantive to be described as liberal international.

Richard M. Nixon (1969–1974)

In contrast to the Kennedy administration's liberal internationalism and the attendant overtures that flowed, toward Africa, the Nixon administration extended an opposite approach. It was based on the theory officially referred to as the "vital interest" doctrine. Its expectations, in essence, seemed narrow and rather inward. Particularly, the "vital interest" doctrine contended that Africa's inherent value to the U.S. was minor and that it was better to spend American resources merely to contain Soviet influences on the continent. Efforts beyond that, the administration further contended, were likely to be unrewarding given the small-sized economies and the rather inefficient and volatile regimes that ran them. Yet, at the same time, the Nixon administration expected Africa to rise toward its potential as "… a healthy and prosperous region in the global community." His reasons for such expectation were rather self-seeking; he expected Africa to be self-reliant soon so as to curtail America's long-term aid commitment to the region. In other words, Africa must not remain "the white man's burden" much longer.

From his inauguration in January 1969 until well after he left office in the mid-1970s, this short-term-interest view became the basis of American policy toward Africa. Debates and challenges, if any, were of strategies and tactics; some were not so easy to understand. For instance, in an effort to improve prevailing dismal relations between official America and the African American community, the Nixon administration sought to relax pressure on apartheid South Africa and the other white minority settler states of Namibia, Southern Rhodesia (now Zimbabwe), Mozambique, and Angola. Pressures had been brought to bear on these white racist states by the preceding Kennedy–Johnson administrations to force them to abandon their despotic and separatist systems of rule. Strangely, the Nixon administration sought to reverse policy with the rather illogical argument that such relaxation of pressure would free the white settlers of their siege mentality and thus help them improve relations with their neighboring black African states, which, in turn, would enhance and secure America's strategic and other interests in the region.

As most Africans saw it, the truth simply was that the Nixon administration saw black Africa as fragmented, powerless, and incapable of organizing itself effectively. On the other hand, it saw apartheid South Africa as a well-organized, well-run nation militarily and economically powerful and, above all, supportive of America's position on important global issues, particularly regarding East/West contentions.

Such dismal views provided the impetus for less-than-favorable policies toward Africa. The Nixon administration felt at ease with strategies it believed it could well get away with or that would at worst elicit feeble and minimal repercussions from antiapartheid African nations and from African American pressure groups and "agitators."

Gerald Ford (1974–1977)

In much the same way Lyndon Johnson replaced John F. Kennedy as U.S. president past the half term of his presidency, Gerald Ford replaced Richard Nixon about halfway into the latter's second term. More or less a caretaker government, the Ford administration made no efforts to advance any new policies or to adopt new positions on Africa. The remaining policy matters were left to State Department bureaucrats. So, a benign form of the "vital interest" doctrine toward Africa prevailed in Washington until the inauguration of Jimmy Carter in January 1977.

James Earl Carter (1977–1981)

Jimmy Carter believed fervently that change to the apartheid system of rule in South Africa was not merely morally right, but also historically inevitable and that, by siding with the inevitable, the United States would enhance its long-term prospects in the whole of Africa.

This prompted a revival of "liberal internationalism." Much like John F. Kennedy's broad- based views, Mr. Carter believed open, friendly relations with Africa that included economic aid and similar incentives were a more effective means to help the continent develop and thus fend off Soviet influences.

His strategy for implementing this new version of the liberalist view on Africa was to focus on two of Africa's four pillar nations: Nigeria and South Africa. Based upon recommendations drafted by Andrew Young, his ambassador at the United Nations aided by Donald McHenry—then Mr. Young's deputy and later to be his successor—the Carter administration adopted an aggressive stance against the southern African white minority regimes with the hope it would appease African and other Third World nations (particularly Nigeria) and thereby sway such countries away from Soviet influence.

The Carter administration saw Nigeria not merely as a potentially important trading partner, but also as the indisputable major player and power in African affairs. Nigeria is large in size and in population. Geographically, it is well positioned and had in fact championed the formation of the Economic Community of West African States (ECOWAS). It is without doubt a pillar, a core nation in Africa. By 1977, Nigeria was among the top five suppliers of U.S. oil imports (Measures of Oil Import Dependence: James M. Kendell, 1998). American major petroleum companies operating in Nigeria included Mobil, Gulf, Texaco, Phillips, and Ashland. These companies were realizing enormous profits in Nigeria, profits they quickly repatriated to America; they ignored opportunities to help transform Nigeria into a strong consumer society capable of higher consumption of American-made goods, which was in fact the vision of John F. Kennedy some fifteen years earlier, and which had been smothered due largely to Africans' nervous perceptions and interpretations of American domestic racism and support for racist South Africa.

Therefore, it was very important that Mr. Carter's administration get it right this time, and, though the chances for success seemed great, they were, nonetheless, conditional. From African perspectives, Mr. Carter did indeed start off quite well. Even his predispositions were favorable. He was a native of Georgia where he had served as governor before his election to the American presidency. His father was a farmer, and his mother served in the Peace Corps. The state of Georgia a decade earlier had elected Julian Bond, an African American, to its legislature in spite of the racial turmoil of the time. Contrary to most expectations, but comforting if not assuring to most Africans, Mr. Carter seemed the most liberal of recent American presidents. He named African Americans to prominent positions in his cabinet.

Names like Andrew Young and Patricia Harris symbolized hope for African American aspirations for high public office. The wave that lifted a number of African Americans to prominent positions in public service started at the local level with the election of several as city mayors - in Los Angeles, California; Detroit, Michigan; Atlanta, Georgia; Gary, Indiana; and Cleveland, Ohio among others. It also ushered into congress representatives that included Shirley Chisholm, Barbara Jordan, and Charles Diggs. On Mr. Carter's watch, the climb finally reached the top, the federal level. The perceived helping hand also seemed indeed friendly. When the Carter administration sought to establish good relations with the North African state of Libya, its foreign minister, Atashier Zahedi, visited Washington more than once. Mr. Zahedi was a black man, and so his prominence as a world statesman was most arousing to Africans everywhere. Not since the days of Dr. Martin Luther King and the American diplomat, Ralph Bunche, had Africans and African Americans seen one of their own so high on the world stage. Mr. Zahedi's position awed and delighted descendants of Africa the world over. It was credited in large part to the outreach of President Carter.

Even more remarkable to Africans was Mr. Carter's own diplomatic appointments, he appointed more African Americans to prominent diplomatic posts; – Andrew Young followed by. Donald McHenry at the UN; he appointed Orison Rudolph Aggrey ambassador to Romania. Jerome H. Holland who had served as ambassador to Sweden under Richard Nixon, was appointed by Mr. Carter to the American Red Cross Board of Directors. These were positions well beyond the then traditional "Negro posts". Such gains and advances, even those that were perhaps not directly attributable to the efforts of Mr. Carter, were considered inspired by the spirit and style of his politics. It was a spirit and style contrary to what many Africans had suspected of a white Anglo-Saxon Southern Protestant.

And so, with the necessary correct moral position thus established, Mr. Carter was on a solid footing to deal on numerous terms with black Africa, especially with Nigeria, which, at the time, was raking in vast revenue from the sale of oil. In 1979, Nigeria's gross domestic product (GDP) was posted at almost fifty billion dollars. Such income could well have afforded Nigeria the finances necessary for all aspects of national development: to fortify the infrastructure, improve education, and improve the health care systems. Nigeria at the time had a population of a little more than eighty million, and, with the rise in oil revenue, there was a corresponding rise in per-capita income. As impressive an output as this economic profile suggests, its details were in fact misleading; for much of the new wealth was concentrated in the hands of the upper brass of military officers, civil servants, traditional authorities, and regional power brokers.

To the extent that the Carter administration was sincerely interested in and morally committed to a developed and strong Africa, this was good cause for a "sit down" to urge and to advise, to redraw plans and perhaps—as did the Kennedy administration—to offer technical and other support for plan implementation. Such an undertaking, even if only partly successful, could well have laid the foundations upon which a strong industrial society could flourish in Nigeria with ripples to neighboring countries.

Instead, as if mainly compelled by a need to satisfy special interests or to fulfill a pre-established agenda, the Carter administration's focus seemed to drift. It sought more investment opportunities for American companies without laying the necessary and proper foundations to absorb the benefits to strengthen Nigeria. At a meeting during a visit to the United States in late 1977, Mr. Carter asked Nigeria's President Obasanjo to make every effort to hold down the price of oil, to which Mr. Obasanjo replied, "I'll consider it if you consider giving us an equivalent break in manufactured goods." Whether this was said in jest or not, the dialogue of the two leaders was, to express it politely, misplaced. What Nigeria needed was a revisit to the drawing board, to plan once again the growth of the economy and society, and to decide how the vast revenues from its oil could be used to establish a strong consumer society, a diversified economy capable of annual surpluses for export. President Obasanjo should have asked for access to America's market for Nigerian manufactured goods, not for price concessions on American manufactured goods into Nigeria. A developed Nigeria would, of course, offer American consumer product and service companies a strong basis to set up shop and operate profitably in Nigeria.

By the time Mr. Carter visited Nigeria from March 29 to April 2, 1978, African suspicions and reservations about American intensions in Africa had subsided, at least somewhat. After all, programs to achieve de-facto desegregation in America were being pursued earnestly and publicly throughout the Union. In addition, the white minority government of Southern Rhodesia had just been replaced by the black majority of Zimbabwe while cries for sanctions against the apartheid government of South Africa reverberated throughout America nearly as much as it did throughout the continent of Africa. Against such backdrop, Mr. Carter was seen by most Africans as a true liberal internationalist and a humanitarian with a spirit for charity and charity had well begun at home. In spite of this, there were still some on the continent who grumbled that Mr. Carter's visit was merely to make sure Nigerian oil continued to flow to America and at even more favorable prices to American oil companies.

What most Africans did not know—what they could not have known—was that the Carter administration had, in fact, made the most gallant effort since JFK to encourage American businesses to develop trade and commercial relations with Nigeria, in particular, and Africa, in general; it was not merely to increase exports of American goods to Africa, but as part of the effort to help Africa up. His pleas and encouragements, however, went virtually unheeded by the American business community. I can only guess the reasons.

You see, American business analysts and strategists assess market potentials not by intuition but by manipulation of hard facts and figures, even if incorrectly perceived. A consumer market like Nigeria's posting an annual per-capita income of $500, at that time, is not likely to interest "serious- minded" American business decision makers. Many lacked the degree of sophistication that recognizes wealth at the bottom of the socioeconomic pyramid. Other factors weighed in:

    a) The volatility of African governments with the attendant prospects of nationalization/indigenization that were political catchphrases in those days

    b) Africa's bureaucracies, fraught with red tapes, fostered by corruption

 c) America's own bureaucratic inertia and general disinterest in Africa
 d) Competition by European and especially Asian businesses for Africa's markets.

Not long after Mr. Carter's visit to Nigeria, his administration was gripped by political upheavals in Iran: Americans held hostage in the face of approaching presidential elections.

Much to everyone's regret, Mr. Carter's vigorous pursuits of interests such as Africa had to be markedly curtailed. Thus, a golden opportunity to begin the process of restoration in Africa fell by the wayside once again. The case of Nigeria is particularly lamentable. With such vast annual revenue and a positive will in Washington to support efforts for Africa's growth, Nigeria's own efforts for self-reliance, if any, were woefully dismal. One can only be consoled by the thought that the establishment in Nigeria had failed to anticipate this opportunity.

And so, in spite of Mr. Carter's noble intentions and gallant efforts, American investments in Nigeria remained confined to the oil sector, and America's trade deficit with Nigeria increased as its market share decreased.

Ronald W. Reagan (1981–1988)

In a *Wall Street Journal* interview in 1980, just before he was elected, Mr. Reagan promised weapons to União Nacional para a Independência Total de Angola (UNITA) rebel forces fighting the government of Angola, weapons to help the rebels' efforts to overthrow the then Marxist-leaning government of Agostino Neto.

This, to a large extent, sums up the Reagan administration's initial interest and priority in sub-Saharan Africa (apart from South Africa). It can indeed be said that several conditions conspired with Mr. Reagan's perceptions and influenced his interest. For one, the elements had not been particularly kind to Africa in those early years of his tenure. Drought had caused widespread famine and a significant drop in earnings from the sale of African raw materials, coupled with a rise in the price of oil that Africans had to import. The result was that most African governments were forced to cut back spending on vital and important services, such as health and education. Such austerities led to a rash of political, economic, and social difficulties for many African nations. As if such catastrophes and the difficulties they posed to governments and people were not enough, the Western press, in typical fashion, hoisted Africa up to the world as the classic bastion of gloom and doom.

Intended or not, such portrayals, which were really nothing new, rendered black Africa less appealing to potential foreign investors with the obvious result of low to no private sector capital for serious development efforts. One effect such conditions have had—particularly in the 1960s, 1970s, and well into the 1980s—was that the debt burden of African nations grew to a point where no external creditor, not even the International Finance Corporation (IFC) of the World Bank, was willing to advance any more credit to African nations. Even worse, it compelled most African nations to yield and submit to Soviet bloc influences. At the very beginning of his first term, there were some 40,000 Soviet bloc and Cuban troops in Africa, mostly in Angola. This fact, perhaps more than any other, influenced Mr. Reagan's priorities toward black Africa.

In fact, by the beginning of his second term, the administration seemed to have all but lost interest in Africa, and so too had the press. Even news about giant Nigeria was more often relegated to the back pages of most major journals. Remarkably, in spite of what might be aptly termed a personal, worldwide crusade to bolster democracy as the only rational form of government, Mr. Reagan showed very little interest in Africa. Whatever the level of interest, it seemed all directed toward only one of the other four core (pillar) states - South Africa. To his administration, it seemed, South Africa was the only bright spot in Africa: pro-Western and "reliable."

Thus, the new policy of "constructive engagement" emerged. Its very reference suggested its aims and goals, and, indeed, when it finally defined itself, it sought to reverse sanctions that had been imposed by the world community against the apartheid regime. Many Africans, however, saw it as nothing more than a rationalized, bolder application of the "vital interest" doctrine, a continuation of the Nixon administration's policy position.

This time, however, there were serious strategic and commercial considerations. Titanium was being developed to replace aluminum and iron in several applications in the global market. God being so good, vast portions of the world's titanium deposits is in southern Africa. Huge investments had already been made to develop titanium alloys and the necessary marketing strategies. Apartheid was in the way of a smooth exploitation of this new wonder metal. Thus, the policy of "constructive engagement" was reframed to accommodate possible political revisions that might avert possible exacerbation of social turmoil and political upheavals in the region. The newly framed policy was placed under the management of Under Secretary of State Chester Crocker.

With much the style of Chester Bowles—his namesake and opposite number in the liberal international–vital interest duel over Africa—Chester Crocker single-handedly managed the Reagan administration's revised policy on Africa. In his introductions,
Mr. Crocker boldly tried to make the case that the broad implication of sanctions was stacked against America's interests. However, in the long, drawn-out tussle that followed between the administration and congress over the issue, congress prevailed by a wide margin. The result was a most impressive show of support for sanctions, which finally forced the South African apartheid regime

to the bargaining table. Thus, clearly, it was the U.S. Congress, not Chester Crocker and the Reagan administration that forced the issue for change in South Africa.

To the extent that even South Africa was but a factor in the broader interest of fending off Soviet influences and expansion in Africa, one clearly discerns the logic behind the pattern of alternating policy positions vis-a-vis liberal internationalism advanced by Presidents Kennedy and Carter in contrast to the "vital interest" positions of Presidents Nixon, Ford, and Reagan. By observation alone, one can only conclude that during the period between the early 1960s to the late 1980s, America was presented with opportunities to help African establish the basis for strong, long-lasting bilateral trade relations. America was at the same time faced with the threats of Soviet influences in Africa. In this dilemma, America's policy priorities seemed driven more by concerns for Soviet bloc influence than by strategies to empower Africans for the good of Africa and of Africa's trade relations with America.

Chapter Four

The New World Order

Post-Cold-War Imperatives—Where does Africa fit in?

George H. W. Bush (1989–1993)

In his inaugural address in January 1989, President George Bush, Sr. ("41," as he is sometimes affectionately referred to) uttered a few one-liners, for which he is quite famous. One in particular reverberated instantly around the world, "This is the beginning of a new world order." It had a rather curious and perplexing aura, more like a proclamation, perhaps a sinister proclamation. The very next day, people were talking about secret societies and conspiracies by secular and religious orders that were well beyond my knowledge, in fact, beyond my imagination.

The one idea I heard a number of times and that I well understood was that the cold war was over. I also understood the inherent implication. America's policy approach to Africa, which had been driven by doctrine, was no longer necessary or relevant. America was to establish a new basis, a new set of imperatives for its future relations with Africa. If, as many people seemed to have interpreted it, a "new world order" necessarily meant a "one- world government" in which Africa would be a mere province, albeit a large one, Africa must still be able to hold its own and contribute its fair share to the economic, political, and social balance of the order. In more positive, proactive terms, Africa must be allowed to regain strength and to assume its proper position that the laws of nature and of nature's God entitles her in this or any future God-approved world order.

To many observers, the foreign policy of the Bush ("41") administration was not well defined. For one thing, his overture to strengthen America's commercial relations with communist China, where he had served as ambassador, aroused curiosity. Mr. Bush's new initiatives on interdiction of the flow of drugs from south of the border were widely applauded. Drug kingpins of the Columbian Madeline cartel were killed or apprehended in openly televised spectacular raids. Before long, such manner of military raids began to appear like standard operation, and its application seemed extended beyond the interdiction of drug supply when the president of Panama, Manuel Noriega, was captured in similar style and flown to America for trial and imprisonment.

And so, for the four years of his tenure, the world waited anxiously, somewhat mesmerized, for further interpretations and explanations of this new and dynamic expression. Not much happened during this time with Africa, not at the federal level. Regarding South Africa, the Bush administration rightfully settled on managing the implementation of revised American policy that called for transition to (black) majority rule. The Bush administration's only other focus in Africa was Somalia, where there was armed civil conflict among several factions. Having seemingly taken sides with one faction, Mr. Bush personally led U.S. troops to the shores of Mogadishu just weeks before he left office, a venture that turned out to be a military fiasco, ending with the now infamous "Black Hawk Down." So, all told, beside attempts to intervene in civil conflicts in one or two selected spots, most American contact with Africa during the tenure of Bush Sr. ("41") was by private individuals like you and me or through churches and civic and small business groups that traveled to Africa to explore for business opportunities, for spiritual reconciliation, or simply for leisure and sight-seeing. What remained clear at the end of the Bush ("41") administration was that with the cold war over, new sets of policy initiatives toward Africa were still required. It was equally clear that such new initiatives would be left to his successors to craft and to implement.

Africans must first clean house.

If, so far, I have given the impression that African ills are all due to the slave trade and to policies in Washington, I must attempt to explain the basis of my argument further. Yes, the slave trade, colonialism, and current policies in Europe and in Washington have all contributed in significant respects, to one degree or another, to what ails Africa today.

However, there is a great deal more on the other side of the equation - about the peoples of Africa; what they do, and what they fail to do. So let us now turn around and take a cursory look at African-specific contributions to the reasons for Africa's low position on the ladder of global society and economics; let us examine why Africa, at least in some parts, offers the highest return on investment—(according to an Overseas Private Investment Corporation (OPIC) 2004 report) yet attracts the least investments. The likely contributions are varied and many. Let us look at the subject of governance and some related factors. In doing this, it is necessary to refer to the impact of intervention by outsiders in Africa's affairs. You may also choose to ignore such fact and regard the issue of African follies and shortcomings at face value. One of the more remarkable features of postcolonial governance in Africa is the quality of leadership. One can express it politely only to a point. The fact is a good number of African leaders between 1965 and 1990 lacked both preparation and temperaments to lead and to manage serious organizations, let alone a nation. Equally remarkable and deeply troubling is the question of how these men got into such positions of power and leadership. I believe we have already touched on that issue, but a whole lot more remains to be said. Let us look briefly at some of the manifestations and the effects they have had on the dispositions of Africa and Africans today. When I remarked that many of the leaders of the period were unprepared, I referred specifically to the fact that they lacked the requisite formal education.

What little education they did have was almost invariably unrelated to the tasks of governing and efficiently managing a developing society. Much of the wisdom and examples they could draw on were traditional African norms of conduct and protocol: essentially feudal or pre- feudal in quality. For instance, I speak of African norms that allowed a ruler to amass wealth and to treat the state treasury and all other state assets and privileges as rights and virtual personal property. These were traditional norms that also did not accommodate criticism, dissent and opposition.

You are right; all these men had advisors, but keep in mind men of such limited abilities and discretion often also lacked the disciplines to fully understand, let alone appreciate, the value of advice. To many such African despots, an advisor was nothing more than a formal nicety. They were, for the most part, unenlightened, inward thinking and took delight in hoarding as much as they believed they could get away with. I must explain a point quite relevant to this subject. When I refer to African leaders, I do not mean just the heads of state and government. I refer broadly to anyone in position of power or responsibility, that include cabinet ministers, regional ministers, senior civil servants, religious leaders, civic leaders, and even those who prefer to lead quietly from behind.

In a number of African countries, political leaders are by definition part of the social elite. Public position and the opportunity for material accumulation are often regarded as one and the same, so a person with a position of importance is also regarded a person of means and influence. Even if such regard is far from the truth the strength of public perception is bound, sooner or later, to reshape his regard of himself. Once set in motion, its manifestations spiral downward and fast. Accumulation, by any means, becomes a measure of his power and prestige. Greater acquisition requires higher position from where he can expedite more lucrative illicit schemes without fear of scrutiny. Before long, such leader begins to attract a cadre of young professionals. These young professionals offer themselves as proxies, agents, and conduits to his numerous deals. To ease their consciences, they prefer to regard corruption as nothing more than a necessary antisocial behavior, a means to cover the margins of the high daily demands of the lifestyle they have set for themselves.

Corruption becomes increasingly prevalent as it spreads and settles in the lower rungs of society. At this level, corrupt practices becomes both absurd and rational. The chasm between supply and demand for the individual wage earner in Africa during the 1960s through the 1990s was readily discernible. Most wages were well below what was minimally necessary for the daily demands of the average worker. However, expectation was high and constantly rising and since 'everybody eats where he works', bribery and similar forms of corruption became compelling means to make ends meet. For example, at airports, a passenger sometimes must offer bribe to secure a seat on a flight. It often got worse as the passenger went on through the process. At destination, the handlers at baggage claim, the customs and agriculture officers, even the police and the soldiers at the exits must all be bribed individually.

It cannot really be overstated; corruption, like a cancer, spread insidiously into every aspect of African society. No sector was spared. School administrators expected bribes to admit students.

The bursar and matron colluded to skim off allocations for student meals.

Nurses, sometimes doctors at state run institutions expected bribes up front before treatment. Bribery became a norm. Even the once highly respected civil service was in. Bureaucrats continued to draw full salary years after their retirement, of course with kickbacks to the paymaster. For example, in a 1991 study in Zambia, it was estimated the government was losing nearly the equivalent of twelve and a half million dollars a year in such dummy payroll schemes. Nigeria's reported losses were worse, almost the equivalent of six hundred million a year in the government sector alone. I recommend you watch the movie

A Good Man in Africa starring Sean Connery and Louis Gossett, Jr. for a general impression.

As the saying in Africa goes, "Once the rot is established at the top, it eats its way anywhere and everywhere on the inside." Padding projects in order to pocket the excess, kickbacks, outright bribery, and diversions were only some of the preferred methods. A World Bank report on Liberia during this period suggested about sixty million dollars was diverted each year from government coffers into private accounts. This occurred in a country where sixty million dollars represented a significant ratio of the annual national budget at that time. What makes the account of such practices truly tragic is the fact that much of the loot was used not for productive ventures but was spent frivolously for conspicuous consumption of imported luxuries, overseas flings with cronies and concubines, or simply stashed in overseas private unnumbered accounts, especially in Europe and America.

If leaders who presided over affairs in these countries had both the will and the ability, they could well have minimized such practices and could have used the looted resources for development and progress. As it were, many of the leaders were busy with their own corrupt schemes and often had no plans or vision for even the most basic development initiatives. The trend started with the civilian regimes that fought for and gained independence. However, both corruption and neglect took on a higher and more fervent pitch when the military engaged itself in the tasks of government. Absolutely unfazed by the moral implications, they ravaged the national treasuries and anything of material value they could lay their hands on.

Estimates worked out in the 1980s suggest that the price of a pre-owned, loaded army tank could provide elementary and secondary education for 40,000 African children. The price of a military helicopter of similar description could have paid the salaries of 15,000 school teachers for a year. Yet, in countries like Ghana, Angola, Congo Brazzaville, Gabon and Mauritania, the military governments spent such sums and often more on itself. In some African countries, military spending was as much as 40 percent of the total annual national budget. In 1983 alone, the total military spending in Africa was about $17 billion, an increase of over 400 percent over the previous decade (1973 figures of a mere $3.8 billion). If they could not readily dip into the country's coffers from outside, then they did so from within the government, in the name of the state and in a manner that enabled them to skim.

Perhaps, one of the two worst culprits in the history of modern African corruption was General Sanni Abacha, who was head of state of Nigeria in the mid to late 1990s and whose personal wealth at the time of his death in 1998 was estimated to have been in the billions of dollars equivalent. His family is said to have been forced to return to government coffers the equivalent of over $2 billion in cash along with some fifty-two luxury cars and thirty-four houses. Yet, even General Abacha's greed and accumulation pales in comparison to that of General Mobutu Sese Seko of Zaire (now Congo DR). Over thirty plus years, General Mobutu was estimated to have accumulated over $20 billion, much of it stashed in private accounts in France, Belgium, Luxembourg, and the United States of America.

Of course, Nigeria and Zaire are giants both in size and in their earning capacities. However, the smaller, less-endowed countries did not spare themselves either. Kenya is a smaller country with far less GDP compared to either Nigeria or Zaire, yet it is estimated that in the first twenty-five years after its independence from Britain (between 1960 and 1985), Kenyans stashed away in overseas private accounts the dollar equivalent of over $5 billion, nearly all of it illicitly acquired. As a result of these rather pernicious practices that started in the late 1960s, many African communities have suffered neglect and decline in productivity, especially in the area of agriculture, the backbone of most African economies. Threats of famine and government curtailment on spending on essential services such as health and education caused unrest and sparked agitations throughout much of Africa.

To preserve themselves against the fury of their peoples, many African military governments resorted to repressive measures, even after they had morphed into civilian forms of government. Worse still, their decline in prestige and the related inability to adequately provide for their peoples further diminished the already low bargaining position of African leaders in global circles. By 1990, twenty-four of the world's poorest thirty-six nations were in Africa, a continent that without argument should be ranked the richest.

It is this paradox most Africans refer to in their outcries against foreign interventions in Africa's affairs. Africans argue that, in addition to the slave trade and colonialism, the worst contributor to Africa's under development has been the overt and, more often, covert interference in Africa's internal affairs by Europe and America. The standard mode of operation seems to have been guided by standard doctrine; a seemingly collaborative effort in which African leaders who appeared enlightened, sensitive, and progressive were—by use of force, economic strangulation, or some other form of treachery—replaced with ones far less competent, far less sensitive, and only marginally, if at all, aware of what was really going on in the world. Some were so uninformed, uninspired, and insensitive that they could not possibly have been considered by their own family clans to serve on the village council. Yet, it seems such deplorable qualities were what qualified and made them most fit and suitable to be imposed over whole African nations.

Most Africans point to leaders like Moise Tshombe and later Mobutu Sese Seko of the Congo, Idi Amin of Uganda, Samuel Doe of Liberia, and J. A. Ankrah of Ghana, to cite but a few. These were men who were widely seen by most Africans as imposed to serve outside interests. Documentaries and recent releases of classified information have supported and confirmed such contentions and suspicions.

If Africa must clean house, as it indeed must, African countries must be spared the stifling encroachments posed by policies of Northern nations toward Africa. Offers of help must be sincere and must be calculated for the benefit of Africa. Regime change and the imposition of leaders on Africa by outsiders for benefits that does not particularly favor the continent and its peoples must be a thing of the past. This, really is the responsibility of the African masses. To demand of their elected leaders refrain from undue external influences.

Chapter Five

The Prophesies

Of Condemnation

"Hopeless Africa" was the title of an article in the May 2000 issue of *The Economist*. Without any reservation, the article listed what, in its view, was wrong with Africa. The list was long. It included disease, poverty and squalor, wars and civil strife, and mismanagement. You too might have similar damning adjectives with reference to Africa: "the dark continent;" "Africa, a basket case;" or "hopeless Africa." Africans tend to interpret such derogatory references as either expressions of frustration when Africa and Africans prove too much to control or expressions of exasperation by truly concerned Africans and Africa's well-wishers. Those who get frustrated because they are unable to get over easy in dealing with Africa and Africans deserve their frustration. No part of Africa is for the taking on the cheap.

I happen to be one of those who lament prevailing conditions in Africa just about every day. Living in Atlanta, thousands of miles from any important African location, I often find myself thinking through African issues as if I could offer some practical advice. What seem to be the obstacles to African unity? What can the regional groups like ECOWAS, the East African Customs Union (EACU), and the South African Development Community (SADC) do to improve the quality of life of the ordinary African? Is Africa really under a curse as some people still say? Lately, I have been reading the Scriptures to familiarize myself with the numerous biblical references to Africa. I have seen some that might well be interpreted as curses, but I have also seen more that can only be predictions of redemption.

Come with me, and let us first take a look at some of what might pass as condemnations for anyone who wishes to interpret them as such. Let us begin at the beginning, in Genesis 9:18–25. Noah planted grapes and made wine, and, when he got drunk from his own wine, he took off his clothes. When his son Ham saw him as such, he summoned his two brothers, Japheth and Shem. The three, with prompt and due respect, attended to their father. Now, as Noah recovered from his drunken stupor, he got into an argument with his grandson Canaan, son of Ham. Thus angered, Noah is said to have cursed Canaan and all his descendants with servitude unto the descendants of Japheth and Shem. For another example, let's fast forward to Egypt before the Asiatic and European occupations: An African ruler (probably of the twenty-fifth dynasty) is said to have promised military support for King Hezekiah's plans to institute religious reforms necessary for the restoration of Judah. The neighboring Assyrians did not like King Hezekiah's intention and threatened to intervene with force. The African ruler of Egypt, having promised to come to the aid of King Hezekiah and Judah against the might of the Assyrians, failed to deliver when the time came, and, for such poor show of integrity, God is said to have directly cursed Africans. There are other examples, but I think these two makes the point.

Whatever their real worth, such references have provided the basis for European attempts to cast Africans as inferior by some divine design. Often presented as scholarly work, Europeans have, since the Middle Ages, attempted to rationalize Africa's dispositions and European exploitations of Africa and Africans with postulates based solely on such biblical mythology; from fifteenth-century Swiss scientist, Karl Von Linne (Linnaeus), to "eugenics" and socio-biology academics like Shockley, Jensen, Abrahamson, and many others of the twentieth century.

In the mid-nineteenth century, Professor G. Curvier, a French socio-biologist, postulated a classification of the human race based solely on the lineage of the three sons of Noah. In it, he assigned Japheth as the father of Caucasian peoples, Shem as father of Mongoloid (Asiatic) peoples, and Ham as father of African people.

Most interesting is that even in his elaborations, he assigned the blackness of Africans to the curse of Noah on Canaan. There are several passages in the Bible that have been painstakingly construed to support such thinking. For example, there are prophesies by Ezekiel and Isaiah that have been interpreted to suggest that God intended punishment for the Assyrians, the Babylonians, and the nations of Africa for the way they behaved during efforts to restore Judah, which itself had fallen out of favor with God on account of its king, Manasseh, who had plunged the kingdom into idolatry and had thus prompted the faithful to move the Ark of the Covenant for safekeeping deep in the heart of Africa.

Such postulates tend to raise even more challenging questions. For instance, why would God give the riches of Africa and other nations to Israel? Was it punishment of Africa? Was it to give Israel vain cause for joy? Even deeper, was such punishment exacted because King Manasseh's father, King Hezekiah, traced his lineage to Africa or could it be that references to "the riches" were, in fact, references to vast wealth and military might that might be realized with help from the power that lies within the Ark of the Covenant in the heart of Africa? We all know that today, America's aid donation to Africa is one dollar per capita compared to over eight hundred per capita to the state of Israel. You will have noticed of late, many have staked claim to the true identity of Israel. Some claims sound, at least, nearly convincing and others not even marginally so. In his book, *The United States and Britain in Prophecy* (Armstrong 1980), the late Herbert W. Armstrong, founder of The World Wide Church of God and publisher of the *Plain Truth* magazine, presented a compelling and convincing thesis about the true identity of modern Israelites. He asserted that the two main houses of Israel (not of Judah)—that is, the houses of Manasseh and of Ephraim having been given the birthright—moved out of Judea and headed for destinations foretold in prophesies by Isaiah, Ezekiel, Jeremiah, and Hezekiah.

According to Mr. Armstrong's thesis, the House of Ephraim settled in the British Isles ("Brit-ish" means Covenant people) and developed a global sovereign sphere in the form of the British Empire and later the British Commonwealth of Nations. The House of Manasseh settled in North America and has developed into the strongest single nation on earth. To the extent that this interpretation is compelling, it is also twice as troubling. For one thing, it raises deeper and more serious issues and questions. From which Israel are we to expect the fulfillment of these prophesies—the Israel of old, of Judah, or from America and Britain? For instance, Isaiah prophesied that

      a.) The Assyrians would enter Egypt and carry Africans into captivity

      b.) The material wealth and human resources of Africa would go to Jerusalem for Israel's use

      c.) As Africans were led by Cyrus in bondage through the trading centers of Israel on their way to captivity, they would finally acknowledge the presence of God.

If we accept this thesis—that in fact all biblical prophesies and other references to Ephraim and Manasseh for present-day fulfillment are references to Britain and America—then we can only infer that

a) African bondage in Israel is in fact the transatlantic slave trade
b) The Assyrians are really Arab middlemen and slave traders ("monkey peddlers") peddling away African human and material resources
c) Africans in the diaspora in America and in the nations of the British Commonwealth have developed a culture steeped in praises to God through the gospels (Negro spirituals) and Reggae and similar forms of praise songs, in addition to a keen interest in the Scriptures of Christian worship. In fact, they have.

Holding up the fulfillment and the manifestations of such biblical prophesies in a modern-day setting does indeed have a profound impact on anyone's mind. So far, I have refrained from any conclusive judgments of these prophesies. In fact, I am not capable of making appreciable assessments on the accuracy and soundness of the references to any of these prophesies and certainly not the validity of their interpretations. I can only observe and remark on their possible impact on the minds and attitudes of those who believe in them.

We must note, in conclusion, however, that both Ephraim and Manasseh were born in Egypt to an Egyptian mother. That, biologically, makes them at least half African. In fact, by European convention (the one-eighth rule that insists that a person with one-eighth African blood is African), Ephraim and Manasseh were Africans.

Also, of mere interest, note that of the lineage of the two sons of Joseph's, the Manasseh's descendants—America—had by far the larger number of slaves and flourished commensurately by it. The descendants of Ephraim—Britain—were first to abolish the slave trade (1807) and slavery (1835) in their empire. America (the descendants of Manasseh) did not abolish slavery until thirty years later (1865). Keep in mind that Manasseh was the older of the two brothers, but their grandfather Jacob blessed Ephraim first with the birthright. We will look at the possible significance to all this a bit later.

Misinterpretations (Errors of Omission)

There is little argument among historians that the name Ethiopia, as used in antiquity, refers to Africa and Africans: those at home as well as those abroad. The attributes of Africans were hailed and widely portrayed in plays, ballads, historic narratives, and other forms of epics by legendary narrators and playwrights like Aeschylus, Herodotus, and Pliny the Elder among others. With time, however, the geographic reference to Ethiopia diminished until it referred only to the areas around Abyssinia. Other terms such as "Punt," "Nehesi," and "Wawaht" were used in reference to different parts of the continent.

The other term most often used to refer to the whole of Africa during and shortly after antiquity was the term "Kush." Like the term "Africa," "Kush" was an Egyptian term used in its various forms of spellings and pronunciations by other cultures of the region, including the Assyrians and the Hebrews. The Hebrews used the terms "Kush" and "Kushites" extensively in their writing and often with high regard. Kushites were often described as tall and smooth-skinned people. Such descriptions were even used as a metaphor (Isaiah 18:2 and Jeremiah 13:23). Moses' wife was referred to as a Kushite, daughter of Jethro, the Ethiopian magician (Numbers 12:15). So too was the messenger who reported the death of Absalom to King David and the Kushite in the Palace of King Zedekiah who rescued Jeremiah from death. Militarily, Kush was compared to Assyria, so Judah expected Kush to rescue its people from the yoke of the Assyrians. When the Queen of Sheba went on a trade mission to Judah, she donated to King Solomon wood for the building of the temple in Jerusalem and gold and ivory for its adornment. Indeed, the Kushites or Ethiopians of Africa were well regarded in times of antiquity.

In prophecies with direct reference to the greater African community, the prophet Zephaniah foretold of conversion of the Kushites who would bring tribute to God (Zephaniah 3:10). The psalmist foretold the day when, "Princes shall come out of Egypt, Ethiopia shall soon stretch forth her hands unto God" (Psalms 68:31) and would be one of the nations that would acknowledge Zion as spiritual home (Psalms 87:4–5 King James).

The question then is, in what ways and to what extent did misinterpretations of records contribute to the decline in fortune of Africa? Let us take a quick look on some of the misinterpretations at issue. Remember, all the glowing remarks and references to Africa and Africans in antiquity were in the original Hebrew text, and, over a period of several hundred years, a number of translated versions were produced.

With perhaps the exception of the Jerusalem Bible and the New International Version, which retained the word "Kush" in reference to the whole continent, other versions translated Kush so it only referred to a much diminished area of Africa. For example, the King James and the Revised Standard versions of the Bible translated Kush to "Ethiopia." The Good News Bible translated Kush to the Arabic "Sudan" (of course, both translations essentially mean "land of the black people"). And so it has been for quite some time now; the terms once used in reference to the whole of Africa are now diminished and used in reference to small, specified areas. If such translations had more accurately referred to Africa instead of one or two of its subsets, the more appropriate impressions of Africa and Africans would have prevailed.

Instead, such mistranslations have done incalculable damage, subjectively as well as objectively, to the esteem of present-day Africans, those at home as well as those abroad. In one sense, it has provided the impetus to Caucasian claims and assertions of superiority and greater favor with God, and, in a pernicious manner, it causes Africans who believe such European claims (and they happen to be the vast majority) to resign and to conduct themselves according to what, they believe, is expected of them by divine design.

Such distortions and their negative influences were duly noted by Bishop Alfred Dunston when he remarked, *"The term - Ethiopia' in the English Bible has misled the Christian world for the past three hundred and sixty odd years and it is highly conceivable that a more proper English term identification of the Kushites might have changed the whole European attitude towards chattel slavery of Black people. The myths of savagery, cannibalism and general debasement would have been re-examined had the Bible reflected the fact that the people under the myth were being called Negros' in the Western world. The color and geography of Kushites would have contributed to a better appreciation all around and the most ignorant, rabid racist would not have pretended to doubt the existence of a soul in any man about whom he read in the pages of the Holy Bible."*

It is powerful and breathtaking indeed. If, in the translations, care had been taken so that Kush and Kushites accurately referred to Africa and Africans, then present-day Africans at home and abroad would be duly recognized for the achievements and praiseworthy roles of their ancestors in the Holy Bible. The words of Bishop Dunston made many years ago remain true today.

If most people were blessed with the insight and sensitivity of Bishop Dunston there would have been no need for ideas and institutions so alienating, so divisive; the slave trade, slavery, colonialism, apartheid, and the prevailing neocolonialism would be humanized. It must not go without notice that, by calculation or by sheer coincidence, the mistranslations and misrepresentations of the texts have well served the spiritual and especially the material quests of those who, by commission and omission, made such important errors in the translations. Even if only a small consolation, modern day films-makers and journalists aptly recognize the African among the Three Wise Men who paid homage to the baby Jesus.

We have, I am sure, all noted the effects of errors in the Scripture that support European racist ethos to this day. We saw the myth of the curses—that all Africans are descended from Canaan, the cursed son of Ham and grandson of Noah. A curse reinforced by other curses down through antiquity and well into modern history. Caucasians, on the other hand, are said to have descended from Japhet the favored son of Noah, the son whose descendants received the express blessings of the divine birthright with which Britain and America now control much of the world.

Mainly through the distortions of the translations, the true image of Africans, their achievements and capabilities, and indeed the very blessed nature of Africans were also distorted. In their many and varied presentations, the modern day Bibles—the King James, the Standard, and the New Jerusalem versions—omitted, slanted, or in some way misrepresented African contributions as recorded in the original Hebrew text.

Thus, for the better part of half a millennium, beginning shortly after capitalism had taken firm root in Western Europe, Christian Europeans organized and used the "divine rationale" to conduct themselves with otherwise callous, unabashed, and unapologetic racist ideas and attitudes toward Africans anywhere and everywhere on earth; this conduct persists to this day. Until quite recently, such conduct was encoded in law in many places: from the segregated American South to apartheid South Africa and subtle, more or less, de-facto forms in between.

In whatever form, at whatever level, when such notions and attitudes are manifested, the intended effects are just as profound. During the second half of the second millennium, Africans, those at home as well as those abroad, were constantly told they were essentially inferior and least favored by God and that by divine will were condemned to subjugation and servitude. Think about it for a moment. To be pummeled with such perverse impressions of your very own self, constantly and with, above all things, the ultimate source and for so many generations. It is more than enough to shrivel the spirits and self-confidence of even the most stalwart group of humans.

Such degradation of character and self-worth have far-reaching effects; for, sooner or later, vicious, entrenched sets of self-fulfilling behavior binds the manipulative exploiter and victim to each other in a depraved and inhumane relationship that holds firm for as long as the myth remains true in the minds of both, and therein lies the importance of the biblical mistranslations. It lies squarely in the beliefs of those it tends to lift up and to benefit on one hand, and, on the other, it denigrates and renders defenseless, hopelessly submissive, and exploitable those who such misinterpretations disfavor. The fact that a set of distortions helped bring down and held down an entire race of people is indeed a good measure of its profundity.

Chapter Six

African Disunity

A Major Obstacle to True Freedom

The diabolical dynamics of the biblical mistranslations on Africa and Africans need not be waved more than they should; the point has been well made. As profound as it is, it alone could not have held so great a people so far down for so long. Other factors must have contributed. Simple deduction suggests there is more than what is on record. In the late 1400s, Europeans had just begun their incursions into Africa in search of gold and perhaps other commodities that would fetch handsomely in Europe and make them wealthy.

They obviously encountered Africans in large numbers and before long began to observe and to notice traits of weakness—a divided people, who would not hesitate to take up arms against each other and a people steeped in idolatry with tendencies for narcissistic pride and other forms of arrogance. It stands to reason that African societies having enjoyed long periods of strength and prosperity had become complacent. Productivity had been allowed to decline while African communities submitted to greed, lust, one-upmanship with and hatred of neighbors, and all sorts of behavior true Christian principles would certainly advise against. Such decline in behavior could not have sustained the favor of God for long. Inevitably, the loss of esteem, influence, and power followed. As is usually the case, once the substantive qualities of

Africans were depleted, arrogance, in all its forms, became important redeeming features to hold on to and to cherish.

Narcissistic arrogance is insidious. It only weakens and weakens further. Once it is allowed to take root in society, it nestles and gradually but surely depletes the society of all its productive and survival capacities. Ethical and moral values begin to degenerate. Other social norms gradually become insignificant, and, before long, political and economic endeavors become similarly unimportant. The people, individually and later collectively, become easily submissive to inducements and coercions, less capable of rational and logical negotiations.

They thus become exploitable and increasingly so with time.

In Ezekiel 29:1–16, Egypt and Africa south of Egypt are condemned for the sins of hubris and arrogance of Pharaoh, when Pharaoh boasted and claimed to be "the creator and possessor of the Nile." Egypt and Africa south of Egypt are further condemned for posing as a reliable military power capable of interceding in Judah's favor in her revolt against the Assyrians. The expected help from Africa did not show up. You remember the other example we discussed earlier, some 500 years ago when the emperor of the West African kingdom of Mali stopped in Egypt on his way to Mecca and gave away so much money it created instant inflation in and around Cairo for a considerable length of time. Some historians believe his apparent charity was in fact an arrogant expression; as if to say, "Ours is a richer nation, we have greater blessings and I, Kankan Mansa Musa, am the absolute ruler of that great and wealthy nation."

Really, arrogance in African societies is far more ordinary than the legendary examples I have just given; however, where it is tolerated, it permeates the society at all levels and all its segments. Some 2,000 years beyond the period of the pharaohs and a little over 500 years ago, not long after the period of Emperor Kankan

Mansa Musa when Europeans began to arrive in West Africa, Africans lived largely in feudal and pre feudal societies with traditions inherently based on arrogant assumptions. By the mere accident of birth, one person might be looked up to as "lord" for life, with boundless rights and privileges, even to exact servitude from "less fortunate souls," to have some of the less fortunate castrated for the benefit of his harem or sacrificed to his God; when he "crossed the river" to the other world, a few of the less fortunate must yet be dispatched along to continue to serve him.

When I think back to my elementary school days, some of the stories of the initial African encounters with Europeans sounds like children stories yet some make perfect sense, if only as metaphor. I remember one particular story we were told over and again – that when the Europeans first landed on the shores of West Africa, they were confronted by throngs of natives. Soldiers and civilians stood behind their chiefs at the shore. The Europeans had noticed African strengths and capabilities and had also noticed, to an even greater extent, African weaknesses, particularly, of arrogance. To pass through the human shield, the European leader merely took out a hand mirror and held it to the face of the African chief, the big chief. So elated and intoxicated with his first impression of himself, he instantly obliged the repeated request and granted the Europeans entry to the kingdom, with unlimited access to the storehouse.

Bear in mind these were not European tourists, and they were certainly not romantic adventurers. These were producers and accumulators who had set out in search of capital and raw materials with which to create wealth for self and country. Thus, when the easily seduced African chief broke down from the mere glimpse of his own face and gleefully opened the doors to the communal storehouses, European opportunists only had to plug in their hoses and siphon off Africa's inherent blessings to Europe. It was really that simple.

To keep the flow, all they needed to do was to reinforce African weaknesses of hatred of neighbors, self-centeredness with gifts of guns and gunpowder for Africans to fight and subjugate each other. Europeans gave African chiefs and their house-holds cheap adornments with which to flaunt their superiority. For a few pounds of condiments and a barrel or two of cheap whiskey to the African chiefs, Europeans could—in addition to the stores—also get the storekeepers plus the storekeepers' relatives and friends, and especially the neighbors they loved so to hate. What was not readily available, the African was often all too willing to undertake dangerous excursions to obtain for the Europeans for measly rewards.

Arrogant pride is as insidious today as it was some 2,000 years ago and 500 years ago.

You have heard references to the disease of hypertension as "the silent killer," so too is arrogance; those who suffer from it are not capable of recognizing it, and it can bring a whole society to its knees and hold it down indefinitely. It is not uncommon to meet an African with a PhD in, let us say, agriculture who will, without reservation or hesitation, tell you that he does not do field work, because field work is menial and only fit for those with less academic laurels. With a PhD, he will only engage in occupations that offer comfortable and prestigious trappings - nicely draped, air-conditioned office with a secretary in front. Such impressionable, if even less productive, use of his talent makes far more sense to him.

The late Robert Woodruff, who built Coca Cola into an international company, was known to say quite often, "You can do anything, as long as you don't care who gets the credit for it." Ordinary folks like you and me are not shielded from or immune to the debilitations of arrogance. While the tendency for quick settlement might suggest Africans are easy to please, a more careful observation might reveal something more serious. The African, in fact, might opt for a quick settlement just to get that money quickly in hand to take care of the overdue payment on his SUV, for that lavish 500-guest party for his wife's fortieth birthday, for that new set of clothes, or any manner of consumption that will give his friends and acquaintances the impressions that he is financially successful, that he "has arrived," "made." To the extent he has friends and acquaintances who are all too willing to applaud such charades and masquerades, his determination to strive for and attract true success remains dulled. He might go through life far less productive than he is capable of.

All through Africa, in the West Indies, and in many parts of the American South, Africans are selling off family lands and other real properties for a fraction of their worth just to buy nicer cars, some clothes, or to emigrate to more glamorous communities. What makes it impossible for any intervention is that, generally, such individuals also regard themselves beyond advice and criticisms. In many parts of the Third World, arrogance manifests in many forms. In societies that still have vestiges of the colonial social order, there remain a significant segment that derives and expects extra privileges simply because of their (high) skin color, because of the school they attended, their family name, the dialect they speak or don't speak, or some similarly flimsy and silly quality. In fact you'll find such debased self- valuation in African societies anywhere; on the mother continent, in the Caribbean, and in North America.

Whatever the basis, wherever and in whatever manner it manifests, this and any form of arrogance are abhorrent in the eyes of God; for it stifles the expression of God-given capabilities and virtues. Until recently, there were a number of heads of state who declared themselves rulers for life based on the assumption they alone had all the plans and answers to govern and to develop their societies, much like Pharaoh's boast (Ezekiel 29:1–16).

In spite of some argument against it, I'd much rather see democracy flourish for the simple reason it discourages arrogance. The arrogance of African rulers as such is not limited to exaggerated beliefs in their rights and abilities to rule. Sheer vanity remain a good part of the regimen. In the 1970s, Americans watched live television coverage of the inauguration of President Bokassa of Central Africa Republic (he was crowned Emperor Bokassa). At his inauguration, the "Emperor" rode a chariot drawn by a dozen or so white horses imported from Europe. Even more recent is the case of Uganda's President Yuweri Museveni. When he got the cash money in aid for Uganda, the very first purchase he made was a presidential jet for his convenience. Ghana's President John Kufour's government is said to have borrowed money to build a palace estimated between $80 to $125 million plus two jet planes at additional costs when abject poverty was dancing all around him. Most of the citizens of these countries live on less than $1 a day. How can others take African leaders seriously?

In Africa, the challenge regarding the exercise of democracy is multilayered. Let us say, for example, the opposition party of a country had been banned by the country's "ruler for life" for a number of years. When finally they are allowed into the process, instead of presenting a solidly unified front necessary for victory at the polls, factions quickly develop. They lock themselves in petty squabbles often based on nothing more than what amounts to arrogant petty assumption and assertions. One ethnic clique within the party, regarding itself superior, begins to make inconsiderate senseless claims and demands.

If I have beaten this horse more than I need to it is probably because of the devil I see in arrogance. In my view, it is the most diabolical force that continues to hold Africans down, and I mean Africans everywhere. I do not argue the fact that a sinful heart and the arrogance of imperialism gave Europeans the impetus to descend upon and exploit the already- weakened peoples in Africa. However, I also believe it is not so much what others have done or continue to do to Africans, and it is not so much what others have failed to do and still hesitate to do for Africans. As I see it—prevailing African difficulties—the problem why Africans everywhere are still down is due more to what Africans do or fail to do for self and much of it is based on sheer arrogance.

Yes, I have heard much of the counterarguments, and I agree with some but only to a short extent. I have often been reminded that Africans everywhere are by nature more spiritual than material, so, for example, spiritual rewards such as personal recognition are often more gratifying than equivalent material rewards, I agree. However, there are some manifestations of difficulties that do not lend themselves well to any side of the "spiritual versus material" argument. Please bear with me a bit longer. I will give you just two examples and rest my case, I promise.

In the west end of Atlanta, there is a cluster of predominantly Black colleges. I have asked more than a dozen times why there seems to be no effort to join them all into one large university, each college semiautonomous at most. Each college will continue to offer specialties in particular disciplines, as it is with European universities like Cambridge, The Sorbonne, Barcelona, or even right here in the U.S. Universities like Harvard, Yale, or UCLA which are made up of semiautonomous schools and colleges, some located considerable distances from the rest. Such a union I have always thought would give the university a far greater name recognition and prestige in academics and in sports. Materially, it will attract much greater endowments.

Even greater might be the spiritual rewards if Morris-Brown College, Interdenominational Theological Center (ITC), Clark-Atlanta University, Spelman College, and Morehouse College were united into one solid university. How great would be the academics, the athletics, the endowments, and the prestige of the very name. Just imagine the dynamics of the sound of a new name like Dubois-King University. The mere sound of such a name conjures up images of a glorious past when Africans were living in well-organized kingdoms, building pyramids, and using their knowledge of the higher sciences for medicine and agriculture and to embalm their dead rulers. The additional and synergistic advantages are innumerable: the sharing of resources, greater ability to attract and conduct contract research, greater ability to serve the community beyond the realm of scholastics, more extensive award of scholarships, and a more robust endowment register from a long list of successful alumni.

Every time I posed the question, "Why are the schools in the west end of Atlanta not united?" the answer has nearly always been one of two. The one I get more often is that various church denominations are behind each school, and none is willing to relinquish its hold on its darling affiliate college. To me, born and raised in mother Africa, such explanation sounds all too familiar. I can only interpret it one way. The simpler answer I get sometimes is "it's a black thing.'" This answer remains both an embarrassment and annoyance, for it exposes my lack of awareness. In spite of my pleas nearly each time, no one has shown mercy to explain what exactly "Black thing" means.

Often, I have wondered whether the two explanations are perhaps one and the same, and I have also wondered whether what is described as the churches' hold on their schools is nothing other than sheer tribalism. I was once tempted to call it out loud as such, but I quickly realized where I was and decided to keep my impression to myself. As for the oh-so-secret

"Black thing," my hunches have begun to tell me it too must be African, hidden deep down in the subconscious after all these years of separation. If it is, then it is only half-comforting to know that some common traits still linger to provide an affectionate basis for a future reunion between Africans in the diaspora and those in the motherland.

However, on the equally serious business of unity or the dire lack of it, again, if my hunch is correct, "The Black thing" must be what also prevents African nations from giving up at least partial sovereignty toward the formation of a more powerful union bound to confer greater clout for global negotiations for Africa; for better representation at world bodies and at world forums such as the UN, WTO, and Davos and Porto Alegre; and for the development of viable intra-African markets and institutions. The United States of America and the European Union are clear examples, and so too is the long list of corporate mergers in Europe and America since the 1960s. Obviously, there is enormous strength in unity. Arrogance is said to be the mother of all sins. I happen to be someone who believes that, *"we are not punished for our sins, we are punished by our sins"*. In my view, arrogance in its many forms stands out as the most formidable obstacle to African unity and prosperity. No wonder some of the schools in the West end of Atlanta suffer problems that are otherwise petty.

One of the more frequent arguments or rather rationalizations I have heard from Africans on the mother continent regarding this issue is "Africans are raised in a communal setting so, by maturity, they have developed an aversion for communalism; they have become individualistic," with difficulties banding to form political or commercial unions, such as corporations or enlarged colleges systems. Maybe so, but personally, I have difficulties with this argument too simply because, as I have observed, Africans in America are not raised with nearly the same degree of communalism as those on the mother continent yet; as I have noted, African Americans show higher traits of individualism and at a very early age. Please pardon me if I am wrong, but I simply cannot accept the basis of that "aversion" argument.

What I have observed with African entities in general is they tend either to remain as they started or to go backward with time—backward in the sense they fragment toward their most elemental identities. For example, in 1987 or thereabout, a young African Methodist minister attempted to establish a nondenominational church for all Africans in the north Georgia area. It failed, and, being from the country of Ghana, he carried on and successfully established a church for all Ghanaians in the Atlanta area. By the end of 2006, less than twenty years after it started, the number of African churches in the north Georgia area is estimated at about one hundred. The estimated number of Christian churchgoers in the metro Atlanta African community is about 12,000, some of whom attend mainstream American churches. Also bear in mind that of those that choose to attend predominantly African churches, not all attend church every Sunday, so congregations are all too often very small.

The point I am trying to make is that most of the nearly one hundred African churches are in fact fragments from the one initially established in 1987. Often, the course for the split is not doctrinal. The causes might be as flimsy as tribal/ethnic differences. A group of, let us say, twenty-six suddenly decides they are tired of being preached to in a dialect they are less than comfortable with or the region they are from back in Africa is less than proportionately represented on the church council, and off they split. The fact that their departure might have spiritually and materially weakened the mother church is of no interest or consideration. The fact that, as a small group of working-class membership, they are hence likely to struggle to meet monthly obligations does not faze them either. All that is important to them as they split is that they can now conduct services in self-gratifying trappings; at least members of their tribe will have position.

The renowned Kenyan political scientist, Ali Mazrui, cogently characterized it when he quoted the late President of Tanzania, Julius Nyerere, "While the European is striving to get to the moon and beyond, the African is striving to get back to his village …" where he might get better recognition, quite likely, with title. Like a key, arrogance can open, and it can close doors. Like medicine, it is a tonic; yet it can also poison. It is in every human descended of Adam and Eve (who committed the original sin of arrogance). What separates those who prosper from it and those who perish by it is rather simple. Those who are served by arrogance are those with the ability to recognize traits of negative arrogance and to use their moral and spiritual strengths to suppress its temptations. On the other hand, those, who like Adam, give in to selfish demands do not remain in the garden for long.

There are even greater rewards for those who recognize positive arrogance, such as the pride to do good things and to do each particularly well and to give it all you've got so the end result might be appealing and praiseworthy. The benchmarks of positive arrogance are to present well, to be principled and to treat others with consideration and humility ("Blessed are the meek for they shall inherit the earth."), and to be recognized with respect for positive, selfless contributions. Do not let me tell you, just look around and see what can be and need to be done. Look at it against the backdrop of what Africans have in their possession: the material resources on one side of the dividing river and on the other side a remarkable level of income, a high degree of knowledge, and sophistication. Regrettably, Africans on both sides of the Sargasso Sea are pinned down by their own self-centeredness; they are far more obsessed with individual pursuits than common efforts that could benefit both sides, hasten their progress, and help establish them in their proper positions in the New World Order of global affairs.

Chapter Seven

Hope for Africa

Is the cup half full or half empty?

"I can still remember my first trip to Africa, two decades ago, when my sister's Volkswagen Beetle broke down," said Senator Barack Obama. "When I went back recently, we had better transportation. But there was another difference. While that first trip was about discovering my past, my recent trip was about Africa's future. And it filled me with hope because while significant obstacles remain, I believe we have the chance to build more equitable and just societies so that all people have the chance to control their own destinies." This, my friends, is a quote in the July 2007 issue of *Vanity Fair* magazine.

Some other journals have not seen the light to notice and recognize the promise Africa holds for itself and for all mankind. The earth-shaking caption, "Hopeless Africa," was published at the end of the last millennium, in the May, 2000 issue of *The Economist* magazine. Africans, the world over, still express displeasure over the article and its characterizations. Personally, I was not really shaken by it. Similar, if not worse comments have been uttered and written, much in the same vein since Africa went into decline some 500 years ago. The German philosopher Hegel boldly remarked in one of his thesis that Africa have no reflective history. Such calculated characterizations have no basis in fact, needless to say.

Africa, as we now know, has a rich history from antiquity to the middle ages from which time African societies began to decline by subjecting themselves to self-destructive behavior and attitudes; we touched upon these behaviors and attitudes earlier: the arrogance of greed and lust and the lack of love for neighbors. These are weaknesses that made African societies vulnerable to plunder and exploitation by European accumulators and fortune seekers.

If, by his comment, Hegel sought to imply that African achievements up to the early nineteenth century had not been chronicled to reflect Africa's position in world history and society, he probably had a point, if only to a limited extent. Up until the middle of the nineteenth century, only a few African societies kept written records with perhaps notable exceptions like the kingdoms along the Nile and the largely Muslim-influenced kingdoms that flourished in the West and applied Arabic scholarship to commerce and government. What writers like Hegel failed to recognize was the fact that even where there were no written records, there were, in fact, oral and similar traditions that chronicled significant events and activities in society. Hegel also failed to recognize the disruptive distortions caused by European fortune seekers as they pillaged and plundered their way into Africa; they deprived African societies the human and material resources necessary to safeguard the very institutions that provided custody for Africa's history.

Hegel's conclusions are rather a reflection of the general tendency to indolently project rather than to make more careful observations. We, in this day and age, have no basis to make such mistakes; for, in spite of the centuries of disruptions and distortions, Africa is still there, with the longest history of mankind on earth. We also must be careful in our judgment of declarations like Hegel's. With his characterization of Africans, Hegel probably merely sought to express a personal opinion that Africans have no conscious, organized recollection of trends in their past and therefore are deprived of necessary references and bearings to inspire and to guide their future and to effectively manage progress for their benefit. I, too, must be careful and must quickly back off from such rationalization; for it also tends to justify prevailing European notions that Africa is too rich and has too much to offer to be left in the hands of Africans (with their inferior management skills and zeal).

This notion is expressed in more or less subtle terms by other acclaimed European thinkers around Hegel's time, in Europe as in the New World; Emmanuel Kant and David Hume expressed similar impressions. So too did Thomas Jefferson, perhaps one of the more distinguished thinkers among the Founding Fathers of America. He is on record to have said of his slaves, "It appears to me that in memory they are equal to whites. In reason, much inferior and in imagination they are dull, tasteless and anomalous."(www.Trivia- Library.com). Such impressions linger, though perhaps well contained and disguised. We cited earlier, *The Economist's* reference to futile attempts at development and to frequent conflicts in Africa as justification to characterize the future of the entire continent and its peoples as "hopeless." Such rash judgment fails to also point out that in fact nearly all the major conflicts in Africa since about the seventeenth century have been started and waged by Europeans, waged on behalf of Europeans, or at least fueled tacitly by Europeans in pursuit of European interests. In other words, Europeans have nearly always been the aggressors, in fact or by proxy, or have fanned the flames of "African on African" conflicts for European gains and advantages.

The list of examples Africans refer to when making this argument is indeed long and include: The campaigns of British military adventurers under the command of Gordon and later

Kitchener in the Sudan; the Zulu wars that resulted from European encroachment on African lands; Cecil Rhodes' rogue aggressions against Bantu communities; The Yaa Asentewaa War of the Gold Coast that was prompted by Baden Powell (founder of the Boy Scout movement) when Ashanti refused to give gold exacted by Britain; the Boer Wars of South Africa; Mussolini's Italian imperialist aggression against Ethiopia, supported by other European colonial powers.

More recent examples of such conflict provoked and spiked by external hands include the Congo crisis between America and her proxy European nations of Belgium, Britain, and France on one side against the Soviet Bloc for control of strategic supplies; land grab schemes in the European settler states of East, Central, and especially southern Africa; the atrocities of European-backed rebel groups: União Nacional para a Independência Total de Angola (UNITA) in Angola and Resistência Nacional Moçambicana (RENAMO) in Mozambique; the Biafra conflict in Nigeria; the displacements of people and destruction of arable lands and fishing grounds by European oil companies pumping in the delta areas of Nigeria; the conflict between Nigeria and Cameroon over Bakassi Island; the decade-long conflicts in Chad, Liberia, and the Ivory Coast; the war between Ethiopia and Somalia; and the callous evacuation of the inhabitants of the island of Diago Garcia. The list is endless; we could go on and on. If *The Economist* is incapable of recognizing European hands—the invisible or the obvious—in all these conflicts, Africans certainly do.

Africans recognize both the absurdity and the irony of *The Economist's* characterization. Europe withstood the devastations of the bubonic plague; years of Napoleonic wars; two great wars among themselves; followed since 1945 by forty plus years of authoritarian and totalitarian despotic rule left and right and yet is able to form and advance the European Union (EU) and to establish some of the strongest economies in the world today. If that could happen for Europe, then Africa's chances are just as good, at least just as hopeful.

Before we allow ourselves to be all worked up and fuming by Hegel and *The Economist*, let us attempt to look at their remarks in broader, perhaps more rational terms. We must bear in mind it was the same Hegel who in one fell swoop provided the logical definitive expressions and the basis for both fascism and communism; these are two diametrically opposite ideologies, one on the far right and the other on the far left; yet, both were rational and logical. Perhaps, in that paradox, within that contradiction, lies the actionable hope that could help set the framework and propel Africa's recovery efforts forward. I am sure you are with me so far. By accurately determining where Africa is at this point in contrast to where it should be at this point in its development agenda, Africa might be better able to formulate logical plans with pragmatic strategies and tactics to help the continent catch up, much like China, much like India, and perhaps to some extent Russia, Germany, Singapore, Brazil, and Chile.

Those not so blessed with a positive mind-set can only see the gloom and doom in Africa and declare it "hopeless." Others see those same conditions against the backdrop of vast, yet untapped, human as well as natural resources and see a continent full of hope; the continent's estimated mineral reserves alone is in the trillions of dollars. They see that indeed Africa can well be helped to renew its strengths, reorganize its history, and to set and manage its own agenda for a better future, "The rational is real", Hagel will argue. Why else would an honorable person like the well-respected former Speaker of the U.S. House, Dr. Newt Gingrich, work so hard for a PhD in history with concentration on African history? Why would two sitting American presidents visit Africa three times within a time frame of less than four years and the subsequent congressional delegations that included notables like the current Speaker of the House Nancy Pelosi and the highly influential Republican representative Jack Kemp of New York? The Mormon Church (of Latter Day Saints) have established themselves firmly in Africa, not merely to evangelize; they are investing well in Africa's economy.

To remind you again, Africa's total landmass is some eleven and a half million square miles, more than three times the size of the forty-eight contiguous states of America. If, as some believe, there is a metaphysical aura around the very geography of Africa, it might lie, at least in part, in the fact that the continent is set at the very center of the world map (according to Marketer's Projection). The two main geometric coordinates, the latitudinal equator and the longitudinal prime (Greenwich) meridian, intersect in Africa.

Below the metaphysics, underground, is where Africa's material potentials abound, and the list of blessings is innumerable. Africa has the bulk of the world's deposits of precious, strategic, and industrial minerals, which includes about half of the world's diamonds and gold, an estimated 90 percent of the world's phosphates, and about 10 percent of petroleum and natural gas. There are also chromium, iron ore, bauxite, copper, cobalt, and manganese, about 80 percent of the world's titanium. Most in demand is the substance coltan (columbite-tantalite), a metal found in the Congo DR and essentially used in cell phones, laptop computers, and pagers. It provides sustenance for desperate African peasants. It funds rebel activities and produces wealth for European, American, and Israeli intermediaries and petty brokers. Fighting over access and control over such industrial and strategic minerals has caused the lives of millions of Africans in the Congo and elsewhere on the continent over the past several years. The list of industrial mineral deposits in Africa is indeed long and worth tens of trillions of dollars in current valuation.

Above ground, there is yet another set of boundless blessings to speak of. Africa has millions of acres of arable and pastoral lands, about 40 percent of the world's hydroelectric potential. The Congo River basin alone has a hydraulic energy capacity of some six hundred and fifty billion kilowatt hours per year in reserve, which equals approximately two-thirds of total global capacity.

And speaking of history, Africa has the longest history of the human race. Louis Leakey's and subsequent discoveries of fossilized remains of the predecessors of man in the East African rift valley confirm that Africa is, in fact, the origin of all mankind and the place where man's efforts toward civilization began. More recent studies on the human genome strongly support this realization. Thus, history irrefutably holds Africa as the place from where the human race and all its cultures evolved. We can only conclude, therefore, that recent remarks suggesting that Africa had no history and thus has a hopeless future are likely the reflection of a conspiracy of three interrelated mental errors and disinformation:

    a)   Disruption of Africa's logical development

    b)   Distortions of its recorded achievements

    c)   Tendencies on the part of non-African observers to project their distorted points of view, biases, and limitations rather than to exercise due diligence in researching the truth.

What Africa and its people need to do at this point in its history, is to forgive all those who have conspired and contributed to the degradation of its essence and character. Africa must take it upon itself to reconstruct its history on a factual and logical basis and to plan for the more important periods: those ahead, a future in which its people will offer opportunities for higher standards of living, not only to Africans but to the global family at large.

At present, Africa produces about 70 percent of the world's cocoa and about 40 percent of coffee, palm oil, and other forest products. The production of these revenue- earning commodities can be increased, at least their global market shares maintained, while new products with potential for both domestic as well as global markets are investigated and developed. Africa can and must improve its economic output and in ways that will improve the consumption propensities of its people. We must recognize that in the fast-approaching trends of globalization, the bolts and nuts of the process will be economics, capitalism—pure and simple. Cross-border investment, trade, labor, and political movements are already in progress and will all be driven by the forces of capitalism.

Most Africans I have talked to do not seem bothered by the notion of globalization or by the forms it will take; the very idea seems to excite most. What many Africans ponder is the quality toward the end of the process. Is it likely to quell much of Africa's ill or will it, like the slave trade, colonialism, and neocolonialism, further marginalize and render Africans only suitable for more sophisticated and disguised forms of exploitations?

Global capitalism can produce prosperity, no doubt. It can lower poverty and much of its attendant social ills. To achieve such ideals, however, the approaches must be well planned and well implemented with sincerity and prudent calculations. Nothing can be left to whim or to chance. Such planned approaches must include skills development, infrastructure development, intra-African as well as external trade initiatives, with considerate and sincere protocols for fair distribution of opportunities in addition to fairer income distribution regimes that reflect built-in safety nets. Without such considerations, African countries might well remain on the margins in spite of the continent's vast potential. These prospects offer no guarantee to Africa or to any of its potential trade partners, not even the United States. That withstanding, such prospects can and must be realized.

Former President Bill Clinton realizes this vast potential and recognized further that every gain must be earned. When he took office in January 1993, trade as well as budget deficits were at their worst. Consumer and corporate debt were at record highs, and equally dismal were the figures on the rate of savings, personal investments, and productivity. Income and wealth disparity had widened in the face of rising expectations, giving rise to widespread scams and outright corruption, homelessness, and vice. Mr. Clinton's administration approached the decline in the economy with intent to renew attitudes toward and to revise policy on trade. Turning the deficits around was all well and good, but to really be good, the benefits must reach the pockets of the average American. High-profile social programs like

"Welfare to Work" are fantastic only if participants are paid livable wages.

The trick here lies mainly in trade, especially consumer trade. Trade in consumer goods is, without argument, the economic lifeblood of any society. It is estimated that in the United States, for every one billion dollars worth of consumer goods exported, about 20,000 jobs are created and maintained.

With this in mind, the Clinton administration sought to liberalize trade, along the terms of the General Agreements on Tariffs and Trade (GATT) / Uruguay round. With reasonably high expectations, the administration promised reduction in the trade deficit to the tune of about $60 billion over ten years. This translated to increases of almost $2,000 per year in family income. Against expectations, the trade deficit worsened—from $105 billion in 1994 to a $140 billion in 1997 with no signs of reversal. In 1998, four years after GATT, new guidelines under the newly formed WTO were adopted as the deficit continued to climb to

$116 billion. It became obvious that to reverse such an unstoppable decline, a reduction in the trade deficit to the tune of about $12 billion a year was necessary. At the end of 2006, the total national budget was about 70 percent of the GDP, a record high.

In fact, exports were on the rise, but it was mostly due to the export of high-end capital goods such as airplanes, military hardware, oil rigs, and spare parts for refineries, such that much of the profits were going to shareholders and not to workers, who are the real spenders in the general economy. Certainly, there is nothing wrong with shareholders getting good dividends. The problem is there are far more wage earners than shareholders, such that significant increases in wages do a lot more for most people and for the economy in general.

If the trade deficit must be reduced to bearable levels, the thrust for exports must be shifted to consumer goods, particularly durable consumer goods such as appliances, automobile spare parts, power tools and gadgets, and goods made up of different parts and put together with a lot of fairly well-paid man-hours. During 1998, of the total U.S. exports to Africa, consumer goods accounted for only 12 percent of the dollar volume, and of that ratio only a tiny fraction was made up of durable goods. That is not good.

With an estimated population of over a billion, Africa should represent a vast market for American companies from General Motors to General Electric and Harley-Davidson motorcycles, Clear Essence Cosmetics to *Essence* magazine, from Marriot Hotels to Six Flags, and the thousands of others in between. Africa should offer a strong market for these companies to sell appliances and other consumer goods and services, earning lots of money for American shareholders as well as wage earners. The unfortunate reality is most people in Africa simply cannot afford such goods as much as they need and want them. At years end 2004, the rate of poverty in Africa, in absolute terms, was between 55 and 60 percent. Now, to make the math simple, let us just use a ratio of 50 percent, that is half of all Africans in Africa live in poverty (less than $2 purchasing power parity), unable to meet the basic requirements of everyday living of at least providing two meals a day for each member of a family of five; not able to provide for local transportation and not enough money to send the kids to school, at least not all at the same time. Now, 50 percent of, let us call it, a billion is about 500 million. That is about the population of the whole of North and Central America combined. In actual fact, the number of people living in Africa in abject poverty is more than the entire population of Canada, the U.S., Mexico, plus the seven Central American republics.

You might be saying to yourself, "But it's the same difference here in America." I can well understand why you might think so, especially if the balance on your bank account plus the balance on your charge accounts equals anything like mine. But, trust me, my friend; it is nowhere nearly the same. When we speak of poverty in Africa, we speak mostly of abject poverty. It is perhaps the lowest form of poverty in which most of the poor do not even have two cents to rub against each other most of the time; what a shame. Can you imagine if all these people had some money and could buy lots of American-made goods? Yes, you are right; it is not all that simple, and that is the unfortunate truth.

But God being merciful, the dire conditions of poverty in Africa, which deprive America of a crucial trade partner, can be reversed to significantly favorable levels and in reasonable time, possible if not likely, in our lifetime. America is most capable of providing the necessary catalyst in the form of debt cancellation, technology transfer, and loans for small business start-ups. Africa's poor—presently only capable of small-scale production such as crafts, art, gathering of forest products, and small-scale cultivation—will begin to accumulate material wealth, primitive at first; however, as more markets open to them locally and beyond, they will undoubtedly strive to produce at levels that will afford them higher propensity for consumption.

America can provide additional help to the African poor by extending preferences to African-made consumer goods and eliminating quotas, tariffs, especially escalating tariffs, and the other trade barriers so as to grant freer access of African-made goods into American markets. The ripple effects are bound to be far reaching. A most comforting fact is Africans will not need such help forever and ever. As the African poor continue to produce and sell their primitive wares, their propensity to save will increase, savings that might be pooled to provide capital for further and bigger investments. As the population grows and as production and consumption and savings and education rise, in five, ten, twenty years, perhaps sooner rather than later, a layer of society will emerge—a class in the middle, no longer poor even if not exactly wealthy.

Better informed, with cultivated tastes and habits, the middle class will indulge in sophisticated consumption. They will often prefer to read *Ebony*, *Time* magazine, *People*, and *O*. They will prefer Clear Essence and Mary Kay cosmetic products and use General Electric appliances in every room in the house, no more of those off-brands from elsewhere. They will prefer to ride Harley-Davidson bikes and drive well-made Ford, General Motors, and Chrysler cars. When they fly to North America, which will likely be often, many will fly Delta and its code-share partners. Now, let us stop and look at the picture for a minute and ask ourselves the obvious question. Who stands to gain the most in such civilized symbiosis, the African poor or American businesses? I'll make you the judge!

Trade by its very definition is an interaction, a two-way proposition of one's supply and another's demands. For Africans to be able to buy American to appreciable extent, Americans must be willing to buy African so that Africa's growth could, in effect, translate to opportunities for American producers and vendors. Opportunities for higher volumes of American exports could create more employment and offer livable wages, handsome dividends, and, yes, taxes for the various levels of government. Opportunities that could lower the trade deficit with ripple effects that could help curb social ills.

At the end of 2001, the beginning of this, the third millennium, America was buying about $16 billion worth of goods a year from Africa, mostly petroleum and minerals. The problem is, what Africa earns from sales to the U.S. goes to pay down the interests on loans forced on African countries by Western institutions, including the International Monetary Fund (IMF) and the World Bank. A significant portion of the remainder ends up in the private banks accounts of rogue African officials. The small fraction that remains, what is spent for Africans, is likely spent on low-priority demands of marginal relevance. What actually benefits African societies as a whole is not much to speak of. So African governments continue to present themselves and those they represent as beggars, when in fact they earn enough to take care of the people's needs and can do so with self-respect and dignity.

If, at this point, you are not quite convinced that something positive and massive, perhaps even dramatic, ought to be done to give Africa a hand up, I will guess you are probably well informed, but need to learn more. Quite likely, you are also wondering why America must go through such strenuous efforts to redress its trade imbalance and in order to give its people a bit more to live on when there are other regions, other emerging economies far advanced and far better prepared to consume American manufactured goods. You are right—Russia, China, India, Pakistan, Indonesia, Malaysia, Brazil, Mexico, Australia, New Zealand, and Eastern

Europe. Together, they offer an appreciably higher capacity to consume and therefore a much larger ready market than Africa.

The bad news is equally simple. Most of these emerging regions also have the capacity to substitute. Whatever they need to import, they can make it themselves. Africa thus stands as the only region, the only large potential market, for American-made goods and services, that does not yet have such capacity and likely will not for quite some time. In this respect, Africa alone has the potential market that might continue to buy American-made consumer goods and services in significant volumes well beyond the foreseeable future.

Realizing such prospects, the Clinton administration's quest and overtures to increase trade with Africa were indeed very sound. It also expressed hope for the continent. Since the year 2000, a number of American celebrities have also demonstrated recognition of this fact and have visited Africa. The list is long. It includes Alicia Keys, Chris Rock, Chris Tucker, Will Smith, Spike Lee, Don Cheedle, and Reverend T. D. Jakes. Isaac Hayes has built a school in Ghana. Oprah Winfrey has built a forty million dollar school for impoverished girls in South Africa. One might well argue that these noble Americans are driven by a sentimental connection with the motherland.

If so, what would you say about those who have no such sentimental attachment but have visited Africa recently? Can you really apply such reason to the interests of Nancy Pelosi, to New York representative Jack Kemp or to the interest of Dr. Newt Gingrich in Africa? These examples point to a trend driven by more than mere sentiment. I am sure you have also heard and read about the contributions of Angelina Jolie and Brad Pitt as well as Madonna. George Clooney has visited and expressed concerns about conditions and events. So too has the world's richest couple, Bill and Melinda Gates. So ask yourself, what is it these people from Capitol Hill, Beverly Hills, and other high places see that you and I do not yet see? Is it because they work and sleep in such lofty places that they can see farther than you and me? Quite likely, they simply see plenty of hope in Africa for Africa and the world—hope, which when realized, will also translate into profound advantages and opportunities for America and Americans. Their insights are well founded.

Just take, for example, the American film industry. Each year since 2003, Hollywood has produced about two to three major films about Africa: *The Constant Gardener*, *Hotel Rwanda*, and *The Last King of Scotland*. These productions have made money for the producers, and, equally important, they have given award-winning job opportunities to American actors, actresses, and production crews, and this is even before any serious business exchanges have begun. If others can see this, why can't you and I?

Chapter Eight

The First Overture

In C Major

What Africa needs most at this point is precisely what Europe got when it needed it, after the Second World War—a Marshall Plan-like outreach, marshaled with good faith and Christian charity. General George Marshall looked at the vast devastation Europeans had inflicted on each other and saw, not hopelessness but the phoenix of hope and renaissance. There was the need then to thwart the threat of a communist takeover of Western Europe by economic means. Africa faces similar threats today. Left to its current state and trends, even sinister organizations like al-Qaida will likely sway away Africa's peasants. General Marshall then convinced his boss, President Truman to ask congress for a $13 billion (approximately 200 billion dollars today) aid package to bail out and rebuild Europe. He got it. Much of the money was spent right here in America to buy the food and materials needed for the rebuilding programs.

The example of the Marshall Plan for Europe is by no means an isolated one. Look at Southeast Asia; less than three decades ago, nearly all the economies of the region were in a rather similar disposition as those in Africa are today. However, a positive, proactive, and preemptive outreach, with investments and market concessions similar in spirit to the Marshall Plan, gave Southeast Asia a success story to write about. So, too, can Africa.

Personally, I do not worry so much about the intensions behind the offers of help as long as it includes fair and equitable returns for Africa and for Africans in the long as well as in the short run. The future of Africa is very hopeful indeed. Do not allow yourself to be discouraged by *The Economist* or by anyone else. The dire profile and conditions they speak about are nothing more than the lower of the two halves of Africa's dynamic paradox—so rich yet so poor. Africa is poor mainly due to the vast wealth that for centuries has attracted relentless manipulations and exploitations from outsiders. Thus, Africa's blessings have also been its curse throughout its long history.

While most of us know about the exploitations, not many know about the subtle and not so subtle manipulations, betrayals, and hypocrisies. Where was the Western press when African leaders were looting African treasuries and emptying African coffers to stash in Europe and America? Monies much needed for Africa's development were diverted to the advantage of European and American financial markets. That was a time when such journals, if they were truly concerned, should have launched investigative campaigns to expose and forestall the drainage of Africa's vital assets.

The Africa Growth and Opportunity Act passed Congress in the final year of the second millennium with bipartisan support. President Bill Clinton, the latest of the liberal international U.S. presidents, signed it into law and then went on a second official visit to Africa. He actually visited Africa twice during the second half of his eight-year tenure. The first was in August 1997, when he visited six sub-Saharan African states, accompanied by his wife who had visited Africa by herself two years earlier. I remember making the remark to a friend that the very spirit of the Clintons' intentions reminded me of the metaphor of the shoe salesmen who was sent to Africa to sell shoes and accessories. On arrival, the salesman noticed all the locals walking around barefooted, and, right on the spot, he saw millions of dollars for himself and for his company. He returned to America years later, a wealthy man having sold hundreds of thousands of pairs of shoes. He could very well, with the classic attitude of the Hegelian right, declared the situation hopeless "Why did you send me here? It's a waste of my precious time; these people don't even wear shoes," he could very well have said, turned around, and returned to "civilization".

The Clintons stopped in Ghana, Uganda, Rwanda, South Africa, Botswana, and Senegal. In Ghana, they were greeted by a throng at the center of the capital where he spoke to an inspired crowd. He urged action instead of despair; he spoke of an African renaissance beginning at the turn of the new millennium and of reconciliation instead of recrimination. He spoke of new partnerships between America and Africa, and he surely did not fail to recognize the "motion of destiny" campaign launched by Ghana's first president, Kwame Nkrumah. Historically, the "motion of destiny" is the forerunner and the present-day counterpart of the Africa Growth and Opportunity Act. www.tradewatch.org

From Ghana, the Clintons went to east central and then on to southern Africa, at every stop affirming with a fervent liberal international spirit America's new commitment to Africa and to the establishment of new levels of goodwill. On the final leg of his trip, in Senegal, Mr. Clinton deemed it necessary and proper to apologize to Africans for America's involvements in slavery and the slave trade. The words of recognition of wrong resonated well with Africans on both sides of the Atlantic. It would sound rather fickle, if not outright silly, for me or anyone else to say, even in jest, that Mr. Clinton's inspired vision is driven by the fact that he is from a town called Hope. Mr. Clinton's recognition of hope for Africa, in my personal view, is based on his understanding and rational appreciation of the logic of history, pure and simple.

Two years after his first trip, Mr. Clinton was back in Africa for a second visit. He arrived in Nigeria on August 26, 2000, where among other initiatives and pledges, he also promised higher financial assistance and other forms of help to develop Nigeria's entrepreneurial capacities. In a speech just before he departed, Mr. Clinton declared, "The world needs Nigeria to succeed; indeed, the world needs Africa to succeed." Such overture, even if ultimately calculated for America's benefit, also promised rational benefits for Africa. It was as visionary as it was inspiring. It was positive, proactive, and preemptive. For its part, Africa must, for its sake and for the sake of the world at large, position itself firmly on the rational side of the Hegelian dialectic, rejecting all vain and superstitious notions of irreversible doom and gloom. In the question of hope for Africa, the real is not rational.

Africa must seek to build bridges for its people to connect those at home with those in the diaspora. It must seek to build bridges with those who can and will help initiate the much- needed and awaited renaissance with offers in areas such as technology transfer, infrastructure development, and agribusiness. In addition, it must seek to do so in ways that will not only spark but will continue to catalyze desirable growth rates that will give the African poor a solid basis for recurring incomes that enable participation in the global economy. In short, the overarching goal of the first wave of the African renaissance must be economic opportunities aimed directly at reduction of poverty.

America, far more than any other country in the world, has the most to offer Africa. America certainly has more to offer Africa than does Europe in spite of Europe's physical proximity and recent colonial relations. By year 2010, most parts of Africa is a mere four- to eight-hour direct flight from most parts of America, a mere hop over the Sargasso

Sea. Consider also the fact that a significantly large number of African nationals are sojourned in North America, and, of course, the fact that America is indeed the primary home to some forty million direct descendants of Africans, descendants of Africa in whom a latent and burning desire to reconnect with Africa, if only for visits, still churns with affection. This is powerful fact. These factors certainly make America stand out as the most logical prime partner for Africa's restoration agenda.

Chapter Nine

Is Kinship Significant?

Like their kin across the Sargasso Sea in the motherland, African-Americans too have a compelling need and desire to free themselves from the traps of relative poverty. It has been quite some time now since most African nations gained independence from colonialism and about the same time since the civil rights and voting rights bills were signed for the benefit of Africans in America. Is this just an interesting coincidence? Since these attainments, most Africans on both sides of the Sargasso sea have lived in poverty—unable to meet basic needs and unable to participate significantly in their local economies. The frequent reference to poverty as a trap suggests that poverty can be escaped. Indeed, it is not a permanent condition. For any plan to succeed in eradicating or reducing poverty, a high level of awareness is required by all, including the poor. Such plans must, of course, offer opportunities with more equitable forms of income distribution.

At the end of 2003, general unemployment in America registered at about 7.1 percent, while unemployment among African Americans was about 12 percent (according to U.S. Bureau of Labor Statistics data), a population of over forty million. That translates to about five million registered unemployed; larger than the entire population of some countries in Africa and certainly some in Europe, Asia, and Central America. Yet, there is a bright side that must be recognized and put to use. Employed African Americans have a total net worth of over $1 trillion, according to recent factoid published in the *American Human Development*

Project and *Wikipedia Encyclopedia*. - Here is an obvious opportunity that, if well recognized with plans to harness its offers, could help eradicate poverty on both sides of the Sargasso Sea, at least reduce it significantly. A $1 trillion plus net worth is more than most countries can boast of.

Can you imagine the dynamics of such spending power if duly recognized and prudently organized and directed? If even a fraction of it was spent in Africa for consumption of leisure on some of what the African poor have to offer, such as crafts, arts, music and similar commodities. Some of the money could be invested in small to midsize businesses. In turn, African institutions, as well as individuals, would be able to offer contracts to African-American vendors and service providers and to patronize mostly African- American businesses when they travel to America.

In a sense, this is like the story of Moses, as he led the Israelites as they sought to cross the sea to the Promised Land. Moses did not even realize the staff with which to part the sea was already firmly in his hand. On any given Friday night, Saturday night, Sunday morning or late morning, go to any of the hospitality businesses on the north side of the Atlanta metro area—the night clubs, restaurants, hotels and motels, and even the retail shops—owned and operated by non-African-Americans. They are all packed with African American patrons, while, on the south side of town where African-Americans live and manage businesses, African American business owners clamor and pray for just enough volume of business to enable them to meet operation overhead and have some money left to build up their business and, if very lucky, a little bit for themselves. I will leave this issue right here and allow you to take it to its logical conclusion.

At the turn of this millennium, the U.S. national debt was estimated at $6 trillion. In his first speech to congress, on February

27, 2001, President George W. Bush projected an economic growth of 4 percent a year over the following ten years, which, if realized, would produce enough of a surplus to reduce the national debt by some two trillion. At the same time, the president announced a tax cut to the tune of almost $2 trillion over the same ten-year period. In late spring that year, after much haggling over the issue, Congress approved a $1.3 trillion tax cut. Many economists remain far less than optimistic, not sure whether the projections are indeed attainable (United States National Debt: An analysis of the Presidents who are Responsible for the Borrowing).

For starters, a four percent growth rate over ten years is not more reliable than what it is, a projection. It offers no guarantees. Even multiple reductions in interest rates might not be as helpful as expected. Additionally, considering the $1.3 trillion tax cut, the margin of the surplus that must be realized from the four percent growth rate must be large enough to cover the $2 trillion proposed debt relief. There are no strong indications it will be enough. Even the stated goals and objectives raise interesting questions. If the cuts and reduction are to stimulate the economy by increasing capital acquisitions for investments, how profitable will it be to the producer if there are not enough people with enough money to patronize the increases in production? The need to balance investments with market potential cannot be ignored. In March 2001, consumer debt was reported at over $7 trillion (wsjclassroom.com). By January 2002, Wall Street was revealing its hidden weaknesses. Between February 2002 and the end of the following summer, the Federal Reserve cut interest rates about nine times.

The cuts mainly benefited the service sector, particularly real estate sales (www.federalreserve.gov). It did not help manufacturing and other productive sectors of the US economy, according to journal reports.

(www.abc.net.au/businessbreakfast/content/2002)

What is happening is that the large markets and potential markets for American goods in Europe, Asia, and South America are themselves putting out products similar to what America wants to sell them. In fact, some even go to the extent of pirating American inventions and creations and then produce and sell them on the world's black market.

If only America makes the conscious efforts to help Africa restore itself with debt cancellation, investments in manufacturing and similarly dynamic offers, by the year 2010— certainly no longer than the year 2025—much of the over 500 million African poor will have acquired the capacity for significant consumption of all sorts of American-made goods. This will inevitably translate into opportunities for exports of goods and services for Americans in general and particularly to African American producers and service providers. The win/win equation is so simple to see, as if on a chalkboard: African growth = American opportunities.

There is a rather pervasive suspicion among Africans that a powerful segment of America—mostly in the higher levels of industry, commerce, and government—imagines and fears that a developed and restored Africa will challenge American interests and compete with Americans for global opportunities. If such fears really exist at such quarters and levels of American society, then we might also believe rumors or at least suspect that there are invisible hands holding back American help to Africa. Personally, I think the world's supply is much too vast to worry about competition to such extent. Secondly, and more importantly, whether a restored Africa becomes a competitor and an adversary or becomes a friend and a partner depends largely on the choices America makes in its relation with Africa, now and in the years leading up to the end stage of Africa's recovery agenda. In more precise terms, it is entirely up to America—it might choose to help

Africa up and waltz into the sunset with a newly found partner or continue to measure and to marginalize its offers and one day feel compelled to march against Africa or be marched against by Africa. Those who allow their imaginations to be saddled with such vain fears will inevitably side with the right of Hegel and rationalize their position with the idea that Africa is what it is by destiny and must therefore remain so.

Personally, I have no worry about such notions especially when they seem confined to the higher circles of government. My trust is more in the ordinary American. America is best known around the world as the bearer of certain principles and ideals, the sort of principles and ideals that rejected slavery and the slave trade. These are the very same principles and ideals that marshaled America's might and popular will against fascism and communism and against segregation in the American south and apartheid in South Africa, the same principles and ideals that continue to uphold freedom of expression and to promote free trade. Such is the spirit of most ordinary informed Americans who, like the metaphoric young, positive- minded shoe salesman outside civilization, saw the locals as they are and chose to recognize the subtle yet profound prospect. Similarly, those who see Africa and recognize that it can be restored so that its people are able to contribute to better trade relations, to good governance and by extension, to world peace.

Henceforth, their position must be championed even more vigorously by liberal international advocates. As for those on the right who seek the vital interests of America, they must realize that for the sake of future trade and other relations between America and Africa, genuine offers of help for Africa, at least initially, are good and necessary, for they will inevitably accrue in favor of America. The Joseph Project which was launched in Ghana in the summer of 2007 is to formally reunite the motherland with its diaspora. With the more than $1 trillion a year in the hands of the African diaspora and the vast resources that remain in the motherland, the two sides together hold firmly in hand, the staff with which to part the water of the Sargasso Sea, to a glorious future.

Chapter Ten

Old Approaches to New Challenges

Referred to by its congressional supporters as the Africa Act and popularly as AGOA, the Africa Growth and Opportunity Act is crafted to lower American trade barriers to commodities from Africa. Before we go any further, let me say I do not see the need to make the reference sub-Saharan Africa, as if to separate one part of Africa from the whole. It only helps to support African suspicions of the age-old divide-and-rule approach to Africa. In order not to confuse you and perhaps myself, I would give in and just go along with the formal language of the document, much as I dislike the very notions of "sub-Sahara Africa."

With the introduction of AGOA, both the U.S. Congress and the administration recognized the importance of a developed Africa to America's economic future. The goal of the Africa Act, therefore, was to set the stage with the following measures:

a) Reduce tariffs and non-tariff barriers to African products entering U.S. markets.
b) Extend U.S. assistance to the sub-Saharan Africa region.
c) Expand and strengthen the African private sector with a bias toward women- owned businesses.
d) Demand, according to the provisions of the AGOA, a U.S.–Africa trade and investment partnership.
e) Increase support for development assistance to African countries attempting to build civil society with accountability and economic reforms.

f) Guide the process forward. The Africa Act calls for a U.S.–Africa annual forum at the ministerial level to discuss and review prevailing trade policies.

g) Eliminate quotas on textiles and apparel from qualified African countries and grant duty-free status for certain products from Africa currently excluded from the list of goods readily allowed into the United States, which is called the generalized system of preference. Such extension of preference must be for ten years.

h) Eradicate or reduce—at least in principle as the Africa Act aims to do— poverty in sub-Saharan Africa, and, instead, establish a strong basis upon which a viable consumer society can be established.

i) Help facilitate these initiatives by directing, according to the act, the Overseas Private Investment Corporation (OPIC) to create $150 million equity fund and a $500 million infrastructure development fund for Africa. OPIC and its sister bank, the Export-Import (Ex-Im) Bank, must have on their boards individuals with extensive private sector experience in Africa. www.tradewatch.org, www.agoa.gov/, www.mbita.org/africa/conference.html

Initial impressions about the Africa Act were quite comforting. At least, it was the very first U.S. trade bill on Africa. More importantly, it was the first official U.S. government recognition of the need to reduce poverty in Africa and set the continent on a short course to its much-needed and much-anticipated renaissance. In a broader global perspective, it is also very historic for several plans for the development of Africa preceding the Africa Act.

The French School of Hygienists, along with a number of mining companies in South Africa, went to great lengths to establish norms for good nutrition, housing, and leisure to improve productivity of African miners. Also, as we referred to earlier in this discussion, the British colonial governor Frederick Guggisberg in the Gold Coast (now Ghana) commissioned noble plans to start developments. Cecil Rhode ("baron of east and southern Africa and monarch of all he surveyed" in Africa) also held the grand vision to develop a highway from the Cape in South Africa all the way to Cairo, Egypt. Noble as these plans were, they all remained nothing more than plans for the most part.

Since independence in the early 1960s, African countries and leaders have continued the efforts, individually and collectively establishing at least broad outlines for developments: The Lome Convention and the Lagos Plan of Action are but two such examples of expression of broad intent for development of Africa. None has produced any significant, discernible results as yet.

AGOA (the Africa Act) for a while at least, seemed different. It seemed broad-based and insightful with charitable offers of opportunity for economic growth for Africa and benefits that will also favor American producers. Without argument, trade is the most viable engine for Africa's growth and prosperity. Trade is the economic lifeblood of any human society. However, it is an engine that must be operated with tact, sincerity, and true consideration if it must serve both sides fully.

Before its passage, as a bill passing through the house, AGOA raised many worrisome questions. Who really stood to gain the most from the AGOA: the poor in Africa and the ordinary American worker or wealthy American companies and their Asian partners? There were worries over implementation strategies: whether they would be comprehensive, cohesive, and viable enough. Everyone hoped that those who would enable and guide the process forward would see the need to first focus all efforts on getting Africa off the ground. After all, doing the right thing the right way is just as important as doing the right thing. By the end of the first half of a recovery agenda for Africa, there should be enough Africans earning sufficient disposable incomes to buy American goods and services liberally.

With such goals and expectations, concerned legislators often intervened to point out flaws and raise relevant issue as the bill made its way through congress. Representative Jesse Jackson, Jr., characterized it as "NAFTA for Africa "(Progressive Secretary.com) perhaps because it was fraught with provisions that were likely to exact African human, as well as material, resources without giving back much in return. Even observers outside of Congress expressed reservations and objections. Trans-Africa President Randall Robinson referred to the act as the "Africa re-colonization Act." (www.ipoaa.com/africa_bill-commentary.htm) The U.S.–Africa Trade Policy working group actively demanded substantive as well as semantic changes. For example, the group demanded cancellation of all debt that still hung over most African countries, a relief necessary to ensure the benefits of American investments to African governments and similar institutions are not consumed by African obligations for debt repayments.

After much haggling and tradeoffs, the bill passed both houses and was immediately signed into law by President Clinton. It was signed in the middle of the transition year between the second and the third millennium. Africa will rise again, and America might play a vital role in its revival. With Mr. Clinton's signature, the idea was recognized in law. The rest was then up to the governments and peoples on both sides.

Chapter Eleven

Second Overture

In B Flat-Minor

Whiles AGOA was still a concept and during its early days as an act, its well-wishers expected reasonable charity in its implementation. African importers and merchants, in particular, expected the United States Department of Agriculture (USDA) and other agencies that regulate the import of consumer goods to recognize and accommodate, at least for a reasonable grace period, the limited capacity of African producers. They hoped such a grace period would give African producers the needed time to improve the quality and presentation of their products.

    Alas! Only months after he signed the bill into law, the Clinton administration's term of office ended and with it the spirit of liberal internationalism. Its successor, the Bush administration, wasted no time in asserting its "vital interest" posture, unyielding and uncompromising. Import regulatory agencies became even more vigilant. Months later— when Homeland Security became both a driving force and an apology for the exercise of "vital interest"—customs and agriculture agents systematically and summarily, for the slightest infraction or deviation, would condemn whole shipments worth thousands of dollars, causing crippling losses and liabilities to importers of African goods, most of whom lacked the reserves with which to recover from any degree of loss. Retailers also suffered (www.webring.com/t/). Often punishment seemed aimed at destroying African-owned businesses rather than correcting them. My own store was treated as such. The Africa Act could have offered some form of assistance to importers of African consumer goods - distributors, wholesalers and retailers, in the form of regulatory and tax moratoriums, low-interest loans, and whatever measures promised to move the process of the Africa act forward.

Of the many factors that stand in the way of AGOA and other forms of American assistance toward African development, none is as stalwart as the May 2002 signing of additional farm subsidy bill, to the tune of some $83 billion over ten years(*New York Times*: *Reversing Course, Bush Signs Bill Raising Farm Subsidies*; May 14, 2002). With the signing of the bill, President Bush raised the level of the tobacco farm subsidy by a whopping 60 percent, establishing the overall farm subsidy provision to $21,000 per American farmer, per year. This, without argument, gives the American farmer a tremendous competitive advantage on the world market. This advantage is at the expense of African farmers, giving them no choice but to charge prices that truly reflect their costs.

Given that 70 percent of Africa's labor force is tied to agriculture, the American farm subsidy bill all but wipes out the entire set of potential benefits AGOA holds for both sides of the Sargasso Sea. I have attempted to point out some of the major flaws in the Africa Act. I could continue in this vein, but let me simply say that for the sake of the ordinary American and the ordinary African—rich or poor and present as well as future generations—it is important to get AGOA and its agenda right, the first time. To keep up with the program, check the following Web site periodically: www.agoa.gov.

Revision and extension of provisions in the Africa Act are necessary if significant manifestations of its goals are to be realized. Similarly, grand and promising development plans for

Africa have been advanced in recent times. In the year 2001, the first year of the third millennium, several African leaders collectively initiated a New Partnership for Africa's Development (NEPAD). Its preamble is based on two broad and closely related assumptions:

      1)   The development of Africa rests with Africans.
      2)   Outside help is necessary on a short-term basis.

To most Africans and to most outside observers, giving help to Africa must begin with the cancellation of the balance on the debt to Northern countries and institutions. Further help must be made up mainly of trade and investments, especially foreign direct investments. This means companies coming to Africa from elsewhere, with their own monies, can establish and operate their businesses and do as they please with the net profits. Many observers hold the view that such help, though necessary, must be sufficient to start and move the process beyond the required threshold. In order to attain a recognizable middle class by year 2020, African economies must strive for an overall growth rate of 7 to 10 percent annually. Africa's resource gap at year end 2004 was about $65 billion. While it is believed that much of what is needed to bridge the gap can be generated from within, it is also clear to most experts that trade and investments from outside are indeed necessary (National Policy Plan Of Action For U.S.-Africa Relations In The 21st Century, Washington D.C., February, 2000) . Once again, it seems Africa is receiving the short end of the stick.

In June 2002, the eight leading industrial nations, also known as the G-8, met in Kananaskis, Canada. The group proposed and adopted what it called the "Africa Action Plan." With it, they pledged corporation with Africa to ensure success of the New Partnership for Africa's Development (canadaonline.about.com). Before long Africans, privately and publicly, began to express doubts about the feasibility of the plan and even an outright dismissal of the G-8 pledge. A cursory inspection was enough to see why. The pledge was fraught with conditions, contradictions, selectivity, and an apparent lack of sincerity:

1) Any new loan to Africa would be advanced with a set of conditions.
2) Each G-8 member would make its own determinations as to which African country to aid regardless of NEPAD's established criteria and priorities.
3) Most G-8 members chose to emphasize secondary factors such as good governance, peace, and security over more basic development needs, such as private investments, education, health, and physical infrastructure development—factors, which on a logical development agenda, must precede good governance, peace, and security. (www.dfa.gov.za/docs/2002/)

The topic remained on the agenda since the summit in Canada, as it should. It was discussed at the Sea Island summit in Georgia and was at the top of the agenda in Scotland in the summer of 2005 with the host and chairman, British Prime Minister Tony Blair, proposing a goodly sum of $50 billion in aid to Africa by year 2010 (news.bbc.co.uk/1/hi/Scotland). The idea was gallantly championed and supported by other Britons: Bono and Bobby Geldorf.

Here again, we see the descendants of Ephraim have taken the lead in pushing for solid contributions to help lift Africa out of poverty. The descendants of Manasseh will sure follow. Regrettably and ironically, the agenda was derailed temporarily by fatal bomb blasts in London, while the conference was in progress in Scotland. At the following G-8 summit, in Germany in June 2007, just days before Mr. Blair left office, the pledge amount was raised to $60 billion (www.g-8.de/content/EN/Artikel/_g8-summit/). The very idea of the pledge and all efforts behind it always sounded noble. Raising the amount from $50 to $60 billion sounded nobler. However, everyone, including the more stalwart champions of the idea, is asking, "When are we going to start seeing some of the pledge money where it is needed?"

If the African renaissance should be led by an economic revival, which in turn would be led by exports, the obstacles have already been planted by European and American farm (and other producer) subsidies and by Asian substitutions and imitations. Much of what the African poor produces for export is simple: primary farm products, utility and decorative artifacts, small-scale handicrafts, recorded music and entertainments, and the expansion of hospitality in Africa. Here too, the potential for even meager earnings is smothered not only by European and American subsidies and import barriers, but also by Asian imitations and substitutions of what is even indigenously and identifiably African: drums, kente cloth patterns, and similar handiworks. As I have said before, at year end of 2003, U.S. subsidies to farmers was $21,000 per American farmer per year. In the European Union (EU), it is about $16,000 per farmer per year. All together, farm subsidies by developed countries to their farmers is about $300 billion a year as at year's end 2005 (www.financialexpress.com/news/), virtually shutting off African producers from world market participation.

It bears repetition that, as farm-related employment accounts for about 70 percent of the African workforce, these subsidies deal a heavy blow to the earnings potential of the African poor. West Africa alone lost about $800 million a year in potential earnings due to subsidies given to farmers in developed countries (www.timesonline.co.uk/tol/new/africa/).

$800 million for a whole region of a continent might strike some Americans as "peanuts." It is megabucks in those parts.

There seems to be no end in sight with these practices. While subsidies to cotton producers in America completely shut out cotton producers in East and West Africa, growers of other cash crops have not fared much better. Coffee growers in Africa got only thirty-five cents for every three dollars of coffee they sold in developed countries as at year end 2003.

By year end 2004, the earnings had improved; they had in fact doubled, not due to inflation, but in real terms. In some countries, it was due largely to external assistance. For instance, the United States Agency for International Development (USAID) helped coffee farmers in Uganda and Rwanda with microloans and planting higher-yield crops that are acceptable to Starbucks and other American companies (www.usaid.gov). Such country-specific offers, though noble and laudable, are selective and fall short of what is necessary to advance a viable agenda to the desired goal of poverty reduction.

In fact, as unfolding events have revealed, much of the supposed gains for African farmer are easily reversed, and they are tenuous at best. Coffee accounts for about 60 percent of Ethiopia's exports. Ethiopian coffee farmers earn less than one dollar per pound, while companies like Starbucks charge up to twenty-five dollars per pound for the same variety. Recently, the government of Ethiopia tried to obtain trademark registrations for coffee varieties grown in Ethiopia to gain better control over global marketing (wwwafricaresource.com). Starbucks resisted the Ethiopian government attempts until American massive public pressure prompted the aid agency Oxfam to intervene and coax Starbucks to a compromised agreement. (www.oxfam.org).

Examples like these prompt Africans to ask whether the offers such as the G-8's "Africa Action Plan" are genuine or merely a well-finessed Machiavellian, neocolonial ploy disguised as a sincere response to Africa's plea for help. Indeed, most Africans see the pledge as nothing more than orchestrated hype. To boot, the loan pledged by the G-8 had also fallen far short of what was needed and expected. Even the $5 billion a year to Africa (with its billion people), pledged by the Bush administration early in its first term remained a promise at the end of 2004, not a penny had been spent (www.blackcommentator.com). What was later given was given piece-meal and was far less than what was necessary to give lasting impact. Ghana was given $547 million in 2006 with conditions for good governance and anti- corruption commitment but without the necessary mechanism for verification. No wonder about 100 million more have been added to the ranks of the African poor, raising the ratio to well over 50 percent, about 600 million people who cannot meet their daily needs (www.saveafrica@cozy.com); this is about twice the entire population of the United States of America. What a sinful waste of potential market, not to speak of cultivation of global insecurities.

What makes it even more alarming is that each year, nearly $1 trillion is spent on military-related transactions, while only $60 billion, a mere 6 percent or so, is spent on poverty-related demands. According to Patrick Bond of the Centre for Civil Society, "Rich countries have shrunk aid by 8.4% in 2007 compared to a 6% rise in arms expenditure." If such ratios were reversed for just one year, many of the ills of the world, including the threat of terror, which necessitates and rationalizes such high military pending, would be dramatically reduced. While this is a noble idea, we must not delude ourselves. Military expenses are highly profitable to many in high and powerful places in this world. Just consider the fact that the five leading countries in arms sales are all members of the United Nations Security Council. The idea of reversing the ratios of expenditure in the sale of arms versus expenditure on poverty-related issues will likely remain nothing more than an ideal unless and until bold steps are taken, without smashing the pork barrels.

African-Americans are suffering from low job prospects as the statistics we discussed earlier reveal. In the first four years of this new millennium, unemployment in the general population of America hovered around 5 and 6 percent, while unemployment in the African- American population was often two to two and a half times higher (www.highbeam.com). As it is on the African motherland, program after program have been established for the African-American poor, with the goal of reducing unemployment and improving earnings.

Each has either failed outright or turned out a disappointment.

From the Manpower Development and Training Act of 1962 to the Comprehensive Employment and Training Act (CETA) of 1973 to the Labor Department administered Job Training Partnership Act (JTPA), these programs were too complex and too rigid to be practical; instead of sincere and objective reviews and reforms, each initiative was replaced with or superimposed on another. For instance, in 1998, the JTPA was replaced with the Workforce Investment Act (WIA), popularly referred to as the "Workforce Centers." Most of these programs were funded through block grants, and, in spite of the good intensions that prompted their establishment, none of them have been able to concretely address the issue of job creation with livable wages for the African-American poor with sustained success.

www.doleta.gov
www.usworkforce.org
www.cet2000.org

The outlook for the poor is not good, and it is getting worse. I had to have my car towed recently. The tow-truck driver and I got into conversation as he drove toward the garage. He told me he was from a small mill town in rural Georgia. The mills moved off shore in the mid-1990s. As there were hardly any decent jobs remaining, his uncle forced him to move to Atlanta as soon as he finished high school. He had not realized how good an uncle he had until he went home to visit after four years in Atlanta. He could not find any of his old high school friends to hang out with. A couple of them had died, and most of the others— those who were still in town—were in jail or on drugs. Most of the women were unwed single mothers. He had planned to stay for twelve days, he only stayed for three.

Better implementation with well thought-out strategies would likely do much more to reverse prevailing trends of stagnation, unemployment, and the social ills they breed.

Chapter Twelve

"The Congo Syndrome"

Earlier, we discussed the mind-set that supported European attitudes and actions toward Africa and Africans. Such thinking, as wrong as it is, influences and guides policy at all levels. In romantic forms, such as in the television *Tarzan* series and in movies like *Birth of a Nation* and the comic character, "Stepinfetchit," Africans have been portrayed as having limited mental capabilities. The divisive and exclusionary quality of such belief was equally well demonstrated in sports and in life. In America, athletes of African descent were not featured in certain positions of popular sports. For example, the position of quarterback in football and the position of catcher in baseball were considered too complex and mentally tasking to be trusted to a person of African descent. In some circles, Europeans and Americans of European descent who subscribe to such notions of inferior African mental capabilities, referred to it as "the Congo syndrome." Others, in more casual circles and in particular reference to Africans referred to it as *"The National Geographic"* phenomenon.

As embarrassing as it is for me, I must admit that indeed the conduct of many postcolonial African officials, especially those that were posted to represent Africa in European and North American capitals, often conducted themselves and their affairs in ways that tended to give credence to such cryptic and laughable notions.

In the years immediately following independence, African diplomats and similarly high-ranking state officials were often selected and posted not by merit but on the basis of familiarity.

Often, they were relatives and cronies of officials in the inner circles of African governments. Some had little or no formal education to aid and guide the conduct of their official and personal affairs. They offered very little savvy, let alone sophistication. A good many tended to preoccupy themselves with prospects that promised to enrich them, members of their families, and their friends. Pitifully, if in any encounter, someone should pull the banana leaves over their heads, all they saw was green. Their display of dismal awareness made it difficult for anyone concerned to dispel or even attempt to challenge the notion of

"the Congo syndrome" or any actions or remarks that stemmed from it.

When then Senator Patrick Moynihan of New York made those humiliating remarks about African diplomats: that United Nations diplomats from Africa became visibly upset at the end of their terms, when they had to return home, because they dreaded losing the luxuries they enjoyed in New York. Africans, even those in high positions, could only register feeble expressions of disappointment. A decade earlier when President Nixon's secretary for agriculture Earl Butz said something to the effect that people of African descent (coloreds) only want three things in life: satisfying sex, loose shoes and a warm place to go to the bathroom; Africans in America could say very little, because that was how Africans in the motherland and in America had allowed themselves to be perceived and portrayed.

From about the beginning of the 1990s, with the advent of satellite communications, the Internet, other advanced modalities of communication and education, there seem to have quietly emerged a radically different breed of Africans. Fully cognizant of their history, they seem more interested in their future than bitter about the past. They show traits and attitudes markedly different from those of their parents and grandparents. To describe their behavior in metaphoric terms; these young Africans (*jeune Afrique*) seem to see themselves not sitting down looking into someone else's handheld mirror for vain impressions of themselves. They are certainly not looking with gleeful expectations for bailouts, handouts, pacifiers, and what often turns out to be nothing more than disguised baits. Rather, they seem to see themselves standing firm and looking out from behind a one-way mirror for opportunities that might enrich and secure their future.

They often appear quiet, yet so aware and alert though not necessarily standing tall, and if out of sheer politeness, they allow someone to pull the wool over their heads, sooner rather than later, they begin to see through the fabric. If the rug is pulled from under them, they quickly regain their balance. You will meet them everywhere these days; in Africa, in the Caribbean, and in every community in North America. They appear in fiction TV shows like *The Cosby Show*, *The West Wing,* or *The Jamie Fox Show* and in similar settings of fiction as well as in real life.

Perhaps the most remarkable feature of these young Africans is that many of them were not quite thirty years old at the turn of this millennium. They were yet to take up positions of power and responsibility in government, enterprise, and society. They talk intelligently and always seem curious and informed. I happened to talk to one on the very day the AGOA was signed into law. I asked her what she thought of AGOA. She replied with a question. "Is the provisions of the law, as structured, capable of getting significant numbers of Africa's poor out of poverty or would it end up a convenient device for Asian and European manufacturers to hurdle over quota limits to the American market".

Remarkable insight and foresight indeed, I had not even thought of it in such terms and to such extent. What she probably noticed was that since the provisions of the AGOA raised the limit on apparel made of value-added cotton grown in Africa to 3.5 percent of overall apparel imports into the U.S., and since African producers lacked the capacity to raise production to such levels within the limited time span of the AGOA, that particular provision was not likely to favor African cotton growers and apparel manufacturers. That is precisely what has happened. All throughout Africa, especially in the smaller republics and kingdoms of east and southern Africa, Asian apparel producers have set up shop in ways that enable them to export to the U.S. large quantities over and above the quota limits set for their respective countries. This occurred in spite of a visa system (to track apparel from source to market). Thus, Asian apparel producers and their Western partners were able to circumvent both the quota and the visa tracking systems. The precipitous rise in production and export in some African countries like Kenya, Ghana, and Lesotho is due to the sudden investments of Asian companies like Daewoo and Hyundai and similar-sized European companies all using Africa to hurdle over U.S. import quota limits into the highly profitable American market. There are high-ranking officials at both the State and Commerce Departments that seem to, at least tacitly, applaud this setup. It is in the long run a disadvantage to African producers.

To boot, the whole idea of the AGOA was to allow 1,800 African manufactured products into the U.S. duty free and was designed to help alleviate poverty. According to the Office of the US Trade Representative, trade increases have been substantial. For example, in 2005 the total volume of trade between Africa and America rose to nearly $65 billion, generating about $340 million in investments and creating thousands of jobs. The benefits had been appreciable in the short period of its implementation, encouraging both congress and the executive branch to extend the original terminal date of 2004 to 2008. In 2006, President Bush extended the privileges further to the year 2015; and the year before he had offered $200 million to improve and expand African trade competitiveness (www.ustr.gov), noble indeed.

But now, as many young Africans see it, the privilege might be circumvented and superseded by the separate arrangement between the U.S. and the Southern African Customs Union (SACU) for a Free Trade Agreement (FTA). It is an arrangement that seems to selectively extend trade, with broader and better rewarding privileges and benefits, indefinitely to a preferred corner and, practically speaking, a preferred segment of the African business community. Africans notice it all with quiet displeasure.

Chapter Thirteen

Trade Not Aid, Not AIDS

In the early summer of 2001, the United Nations convened in New York a meeting of African leaders to discuss, in particular, the issue of aid. When it was over, President Bush invited three of the African leaders to the White House for further discussions. Instead of trade, investment and similar economic issues, the meeting focused on the fight against AIDS as a basis for continuing monetary and economic assistance for African development. Young Africans were quick to take issue. I heard many things I had never heard before. Many people asked why there was such a dogged insistence on AIDS instead of aid and trade, which might offer Africans a better chance to fight against AIDS and other ills.

Young Africans raised even more fundamental questions. They challenged the origins of AIDS and why Africa. I heard talk about the Tuskegee Experiment (with syphilis) and about the affliction of native Indian populations with syphilis and tuberculosis, which left the Indians weakened and vulnerable. I even heard someone suggest the whole discipline of obstetrics was developed with experimentation on African women slaves. These stories are hair-raising indeed, to say the least. Many young Africans asked whether the proliferation of AIDS is with similar motives. That was the first time I even learned there is a popular belief about the development of AIDS. According to word on the streets, experimentations on humans in New Guinea and elsewhere with viruses were conducted decades ago. I heard about a U.S. federally run program—"MK-NAOMI"—about the trial of a South African medical biologist, who on trial for his involvement in such experimentations, had claimed that he had acted with the blessing and collaboration of the American CIA.

Though I do not know much, a great deal of what I heard, by its sheer popularity, sounded possible, at least plausible. African communities suffer a wide range of diseases, many with high rates of mortality and morbidity; diseases such as alcoholism, morbid depression, malnutrition, tuberculosis, malaria, hepatitis, dracunculosis, schistozomiasis, and a host of other vector and waterborne diseases endemic to Africa. Really, these are diseases that thrive on sheer poverty and ignorance. A serious attack and a full-scale, broad-based frontal assault on poverty and illiteracy, even if only partially successful, will also enable Africans to reduce many of these diseases, including AIDS.

The Global Fund (administered by the World Bank), the Millennium Challenge Account, and similar allocations pledged to fight AIDS in Africa will do much, much more for Africans and for the global community at large if extended to more fundamental African development needs that include education, poverty eradication, and eradication of malnutrition. The present form, the present ways, and means of extending aid to Africa that seem to drag—to be selective—and often so rigidly tied to specific interests and expectation not particularly to the benefit of Africa, opens up chances for failures and disappointments on both sides. What many young Africans fear the most is that, decades later when the ways and means are all forgotten, it might be said, "Africans were given so much and so many chances, yet there is not much to show for it." I agree with such fears.

What Africans hoped for were offers from the American pharmaceutical companies to search and research for cures within Africa—working with African botanists, chemists, physicians, and traditional healers combing the African flora for cures and potential cures that might be more effective, affordable and safe.

Costs have, in fact, plunged the Global Fund's aid for the AIDS program into contention. At year end 2004, a year's regimen of AIDS drugs in America cost approximately $12,000 to $20,000. The same exact combination from elsewhere, from India for example, costs a mere $300 to $400 a year. That is nearly sixty times cheaper. When it was proposed that the Global Fund's money should be used to pay for purchases from India to treat AIDS in Africa, America vehemently objected, suggesting that drugs from non-American companies are suspect, in efficacy as well as safety. The drugs from India, however, had been independently assayed and tested in three different Western countries, and each set of tests determined the Indian drugs had the right degree of efficacy and safety. This was much to the displeasure of the American pharmaceutical manufacturers and the Bush administration.

America, the largest contributor to the Global Fund, threatened to permanently withhold its contributions.

Young Africans' suspicions and misgivings about America's attitude toward Africa and Africans are based mainly on what they see as a certain disregard for what passes for news on Africa. To most young Africans, beyond Tarzan and Daktari, the only good news about Africa offered by the Western press is no news. By definition, the formula for coverage on Africa must entail gloom and doom, savagery, and some suggestion of backwardness. I believe I understand what young Africans mean by their reservations. A classic case in point was the American press coverage of the crisis in the West African country of Liberia. All through the summer of 2003, there were daily reports of bloody fighting among young Liberians of opposing factions. Throughout much of the day, CNN, PBS, and the networks presented accounts that were bound to give viewers the impression that Africans alone are responsible for African sufferings. America was carefully portrayed as the benevolent and humble peacemaker. Several weeks later, when under the auspices of ECOWAS and the African Union, an interim government was peacefully installed in Liberia; CNN, the networks, and even PBS gave virtually no coverage of the positive change of events, certainly nothing compared to the extensive coverage weeks earlier when young Africans were killing other young Africans.

Equally worrisome to most Africans is the benign contagion with which the American press continue to report on Africa. The entire continent, it seems, is painted as one continuous background. It is painted with the same brush so bad news about one country necessarily affects just about every other African country almost to the same extent. For a long time, Africans have held the belief that most northern overtures and offers of help are strategic and quite likely not in their favor. So when President George Bush so boldly announced his position on Africa during the campaign debates in 2000 telling the world in effect that Africa was the least of his interests, most Africans were not so surprised. What did ruffle most Africans was the unabashed, unreserved tone with which he made the pronouncement, as if he really expected Africans to take such a confession as a matter of course. Some twenty years earlier maybe, but these days, with the level of awareness and the demand for integrity accompanied by higher expectations, Africans on both sides of the Sargasso Sea take such affronts with quiet exception. Mr. Bush's ticket gained a measly 8 percent of the African-American vote.

In reaction to what most Africans saw as a desperate attempt to smooth ruffled feathers, President Bush's Secretary of State, General Colin Powell, flew to Nigeria, to South Africa, and one or two other African states. From what acquaintances told me shortly after his trip, he was greeted with due formality and with characteristic African politeness, nothing more. He neither impressed nor pacified many, if anyone.

Personally, I think it is important for America to strive to avoid further erosion of respect and credibility. Policy managers must begin to appreciate the fact that often it is not so much what is done but how it is done. That is what gets the right message across. Africans need not continue to fear what they see and interpret as hidden American intentions to neo colonize and further exploit the continent, directly or through proxies, lackeys, and ploys.

Presently, most Africans, right or wrong, see institutions like the IMF and the World Bank as proxies for American interests in the "Third World." The recent construction of embassy complexes that look more like fortresses plus establishment of the military unit Africom have only served to heighten African fears. Now, how does any of this affect Africa, America, and the relations between them?

The 2000 signing of the AGOA trade act by President Clinton will go down as a landmark event in the history of African and American relations. It was, for one thing, the first formal recognition of the need for improved trade relations between the two sides of the Sargasso Sea. Secondly, it expressed recognition of error in previous policies and approaches designed to address poverty and related issues in Africa. As Ugandan president, Yuweri Museveni, so cogently expressed it, "By itself, aid cannot transform societies. Only trade can foster the sustained economic growth necessary for such transformation." The implementation of the provisions of the act started earnestly in the jubilee year of 2000. It has yielded many successes stories, but none quite to its full potential. Would the level of success have been higher if much of its implementation had remained on the watch of the Clinton Administration?

As we said before, by 2004, only three and a half years after the AGOA trade act started, it had generated $340 million in investments and created thousands of jobs on both sides of the Sargasso Sea. It did so well that congress and President Bush decided on a four- year extension, and the positive trend continued. In 2005, the total volume of trade between America and sub-Saharan Africa was over $60 billion. Imports were over $38 billion, an increase of 44 percent from the previous year. Even though much of this increase was due to an increase in petroleum imports, nonpetroleum imports have also done well (www.ustr.gov). It has not been exports per se alone that merit mention. The AGOA have compelled American inputs to enable both quantitative and qualitative increases in African nonpetroleum and non- mineral exports. Cattle farmers in Botswana were given technical and financial assistance to help beef up their production. Similar assistance in Rwanda from USAID helped coffee farmers increase quality and yield and to enter Western markets. Some of the leading coffee buyers from Rwanda now include Green Mountain Coffee Roasters of Vermont, Community Coffee of Louisiana, and Starbucks among others.

This assistance has not been limited to farm and factory productions. It extends into commerce and other sectors. Global competitiveness hubs have been established in West Africa to provide sound business and financial consultation. USAID has also partnered with ECOWAS to help improve the supply of energy. In keeping with the original goals of poverty reduction, the act has given special privileges and benefits to sub-Saharan African countries designated as less developed. These are countries with per-capita GNP of less than $1,500 in 1998, as measured by the Bank for Construction and Development (www.uneca.org/aisi). The future is indeed only half full, and I can only echo President Bush's expression of optimism when, in 2006, he signed a further extension of AGOA provisions (AGOA-3) to the year 2015. The gains have not been all material. On one side, it has strengthened African hopes and reduced suspicions, and, on the other, the AGOA has given American businesses greater confidence to invest in Africa. Americans are increasingly traveling to Africa for leisure, for evangelism, and for business prospects with benefits to American and European air carriers and to the African hospitality industry.

First of all, the only formidable obstacles I see are the lingering mind-sets that still portray Africa as a bastion of doom and gloom, they must change. The extent of negative reporting, with the focus on negative news out of Africa, is bound to frighten off potential direct investors. Who would want to put any serious money in a system rife with stories of gloom and doom? I know I wouldn't, and I don't think you would either. Thirdly, the lack of needed capital investments, from within and from the outside, creates a culture of hardship, which, in turn, encourages the flight of capital from poor African countries, some at a time when they have just managed to accumulate such assets. Often, ahead of capital go the skills. It is estimated that some 20,000 professionals a year from Africa alone immigrate to developed countries. It is called the "brain drain." Go to your nearby hospital, particularly a county or metropolitan hospital, community health center, or a nursing home especially the night shift. Look at the roster of health professionals—doctors, pharmacists, nurses, nurses' aides, technicians, and technologists. You will recognize many African names. There is an estimated 90,000 African health care professionals in America as of January 2007. The majority of them are from Egypt, Nigeria, Sudan, and South Africa. This, by itself, further weakens and renders Africa most vulnerable.

Finally, and certainly most importantly, such negative trends additionally provide "rational reasons" for those to the right of

Hegel, who favored a postponement of the African renaissance. Such postponement would cause a fulfillment of the very prophesy of Africa as nonredeemable. As I said before, the fear I most often hear from young Africans is that, decades from now, Americans and Europeans might say, "Africans were given fair opportunities, but made nothing of it." Such tendency for self-fulfilling prophesies dates back centuries and has also influenced official policies and presentations of the arts, which has shaped our mind-sets and attitudes. These tendencies have been propagated in time, through theoretical thinkers like Hans Morgenthau and Ayan Rand and through more popular, sublime notions such as the "Congo syndrome." The success of the AGOA and any American plan for Africa's development certainly require new thinking and new approaches and new champions.

Chapter Fourteen

Much Has Changed; Much Remains the Same

In 1960, the number of universities in all of Africa—from Cairo to Cape Town, from Dakar to Der-es-Salam, and in between—was less than twenty-five. By the turn of the third millennium, Nigeria alone had some sixteen universities, with plans to establish more in the near future. Education is always good. At one level, it raises awareness and expectations and enables individuals to make good choices and better manage their affairs. At the level of society, education helps to establish the foundations upon which a middle class can thrive. If education is not developed within or along with economic policies and programs that promises fulfillment of expectations, then social turmoil is inevitable. Fraud, extortions, and larceny—domestic as well as international—will create mistrust and generalize fears.

   A caption in a recent issue of the biweekly publication, *Africans Abroad* read, "Encounters with Graduate Robbers." Here, the word "graduate" simply means a person with a college or university degree. I read on, and the very first paragraph of the article gave the gist of the whole story, "They are educated yet mean and they kill if they have to ... the country's underperforming economy *[sic]* have greatly reduced the purchasing power of the average Nigerian. There is much hunger in the land. There are no jobs. Where jobs are available they are too few to go around. Those who are lucky to be employed do not earn enough to eke out a decent living. The story is that of misery." Some of us might feel somewhat indifferent, because Nigeria is too far away or because it is, after all, news about Africa, not inconsistent with our expectations or what we are accustomed to. However, just turn around and take a close look; the same conditions are being reported in parts of America.

A November 2, 2003, article in the *Atlanta Journal and Constitution* was captioned, "Hunger, no stranger to millions in US." It was a very short article, and perhaps we can look at the full text: "Despite the nation's struggle with obesity, the agricultural department says more and more American families are hungry or unsure whether they can afford to buy food, about twelve million families last year worried they did not have enough money to buy food and 32 percent of them actually experienced someone going hungry at one time or another, said a USDA report released last week. Nearly four million families were hungry to the point that someone in the household skipped meals because they could not afford them."

That is over 8.6 percent more families than in the year 2001 when 3.5 million families were hungry and a 13 percent increase from year 2000. The prevalence of hunger in America seems to be on the rise. The report was based on a Census Bureau survey of 55,000 households (www.bread.org). When you read between the lines of the two articles, something rather striking reveals itself. You see America, the richest country in the world, and Nigeria, the richest country in Africa (at least on the basis of GDP), subjects of public commentaries on poverty and hunger in the midst of plenty. Obviously, availability alone is not enough. It is not even the main determinant of supply and satisfaction.

About three weeks later, the same journal published what seemed a follow-up. The author of the article was David Beckman, president of *Bread for the World*, a Christian anti-hunger advocacy group based in D.C. He remarked that the prevailing encouraging economic statistics may well be hiding more than it reveals. He suggested such statistics might in fact be driving down a wedge between "the favored few and the left outs." He repeated much of the statistical figures of earlier reports and poignantly added that thirteen million of those living in households below the poverty level are children. He went on to note that, since February 2002, the U.S. lost about two and a half million jobs, and, in fact, since the year 2000, no new sources of jobs have been created to replace those lost. "Our economy has never experienced such a job creation drought since monthly job numbers began being reported in 1939," he concluded in (www.bread.org/about_us//annual_reports/annual_report_2003.pdf When we happily point to more comforting gains, attendant losses seem overwhelming. Between the signing of the Civil Rights bill, which gave rise to affirmative action in the late 1960s and the year 2000, the African-American middle class had nearly quadrupled. This is praise worthy and pleasing. We all can boast of knowing someone like the Huxtables. However, if you should ever go to visit them—as you stand on the top step, waiting for the door to open after you have rung the bell—just turn around and look across the tracks at the yard of Sanford and Son. Look at the homes in their neighbors. Not much has changed on that side. The ratio of African-Americans living at or below the poverty line remains virtually the same, about 40 percent of the African-American population, just about the same ratio at the time of the civil rights movement of the 1960s.

Whereas African-Americans constitute about 15 percent of the general population, their total material wealth is less than 1 percent, and, whereas general unemployment in America hovers around 5 and 6 percent, unemployment for African-Americans is about 12 to 15 percent (data from jobs reported to the Labor Department). It was recently reported that in the Chicago area, about one out of every ten African-American men in their early to mid- twenties are unemployed and not enrolled in school either (www.bls.gov). These are conditions that compel people to resort to self-employment, even if illicit. Equally, if not more disturbing, those lucky to be gainfully and formally employed often must work with great sacrifices or without benefits or both. Many young, single mothers are compelled to work two jobs just to make ends meet, and, in so doing, they deprive their children of the quality of care, love, and parental attention they need at the most impressionable stages of their development, a fact that contributes immeasurably to delinquencies.

Before we go any further, let us take a quick look at African-American history, in a nutshell, just to see where Africans are in their progress to Middle America. Most historic records suggest Africans arrived in America in 1619 (Jamestown, Virginia). More convincing records suggest the arrival of Africans was much earlier, perhaps as early as the year 1526 (South Carolina). That would make it some ninety-three years before the arrival of the *Mayflower*. The forcible removal of Africans from their native lands in Africa and being bound in America as chattel were without argument one of the most diabolical periods in the history of human society. In intensity and scope, it ranks above even the enslavement of the Israelites in Egypt. Destruction was the lot of those who were snatched and taken away as well as those left behind to grieve the losses of their loved ones. The loss to Africa was incalculable, sons and daughters of vast productive lands; innovators, laborers, managers, merchants, and craftsmen who would have made a tremendous difference between Africa as we know it now and Africa as it should be today, had its logical progress not so profoundly interrupted by the slave-trade (as suggested by Basil Davidson in *The Growth of African Civilization: A history of West Africa 1000 - 1800).*

The spirits of Africans, who remained as well as those taken across the "middle- passage", may take comfort in knowing that divine destiny does not always follow a pleasant and comforting path. To many Africans, the divine purpose of the forced separation and of the presence of Africans in America remain obscured by African tears and by the wedge planted by non-Africans who recognize and fear the positive forces and power with which those on the opposite ends of such a separation are blessed. The trials and tribulations African- Americans continue to suffer in America, like Africans in the motherland, are part of the preparations for a glorious destiny that will soon be set in motion. It remains to yet be fully recognized and realized by Africans on both sides of the Sargasso Sea.

When Africans landed on the eastern shores of America in 1526 or 1619, whichever date is accurate, they were spiritually, if not physically, ready for a steady march to Middle America and beyond. Africans were forced to settle throughout the American South. From there, they fanned out throughout the land. Some followed "The Drinking Gourd" (constellation of stars shaped like a gourd that appears in the northern sky) to northern parts. Others trekked to settle the West Coast. Over time and space, throughout the land and through the entire length of the history of the United States, African contributions in blood, sweat, and tears have been immeasurable. African blood was shed in the first volley of gun shots in 1770 when Crispus Attucks and four other non-African patriots were killed in the Boston Massacre, the prelude to the American War of Independence.
(www.americanrevolution.com/Crispus_Attucks.htm)

There is no basis to argue against the fact that African hands and endurance are what established the foundations upon which this great economy of the United States was built.

Instead of due recognition and appreciation, African contributions, material and otherwise, have largely been suppressed and often denigrated. Africans have been constantly told they brought nothing, have contributed nothing, and, therefore—at least by implication— deserved nothing. However, those who know that supreme knowledge also acquired from Africa guided the founding fathers, the engineers, and scientists in establishing both the material and spiritual foundations that were destined to make the United States the strongest, the most affluent and most flamboyant society in the history of mankind. Let us not even talk about contributions to ordinary life—rhythm and blues, pleasures and thrills, and America's other cultural modalities. And so, for nearly 400 years, Africans in America endured generation after generation of slavery, the charades and the treacheries of reconstruction, and the suppressive and demeaning practices of segregation. The Civil Rights and Voting Rights bills and the affirmative action provisions that followed merely ended segregation as recognized in law. Segregations as practiced persist. Segregation thrives, often suppressed and disguised, and is nestled well within the collective mind-set.

During the 1990s, African-American professionals increased in numbers dramatically. The number of medical doctors increased by about 12,000 and the number of lawyers increased by some 9,000. Other African-American professions fared just as well. The number of college professors increased by some 35,000, and the number of engineers increased by close to 18,000 (en.wikipedia.org/wiki/African American). Even more remarkable is the increases in the ranks of African Americans in mainstream, higher-paying professions of sports and entertainments.

In the 1970s, an African-American quarterback in professional football, even in the college ranks, was news of fantastic dimensions. This was the time when an African American by the name of Joe Gallium tried out for the position in the professional ranks. Weighed down perhaps by his own submission to the expectations of society, he struggled endlessly. In those days, an athlete of African descent with the ability and desire to play the position of quarterback in the professional ranks had to go north, across the border, to sign up in the Canadian league. When Doug Williams was given the quarterback position with the Washington Redskins, a seasoned mainstream newspaper reporter asked him, with genuine perplexity, how long he had been "the black quarterback?" (ESPN: The Third and a Mile) Such was the prevailing ethos, the mind-set of the time. At the end of the 1987 season, Doug Williams led his team to a most sensational and spectacular Super Bowl victory over John Elway and the Denver Broncos.

By the year 2000, however—some twelve short years after Doug Williams' stunning, game-winning, and barrier-shattering historic performance in 1988—the field was leveled.

About ten African-American quarterbacks were in the National Football League each season from then on. That is about 30 percent of the league's starting quarterbacks, and each was commanding hefty seven-figure salaries. At the end of the 2004 season, Michael Vick of the Atlanta Falcons signed a ten-year contract, worth over $100 million, to continue to quarterback the Falcons. The coaching ranks, at both college and professional levels, also show a steady rise in numbers of African-Americans.

In popular entertainment, the story is even more dramatic. In the theater, stage as well as cinema, you will always find presentations featuring African-Americans, some by African- American producers, writers, and directors, in addition to the artists. Cable television, along with the networks, has vastly expanded the scope of opportunity for African-Americans. It started when America was awed by the appearance of Diahann Carroll in a mainstream sitcom back in the early 1970s. It has grown steadily since. Now, there are African American sitcoms or an epic presentation of sorts on television at all hours, especially in prime time. All this happened, because the playing field was lowered to some extent. The satiric movie, *Coming to America* (from Africa), demonstrated convincingly that an all African-American cast can yield for producers some very serious profits. This recognition, perhaps more than any other, helped level the playing field all the way. And who could have imagined, even by the mid- 1980s, that there would ever be a day when three Americans, all of African descent would receive the highest awards in the entertainment industry, all on the same stage on the same night: Halle Berry, Denzel Washington, and Sidney Poitier? It happened. It was a milestone. These are achievements that, with proper planning, can translate into significant, long lasting, economic, political and social opportunities for a people. These are gains that can propel a whole society upward and forward. Soon, African-Americans will be telling more and more of their own stories as writers, producers, directors, technicians, and performers. African Americans will be taking care of the business side as well, as distributors, theater owners, and TV station and network owners and managers.

In spite of the wealth gap and in spite of the fact that Africans in America own less than one tenth the wealth of white Americans, Africans-Americans on the whole have come very far in America (www.blackcommentator.com). With an estimated spending power of over $1 trillion each year, it is no wonder all the television networks, cable programmers, and movie producers are vying for a greater share of the African-American market. It is a market that can no longer be ignored or pushed to the side. However, as gratifying and inspiring as such advancements are, they are not without their contradictions. As Africans forge on toward Middle America, the vestiges and trappings of segregation and bigotry still loom large. Tragically, many Africans who have 'arrived' or imagine themselves to have 'arrived', also seem to have forgotten the tribulations of their forbearers just a generation or two earlier, the forbearers who bore the brunt of the suffering as they blazed the trails. In spite of the centuries of toils and sacrifices and the few generations of steady gains, there are still some who are struggling at the back of the trails.

For those at the back, efforts to get ahead—sometimes to meet mere daily demands for sustenance or for enlightenment and amusement—present challenges with reminders of bygone years: memories of treachery and callous sufferings. Turning the dial merely changes the station; the tune remains the same—blue grass / honky-tonk. Tunes that Africans do not dance to particularly well. Yet, Africans, even those who feel left out, also know the road does not have to be easy, the end must only be good, for when they worship with praises to their maker, they acknowledge his goodness and mercy, "He will not bring us this far to leave us." Their faith remains strong. Indeed, the road ahead—however much of it remains— might be but a bus, a train, or a cab ride away. And so, in spite of persistent hardship, Africans in America forge on undaunted, forward ever, backward never. How much ground is gained and how fast depend largely, not only on their faith but also on the habit of planning for the future. Not much must be left to chance.

Really, I do not see anyone in the way. Africans and African Americans are free to get together to design and implement plans for a common glorious future, plans that could benefit even the least fortunate with bold creation and prudent distribution of opportunities. Africans in America have the unacknowledged power within them to hasten the positive manifestations of efforts that could broaden and strengthen their ranks. If those who have already arrived in Middle America are truly at home and awake, they may double back to give those at the rear of the trail a ride, at least part of the way, perhaps a helping hand over some of the rough terrain. It would be sinful for me to discuss this issue and not mention some who are doing just that: Dr. Bill Cosby, Oprah Winfrey, General Colin Powell, Oral Lee Brown, Dr. Paul King, and the Metro Atlanta Neurosurgery Foundation. There are thousands of others, past and present. Yet, it is not nearly enough; there is still a lot to be done. What about you and me? What have we done? What can't we do? One thing that remains true and remarkable is that Africans have come this far by faith, and faith alone can guide and move Africans through to the promised-land with inspired, planned action. Africans only need to recognize the good that God still holds out for their blessings through their separation.

Lamentably, even though Africans hold the keys to their future, they still behave as though they remain in bondage, as though they need permission to do for self. Since independence in the motherland and civil rights in America, what Africans on both sides of the Atlantic seem to demonstrably lack is that quiet but fierce inner resolve necessary to drive and enable planning for future successes; the zeal and forward thinking to recognize and seize opportunities, even those that might at first appear to be adversities and disadvantages. Even when African names, faces, and lips are hijacked for less than honorable purposes of others, astute- minded Africans must recognize the opportunities therein, We must recognize positive contradictions and then devise plans to extract advantages from such otherwise disadvantageous encounters..

The achievements and performances of such prominent names as the Jubilee Singers, George Washington Carver; The Tuskegee airmen who served so gallantly as a unit in world war two are well recognized. Many more African Americans including: Dr. Charles Drew, Dr. Percy Julian, Hank Aaron, Shirley Chisholm, Kofi Annan, Michael Jackson, General Colin Powell, Whoopi Goldberg, Ruby Dee, Roman Catholic Cardinal Arinze,

Ambassadors Ralph Bunch and Andrew Young and baseball "say hay kid", Willie Mays; broke down high barriers and set the stage upon which Africans dance in America today. All of them, helped establish the necessary degree of recognition that will make Africans anywhere and everywhere a most formidable and respected people once again.

Over $1 trillion a year spending power on one side of the Sargasso Sea when connected to the near-infinite supply of resources that remains on the other side can only produce power dwarfed only by the power that flows from above.

Chapter Fifteen

The Debt Burden

A Sincere Bail out or a Means to Re-Colonize Africa?

In a September 6, 2000, address at the UN Millennium Summit, British Prime Minister Tony Blair made remarks that caught the attention of everyone in Africa and in most other centers of the world, including Washington D.C. "There is a dismal record of failure in Africa on the part of the developed world that shocks and shames our civilizations." (www.unwire.org/unwire/20000907).

It was indeed confrontational, yet true and to the point. Curiously, such considerations for Africa have been expressed time and again, by individuals and by institutions in positions to act effectively and favorably and to commit, with utmost sincerity and with the right amount of resources, to any of the many agendas already proposed for Africa's development: the Lagos Plan of Action, the Lome Convention, the United Nations New Agenda for Development of Africa (UN-NADAF), the G-8 action plan, NEPAD, other initiatives by the IMF and World Bank, and the more recent Africa Act (AGOA) of the U.S., to list just a few. These are all plans for Africa's development, mostly with external support..

Thus far, none have been able to generate any sustained and appreciable response. The reasons might, in fact, lie somewhere between two sides for while Africans often point to half-hearted offers from the North that are only seldom delivered, Northerners in turn cite factors such as African mismanagement manifested largely in poor governance, corruption, conflict, and the lack of plans to properly absorb whatever good is delivered. While both sides have merits, many Africans, including myself, believe the blame for aid failure is, for the most part, disproportionately placed on Africans. I'll tell you why. Let us look at the issue of governance. During the decade of the 1960s up into the 1990s, many African leaders were, in fact, imposed on their peoples by outsiders. Such leaders were imposed or helped into power to serve the interests. As we said earlier, many such African leaders ordinarily would not even have qualified to represent their clan on their village council. Yet, such poor qualifications seemed the very qualities that endeared and made them most suitable to their foreign sponsors. They were imposed for long and critical periods of time, the post-independence formative period.

Invariably, they were imposed as unwitting conduits in the now well establish neo-colonial model of aid and development. These aid and development packages often imposed on the recipient nation by proxy organizations like the IMF and World Bank, often with conditionalities, enables developed nations of the North to exact resources from developing nations at prices favorable to the developed nations. The modality of these aid and development packages leaves the recipient nations poorer, mortgaged, and hostage.

If you have not had the chance, rent the movies I recommended earlier: *A Good Man in Africa*, starring Louis Gossett, Jr. and Sean Connery and *Critical Assignment* starring Michael Power. Another good one to watch is *Wild Geese* with Richard Harris. Perhaps, for mere entertainment, watch *The Last King of Scotland*. In this last story, Uganda's former president, Idi Amin Dada, admitted that the British helped him overthrow his predecessor (Milton Obote) and grab power, an admission that raises a near-infinite number of questions: Why was Obote overthrown? Why did the British help Idi Amin Dada? What gave the British the moral and legal authority, the audacity? Of all the high-ranking military officers in Uganda, of all the intellectuals and the trained and efficient managers in Uganda who were far more capable of organizing and managing a comprehensive development agenda, why did they help Idi Amin Dada to capture power? Was his tendency to buffoonery a total surprise to his sponsors or a suitable and necessary qualification? Finally, why did General Amin Dada fall out with the British? Are we really to believe that this is a story about a "happy-go-lucky" Scottish lad who was stumbled upon by a buffoon African dictator or was he in fact a plant? A Trojan sunflower planted at the center of African government for the benefit of those who believe they have a mandate to control and direct African progress and destiny.

We can ask twenty or more similar questions. Toward the end, a totally different story begins to emerge. That is why we say in West Africa, "As the storyteller is telling you a story, you are telling yourself the story." You will get a good impression of what I am talking about when you watch the movie. You will notice that, invariably, the sole purpose of such interventions was for easy influence and manipulations for maximum exploitation of African goods and for other strategic advantages. The imposed African leader's priorities are always all stacked in favor of his foreign sponsors with little left over for his own people. Any suggestion that African mismanagement is solely African is, at best, only half true.

Ordinarily, Americans are not superstitious, but I feel compelled to cite this example. There might, in fact, be a spiritual, nonmaterial cost to the sponsors of such interference and manipulations of Africa by outside forces. When General Amin died in Saudi Arabia in 2005, word on the streets was that the general's power of sorcery had caused the "stone of destiny," which had laid under the British (descendants of Ephraim) throne in London for centuries, to be removed and hidden in his favorite Scotland. That he had also caused removal of the seat of the Anglican Episcopal church, that serves America (the descendants of Manasseh), to be moved from America to his beloved Uganda. Make of it whatever you will.

In my view—a view shared by many Africans—there are three, perhaps four, main obstacles to Africa's recovery efforts. Each might be eliminated, suppressed, or averted with the right degree of commitment by all concerned, and all concerned are really the world at large, but the bulk of the burden is on Africa and America.

By far, the most rigid of these obstacles is the debt burden. In the 1970s and 1980s, the World Bank and especially the International Monetary Fund (IMF) persuaded several African nations almost to the point of coercion to accept these interest-bearing loan packages. It was by all accounts offers African countries "could not refuse," regardless of the tone of their voices of protests. When the IMF came calling with these loan offers Africa leaders felt they were "between the rock and the hard place." They needed the money for development, but they were also afraid of the terms. While the bases for many of these loans were fairly broad, many more were what are called tie loans, earmarked for specific projects, which often had little or no rational significance to the development needs of those who must toil to generate the money with which to pay back the loans. A case in point is the country of Somalia, which was given a lot of tie loans to buy arms from Western Suppliers instead of loans for the development of roads and agricultural schemes it needed back in the 1970s. The supplied military hardware was used in fighting neighboring Ethiopia. As a result, by the mid-1990s, Somalia was practically a well-armed, failed state. You could walk into an open-air market and buy arms perhaps much easier than you could buy coconuts or a pair of pants. In most African countries, the burden of such loans still hangs over the country without the benefit of the developments, proceeds of which were expected and are still needed to pay off the loan.

Some African leaders resisted the initial offers. They foresaw the likelihood that the loans would hold hostage the development of their countries and with it the inevitability of a "neo colonial" relationship with the same Northern countries that effectively control both the World Bank and the IMF. Their fears were well founded.

The other African leaders, many of whom were lackeys and had seized power with help and encouragement from outside Africa, borrowed an estimated $540 billion between the years 1980 and 2000 (www.afrodad.org). As I mentioned earlier, significant portions of the loan were tied to irrational, nonproductive schemes. Some were willfully mismanaged by corrupt African leaders who indulged in boundless personal luxuries for themselves, family and friends. They fattened their overseas private bank accounts, doing relatively very little, if anything for their peoples.

The loan repayment schedules were often structured such that, for years, profits from the sale of African products were to be used to service the loan. Till this day, proceeds from the sales of oil, gold, diamonds, cocoa, coffee, and timber are used to merely keep up with the repayments schedules, a heavy burden with which African countries remain saddled and shackled; these proceeds should have otherwise been directed for the development of schools, hospitals, roads, irrigation for significant agricultural schemes, and institutions for good and effective governance.

Corrupt African leaders saw in the loan package opportunities for themselves.

However, well-meaning and well-grounded African leaders resisted the initial offers and protested the obligations. Yes, they saw the signs of trouble and recognized the long-term implications. In fact, much of it was quite obvious.

Northern lenders, bilateral and multilateral, showed less-than-normal interest in whether African borrowers had the right combination of policy, productive capacities, plans, or the will to pay back such loans. Many of these loan packages were advanced without adequately assessing prevailing and future African needs, weaknesses, and constraint.

Soon after the first few packages were disbursed, it became apparent the loans also had the tendency to rather widen the gap between the haves and the have-nots, as they were likely to put more money into the hands of a few corrupt leaders and aggressive business individuals and public officials, thus widening prevailing disparities and adding more layers to social, economic, and political problems.

Often, government-to-government loans were offered with clear earmarks for the recipient country to buy specified goods from the donor country even if the recipient country could easily obtain better quality or cheaper prices for the same product elsewhere. This left many Africans wondering whether these were indeed loans to benefit Africa or indirect subsidies and government patronage to favored exporters of donor countries.

The one-size-fit-all approach, typical in dealings with Africa, was quite evident in these exercises. Even in those instances where African governments seemed compelled and sincere in doing good for their peoples, income and opportunities were often allowed to concentrate in a few urban centers, creating yet additional layers of problems. In a number of cases, Africans noticed that even when "expert advice" and technical assistance were offered instead of or in addition to loans, the quality of such assistance often seemed not up to what was needed and expected; it was not quite up to the task and lacked knowledge, experience, or the deftness necessary to adequately address specific African needs to a useful degree. Yet, recipient African countries, directly or indirectly, had to pay for such shoddy services and to pay back the loan fully with all interest.

Of the $540 billion Africans borrowed between 1980 and the jubilee year of 2000, nearly all have been paid back. Much of what remains is interest. At the end of 2004, that balance was said to be about $200 billion, and, in June 2005, President Bush forgave another $40 billion, the balance as at midyear 2005 was about $160 billion (www.africaaction.org). This is still a lot of a burden for Africa.

The year 2000 was a jubilee year in the Christian calendar, a year of forgiveness expected of all Christians. As Christian as Northern nations are, not much was heard in favor of forgiveness of the balance on the loan to Africa except perhaps the lone and faint voice of British Prime Minister Tony Blair. One thing to keep in mind, don't let the word "aid" misinform you. It is just a euphemism, just as you have student loans referred to as financial aid. These loans to Africa are strictly designed as business loans to attract the African borrower and to benefit the American and European lenders. The recipient (not really a borrower in the conventional sense) often ends up mortgaged and hostage, unable to meet even the ordinary needs of their populations, let alone institute programs for developments. However one looks at it, materially or spiritually, forgiveness of the balance on the loan should not be a problem for the donors, unless, as many Africans contend, this whole scheme is nothing less than an effort to weaken and colonize Africa again, establish a neo colonial relation with all the trappings and advantages of colonization without the inconvenience of physical presence, occupation with oppression. The cost / benefit ratio for the colonizer is indeed quite favorable.

To place all blame and burden on Northern donors is less than fair. As many have argued, colonialism, in fact, is a conspiracy between the colonized and their colonizers. Monies given to African countries often go through three, sometimes four or five, vetting processes. At every vetting station, about 10 percent may be skimmed off. By the time the money reached the point of task, not much remain in the sack. Yet, the country's resources have to be mobilized and diverted for repayment. In this too, African officials often sought advantages for spurious gains. Repayment amounts were often padded such that it provided cover for the transfer of the fraudulent, ill-gotten gains to personal foreign bank accounts. Often, such fraud netted the rouge the equivalent of millions of dollars, sometimes tens of millions.

Such thefts ultimately favored the institutions and countries where the loot is deposited, it provides useful capital. The loot, the profits, and interests it yields is never applied to the benefit of Africa. This prompted Africans to wonder out loud. An ordinary African cannot carry or transfer more than $10,000 without query or outright seizure of the cash. Yet, an African rogue official can transfer or carry millions of dollars looted from an African treasury and deposited in a European or an American bank with no questions asked. Where are the investigative journalists? We simply do not have the time or space to discuss this, but I am sure you can take it from here.

As far as the loans are concerned, let's just say, they have served. They have helped some African countries build needed infrastructure and developed some sectors of their economy. What remain on the repayment schedule, much of which is mere interest, may be forgiven—not just those of the "poorest nations" but across the board. What Africa needs most at this point is greater participation in world trade.

Chapter Sixteen

The Way Out

In order for African countries to embark on any effective and sustainable recovery programs, a number of key obstacles must first be removed. As we have just discussed, perhaps the number one obstacle is the debt burden. There are other obstacles that are nearly, if not equally, important. Let us look at three of them.

Good Governance

Let us step back for a good view of the road ahead. By now, it is clear that Africa presents a potentially vast and vibrant market for American goods and services, if only there are enough Africans who can afford such purchases and can afford to buy them fairly often. In order to develop Africa to that point, an economic growth rate higher than what is current must be maintained to the year for twelve years or more. A rate of 7 percent or better is what has often been suggested. At such rate, most African economies would attain middle-class status with appreciable annual per-capita GDP of about $8,000 (adjusted for inflation). At such level, the African human development index (HDI), which measures the ability of the average African to consume goods and services of all descriptions, would be appreciably high. If we are to arrive at such levels in 12 to 15 years, then the process must start soon, not much later (www.africaaction.org). It must start by putting the subunits, the smaller parts in place: how to avoid and defuse conflicts, planning the various sectors of economies for sustainable development, and building the institutions necessary to support good governance.

Good and responsible political as well as bureaucratic management is important to encourage investment flow which might help African producers rapidly get to the point where they can save substantially and reinvest their own resources to increase production for domestic consumption and export of surpluses. This is not a new idea; it has been discussed repeatedly, and the broad framework for implementation has been worked out by the Organization of African Unity (OAU) and spelt out in the Lagos Plan of Action. Exports trade is what will drive Africa's developmental efforts. That is why more responsible African leaders continually plead with their Northern counterparts to allow more African goods into American, European, and other Northern markets.

Current African exports to America and Europe comprise mainly fossil fuel; precious, strategic, and industrial minerals; cash crops, such as cocoa, coffee, edible tubers, and other forest products. There is vast potential for increases in the level of African exports, but the potential benefit will remain narrow unless deliberate steps are taken to realize it and to turn the gains into means of improving the quality of life of the average African. It is estimated that Africa will soon provide about 30 percent of America's oil import needs, assuming America is still so heavily dependent on fossil fuel. The problem with such prospect is the present order of government, revenue from sale of such commodities hardly benefits the ordinary African. This could be corrected with plans and policies to infuse profits prudently into the various sectors of African economies.

Remember the American and European farm subsidies we discussed earlier? They shut out African farm products from any significant earnings on the world market; thus, they rob about 70 percent of Africa's workforce of decent earnings. Africa has about *18* percent of the world's population; yet, it has only a mere 2 percent share of world trade, much of it strategic and commercial commodities, and the revenue hardly trickles down to the lower and more vigorous levels of African consumer society. America, on the other hand, has only 5 percent of the world's population; yet, it consumes about 25 percent of the world's resources. Good African politics backed by steadfast trade and diplomatic negotiations should forge better symbiotic and equitable relations between these two sets of facts. I have often suggested that the regional groups can help individual African states cut back their diplomatic postings and rather develop trade ambassadors who can seek and negotiate favorable trade terms.

Producers of the few consumer goods for sale are often underpaid for the sale of their goods. Let us look again at the example of coffee production and sale. At the end of 2000, for every three dollars worth of coffee beans sold in Europe or America, the African grower got only about thirty cents (a mere one-tenth), out of which he or she must pay the workers and all other overhead necessary to plant, harvest, and make ready for shipment. How can the African farmer and his workers earn enough to take care of themselves and their families? Yet, everybody wonders why Africa has more than its fair share of corruption, low capacity, and other problems. Coffee growers in Uganda, and a few other countries like Rwanda, enjoyed a brief period of higher yields and higher prices thanks in part to Western aid agencies, including US-AID.

Now, the disparity in earnings is even more pronounced. East African coffee farmers get about one dollar or less for every twenty-five dollars gained by American and European companies, like Starbucks. As selective and as temporary the benefits from such help as was offered by US-AID, there will be little momentum to start and sustain the engines that will move the African renaissance upward and forward.

This is an important area where African leadership has fallen short on behalf of the African farmer and worker. African leader have accepted the Africa Act (AGOA) wholesale, without any appreciable and concerted efforts to negotiate important details for the benefit of African producers. For instance, compulsory requirements of the African producer to modernize right from the start with bar coding on fancy paper only ended up enriching the rich nations that produce such supplies and equipment with which the African producer must modernize. To boot, the African producer is not guaranteed entry into American or other Northern markets for complying with such expensive requirements.

Revenue from oil might not bridge the gap, not as subsidies and, quite likely, not as development expenditure for irrigation and roads or even the acquisition and transfer of technologies necessary for development. Oil revenues always end up high in the national coffers, well above even the African middle class. After government pays down the huge external debt, the balance is subjected to what I call "creative shrinkage." The net left over could be used on projects that are likely to contribute little, if anything at all, to the more pressing needs of the ordinary African.

For a way out of dire poverty, the African poor have but two things to rely on: their faith and their hands, the African poor can sell their services. The poor African can cultivate and gather produce that might fetch a decent income in their primary forms or can, with little capital and the application of local technology, produce sellable, even exportable, secondary and tertiary value-added commodities such as fabric, strings of beads, wooden and woven utensils, reed, rattan, and raffia artifacts. Offers of help might come in the form of soft microloans. They must include help for both domestic as well as foreign marketing. The importance of salesmanship must not be discounted. Help might be offered for qualities and methods such as presentation and pricing.

Talent for entertainment is another asset the poor could draw upon for a way out of poverty. Sports, drama, music, and comedy can offer significant rewards for the talented and their managers and other handlers. Here, too, government and other concerns could help with facilities that could encourage the development and recognition of talents.

Tourism is yet another way of helping the poor. It offers a wide range of opportunities in which the African poor can participate, with low skills and little or no material input.

Carnival-like traditional festivals; history and lineage; eco-tourism are some of the specific areas that would likely attract high patronage. Investments, from within Africa and from foreign sources, could provide impetus for many of these considerations.

Much has been said about the need for better governance in Africa. In my personal view, the ultimate burden rests with the masses of the continent. The prevailing tendency to favor a government based largely on sentiments must be replaced with more rational assessments of what a candidate for government is likely and willing to do on behalf of the ordinary African. External interventions, in its many and various guises in African governance must stop. Yes, indeed this must be the primary, perhaps the sole responsibility of the African electorate – favor the candidate who presents the more sincere and realistic plans for equitable distribution of opportunity; favor the candidate who seem less likely to be unduly influenced by foreign concerns. African societies and countries are doing quite well under the umbrella of the African Union, which has thus far proven sincere. The African Union only needs offers of help to increase its capacity.

Conflict

As I said earlier, the debt burden is a most depressing issue. So, too, is the less-than- impressive representation of African needs by many African governments. Some detractors of an African renaissance prefer to cite and dwell on issues that are not likely to impact any well- planned and seriously implemented African economic and social recovery efforts. Conflict is one such issue. For those who only see gloom and doom in the continent, you will often hear them say, "Africa is too volatile to be seriously considered for ..." The list of conflicts in Africa within the last half of the twentieth century is long. Conflicts rage or have raged recently in Rwanda, in the Darfur region of the Sudan, in Nigeria especially in the delta region, between Algeria and Morocco, between Nigeria and Cameroon (Bakasi Island), between Somalia and Ethiopia, and between Ethiopia and Eritrea. We are all too familiar with what is going on in Congo Kinshasa, in Congo Brazzaville, Chad, Ghana, Senegal, and Cote D'Ivoire. To one degree or another, in latent or active form, they present cause for concern, if not alarm. You are probably familiar with many of them, perhaps more than I am. A cursory view might suggest the causes are many and varied. In fact, they often appear ethnic, national, class, or similarly sectarian.

Closer and more careful examination reveals a common denominator; it is seldom sectarian. It is most often economics, plain and simple. Further probing reveals land (real estate), and what is in or on the land, as the cause of all conflicts in Africa, as it is everywhere else in the world. By encroachment, displacement or some form of dispossession, the seeds of conflicts in Africa are in the soil. Currently, in many parts of Africa—in the Cassamance region of Senegal, in the Ga-Adangbe areas of Ghana, in parts of the Congo DR, in the Sudan, in Zimbabwe, Somalia, South Africa, and the Western Sahara—the seeds of discord are slowly germinating or remain dormant waiting for the right set of circumstances to manifest the great displeasure at those who, on the one hand, have custody, but failed to exercise diligence and to husband their lands and, on the other hand, those who with contempt, avarice, and the arrogance of power or position seek to possess the same land. Of the conflicts listed above, the example of Ghana is perhaps not the best, but it is the one I am personally familiar with. I will use it to try to explain this phenomenon of conflict development in Africa a bit further.

The city of Accra and the lands that surround it (stretching some sixty miles east/west and perhaps fifty miles north/south) have been the traditional home and domain of the Ga-Adangbe people, long before any written records for reference. The land does not readily offer opportunities or encouraged efforts for wealth generation. The soil is loamy, and rainfall is just enough to support grass and shrubs and some livestock. Nothing of value, as far as we know today, is beneath the earth. The only value that offers the Ga-Adangbe any significant basis for generating wealth and for making some material contributions to the progress of Ghana is the chattel and real value in the traditional titles to their lands, as allodia owners.

In contrast, the other communities that almost entirely surround them, are well endowed with wealth-generating commodities below and above ground. By most estimates, one of the largest deposits of gold in the world lies beneath that part of the country. There are diamonds, bauxite, and manganese too. Above ground is the rain forest teeming with a wide array of forest products, including timber, which offers tremendous basis for wealth generation. Well-drained and capable of holding moisture, they are also highly productive farmlands.

Being the capital, the city of Accra has had the benefit of government-sponsored developments such that it is increasingly attractive to all Ghanaians. Recognizing opportunities encouraged steady influx, Ga-Adangbe elders began to parcel out and sell or to lease their lands. So far so good, there is nothing wrong with selling and buying or leasing land, and that is precisely how the devil creeps into the details.

1) The sale of lands is often conducted by individuals who do not have the proper authority. Such imposters often also lack the ability to price the property.

2) Structures of traditional authority have broken down in many Ga-Adangbe traditional areas such that proceeds from land sales are conveniently not used for stakeholder's needs: children not enrolled in school, young men and women without means of livelihood, and basic social essentials and conveniences woefully lacking. When people are made to feel left out and behind, they become so busy surviving such that even sincere offers to help lift them out of their condition seem to them a distraction they can ill afford. Even though they are young, neglected Ga-Adangbe youth are fully aware of all that is happening to them and to their ancestral lands; what they regard as the bedrock of any future material salvation.

3) The perception or rumor is that some of the sales are transacted surreptitiously (here, it is important to note that perception is all that is real and dynamic). In many cases, the land is leased by the government or by a large company. At the end of the lease period, instead of the title reverting to

original Ga-Adangbe allodia owners, individuals, with position in government or with the company, would parcel out and sell off the land to relatives, friends, or to themselves. So you have Ga-Adangbes sitting on their land while it is being sold from under them, the culprits shielding themselves with the power of the state and with the insulting, convenient but dangerous invocation, "It is the capital city." There is still much talk on the streets of Accra about a parcel of land that the Church of Latter Day Saints (the Mormons) acquired at the turn of this millennium. Word is that the rightful stakeholders are still grumbling over the terms and settlement of the lease.

4) Wealth transferred to Accra for the exploitation of local opportunities is not available to Ga-Adangbe youth. Instead, as they see it, the inflow of capital only helps to dislodge them further from what they know as their "natural endowment," and all this happening in a society that claims to champion the ethics of care. Ga-Adangbe youth often feel totally abandoned, for they believe instead of standing up for them, their own leaders easily and quickly sells out for measly pacifiers may include offers of position and diplomatic postings.

5) To boot, the manifestation of their frustrations—of hopelessness and resignation—are preferably construed as evidence of inherent traits of low ambition and of delinquency. The classic, all too familiar offense of blaming the victim. It is often stated as, "They are shiftless, not very smart and deserve to be left behind." Ga-Adangbe youth

helplessly feel distraught by such deprivations, alienation, and disparaging references. They take it all in with quiet but deadly resentment.

6) Leaders, especially political leaders, are often reluctant to intervene for fear they will alienate themselves or weaken their position, privileges and perks.

7) However, like everything else on earth, societies advance through time in cyclical progression. At the low end of their cycle, Ga-Adangbe youth are weak and helpless and might therefore appear resigned to prevailing circumstances. However, in 60, 120, perhaps as long as 240 years from now when fourth, seventh, and twelfth generations are at or near the upper crusts of the Ga-Adangbe cycle, manifesting totally different sets of traits, Ga- Adangbe youths will begin to act out their long-suppressed faith-redemption, a deep-seated belief based on no tangible evidence that "it will all come back to us someday", a belief they have held and repressed for generations.

8) By then, the fortunes of those they perceived to have shortchanged them might be on the decline, and tension between the two groups, subdued in the past, might become readily expressed. An unguarded inflammatory reference to Ga- Adangbe ancestral lands, an unintended slight, or some otherwise insignificant provocation might be all it takes to start trouble with needless and endless destruction of lives and property. The movie *Hotel Rwanda* attempted but only told a fraction of the whole story - typical Hollywood style of course.

Rent and watch the movies *Sometimes in April* and *Red Dawn*. Conflict in Africa as elsewhere in the world might appear sectarian or political. A closer look reveals the seeds of discord are always in the soil. The land, with its drainage and its economic potential to its indigenous inhabitants are always the points of contention such as they are in Sri Lanka. The Irish "troubles," are another example; their seeds were sown in the mid-1800s, but they did not germinate until about 1916, some 60 years later, and look how long it lasted and the damage it caused. Its beginnings, in many ways, parallel what is happening with Ga-Adangbe lands right now.

During apartheid, black South Africans were forcibly moved from fertile lands and resettled, confined to a mere 15 percent of South African land - the poorest. White South Africans took and retained the more fertile 85 percent of the most arable lands. The latent rage in black South Africans stemming from this land grab was the fuse that lit the final upheaval to bring down apartheid. The McCoy / Hatfield feud in Kentucky and West Virginia is another good example and so too are the "Trail of Tears," Darfur, Palestine, Zimbabwe, Guatemala, indeed much of Central America, and the Tamil region of Sri Lanka.

In the late1980s / early 1990s, the price of most real properties in downtown Tokyo, Japan was worth the equivalent of about $25,000 per square foot (www.nytimes.com/2005/25japan.htm); yes, you read it right - 25,000 bucks per square foot. I do not imagine real property values in Accra will reach such levels any time soon, but even a value of fifty dollars or even five dollars per square foot of land space, might be more than enough to make people consider extreme and extraordinary means and measure to hold on to land or to rustle for the same.

There is an area of about sixteen to twenty square miles that includes the old commercial center of Accra by the sea and the areas immediately adjacent. It stretches for about four to five miles in all three directions from the center. The value of this parcel could well exceed one hundred dollars per square foot by the year 2040. There are approximately 43,500 square feet in an acre and 640 acres in a square mile; then, multiply by sixteen, to be conservative, and by one hundred, and place a dollar sign in front. You do the math as I am sure, you are better at it than I am. Now, I hope you begin to see what is at stake, and keep in mind this represents a mere fraction of total Ga-Adangbe lands. This is precisely why in the 1960s through the 1980s, governments around the developing world spent resources and made strong efforts to revise, standardize, and harmonize their land laws, with safeguards for allodia land owners.

The prominent question that sticks out of this discussion is why such population influx to Accra, why not to the other principal cities and towns? The answer, I think, is very simple - the heavy concentration of opportunities in Accra. Since independence, approximately half a century ago, most African states do not yet have defined policies and structured mechanisms for distribution of opportunities. A disproportionately large ratio of the investments that have come into most African countries in addition to developments sponsored by government and other domestic institutions are located in the capital. To boot, American and European farm subsidies plus foreign fishing trawlers that now encroach African fishing grounds with impunity and with tacit support of local authorities, have displaced large numbers of African farm and maritime workers with no other hope of opportunity near their native communities. This twin conditions is what spurs the radical population shifts in favor of the capital and surrounding communities adding layers upon layers to existing problems—horrific traffic jams, land encroachment, crime, frequent shortages of essential amenities, filth and squalor, and, above all, development of ethnic resentment and tension. In terms of human population dynamics, this is a giant keg of trinitrotoluene (TNT) just waiting for the flash point. In the hot African atmosphere, it does not take much.

The time to avert conflict is in its formative stages, it is the point at which it is easiest to settle disputes. Government, and organizations that sincerely advocate care, should step in and collaborate to identify legitimate stakeholders. In such civilized settings, what is often required is the mere revision of the terms of sale. It becomes tragic if, for the benefit of a few, nothing is done. It will be most tragic if this should be allowed to develop into open conflict, for this seems an instance where all concerned can keep their stake and eat it too. Ga-Adangbe title holders might be encouraged to lease their lands for private and public developments in considerations of royalty and equity in the development. The use, the sharing, and distribution of all that is realized from such transactions should be well documented and recorded with transparency. Also paramount chiefs and elders with proper authority of Ga-Adangbe clans could leverage out equity in their real assets to acquire debt (bonds or other private equity instruments) for their own developments initiatives, not only of their lands. The establishment of agricultural cooperatives and similar productive enterprises on the more arable lands will also be prudent and helpful.

The center of Accra is obviously in dire need of modernization. Multiuse developments that offer residence for Ga-Adangbe communities with offices and store fronts that can be rented out by the chiefs and elders for steady and much needed income may be considered and encouraged. After all, the idea of leveraging assets and equity by a paramount chief to acquire investments or debt for development is not without precedence in Ghana.

To some extent, conflict is part of human experience. It seems to rage everywhere in the world, in places where and at times when progress is evident. However, to the extent that conflict is very preventable and reversible, it should not be used as an excuse for holding back help for Africa's development. What might be most helpful for Africa is to craft (generally speaking) protocols and policies at national and African Union levels that will detect and avert likely conflicts, before they reach the flash point, such as we now have in the Congo, Nigeria's delta region, and in Cote d'Ivoire.

Corruption

Of the three main arguments often used to rationalize holding back help for Africa's recovery, corruption in my view is the weakest, weaker even than the arguments against conflict and against poor governance. A cursory look at the history of developed and developing economies will support my contention. Let us go back a hundred or 150 years and look at a few examples. Let us look at China, Indonesia, India, Pakistan, Italy, Mexico, Latin America, and the United States of America.

By the end of World War II, Italy's economy was made up largely of small mom-and- pop-type businesses (www.economywatch.com/world_economy/italy). Its forces had been beaten back by the "primitive" Ethiopian militia in East Africa. The entire army, as part of the axis, was later crushed by American and allied forces. General morale was low; corruption, in all its forms, was the order of the day in private and public sectors, jurors and legislators, bank officials, and family businesses, large and small. A top Milan bank official was found hanging under a bridge in London one morning following his publicized implication in massive fraud. A respectable prime minister was found assassinated in a car after failed extortion attempts.

Tourists dared not go to certain parts of Italy for fear of highway robbers. Almost every time I tuned in to the news of Italy, there was a new prime minister or a new cabinet being sworn in. So contagious was corruption, it even infected the Vatican Bank, if only by rumor. The mafia reigned supreme, as it was protected by a total and pervasive code of silence. Currently, a respectable milk distribution family business, with global concessions, is accused of fraudulent practices involving billions of dollars. Yet, as we can see, Italy has steadily climbed to become a formidable and respected member of the self-acclaimed college of the eight highest industrialized nations in the world also known as the G-8.

Now, let us go a few steps higher on the ladder of corrupt societies. From as far back as feudal times, Chinese societies indulged deeply in corruption. The feudal lords exacted heavily and at will from the peasants. By all accounts, the periods that followed the feudal dynasties were worse, and the communist era that followed it in the late 1940s offered no significant difference in spite of its utopian ideals and claims. To say that corruption still thrives in China might be the understatement of the millennium. Some Chinese businesses have shown little if any respect for what belongs to others, intellectual property rights not excluded. They copy anything they believe they can make money on, much of it American, costing legitimate patent owners billions of dollars each year. Some estimates have it at over $50 billion in 2004 alone (www.msnbc.msn.com) Even worse, the Chinese government itself, while it claims it cannot stop the practice of patent infringements, is accused by Western governments of engaging in less-than-honorable practices. Allegedly, it pegged the Yuan (the Chinese currency) to the America dollar and manipulates the currency exchange rates, whenever it can, to maintain a competitive advantage in the export/import exchange.

I know a businessman in West Africa personally, who was swindled with fake letters of credit by Chinese buyers to the tune of about one million dollars. Since 2000, he has since been trying to collect through official Chinese channels. The last time I spoke to him, he was still trying. In spite of such examples, we saw China continue to grow at an impressive 9 to 11 percent a year between 2000 and 2007, and China has just been projected to become the main driving force behind the global economy by year 2025. If indeed corruption is reason not to engage positively with a nation that tolerates rogue activities, then why do giant American and European companies continue to do high-volume business with China? Annual purchases of the American retailers Wal-Mart, K-Mart, Target, and the Federated Group, from China alone, are enough to make any nation on earth wealthy. The technology giants make sure they are not left out; Intel, IBM, Cisco, Yahoo, AOL, and others are all too eager to sell the communists all the software and hardware they need to maintain their upward and forward climb to global dominance. Giant investment banks like Goldman-Sachs and Lehman Brothers were all in China doing high-volume business in a market fraught with all sorts of economic malfeasance.

Even America has had its periods of corruption in its short history. The period immediately following the Civil War to about the end of the first quarter of the twentieth century was indeed a most prosperous one. Exports of raw materials to Europe were endless. There was plenty of capital around. This was the period when many of the robber barons established their wealth and dynasties, and a good many of the present-day Fortune 500 companies were started - J.P. Morgan, Coke, Pepsico, Ford Motors, and Marshall Fields, to name just a few. This was, without argument, the second wave of the Industrial Revolution, and it was also the period that witnessed high and rampant corruption in government, at all levels. From the tenure of President Grant on through Rutherford B. Hayes, James Garfield, Chester Arthur and beyond, federal as well as local governments were rife with corruption, scandals, and even assassinations. Public services and agencies, like the fire and customs departments, were better known for their corruption and tendencies to extort.

The recent cases involving Enron, Global Crossings, World Com, need no elaboration. The corrupt practices in Louisiana that led to the demise of its senator, Huey Long, and those in Tennessee that made Sheriff Buford Pusser a legendary, lone crusader are well known in America and around the world. An African acquaintance of mine was telling me recently it has been alleged that Jack Abramoff, or a close associate of his, approached the president of the West African nation of Gabon (one of America's foremost suppliers of oil) with the promise to arrange a meeting with President George Bush. The president of Gabon promptly paid the American solicitor the requested fee and within weeks was an honored guest at the White House.

In this argument, it is important to note that in an atmosphere with widespread tendencies toward corruption, poor accountability—often due to poor capacity—could very well be mistaken for corruption. For example, in early 2005, an auditor at the Los Alamos National Laboratory was severely beaten in a fistfight days before he was to testify to Congress on the issue of misappropriations at the center (msnbc.msn.com/id/8123885). If this had happened in Africa, there would have been hasty conclusions of an attempt to silence the witness, merely because it appeared so. Methods for awarding defense contracts with no bid and no price ceiling in America are topics for discussions around the world.

Anytime we are tempted to condemn African for corruption, we must bear in mind, "It takes two to tango." Africans cannot be corrupt to such level without the aid and complicity of others. Until quite recently, there were hardly any laws in America that barred proven or suspected loots from Africa or elsewhere from being sequestered in America or Europe. It is also common knowledge in Africa that some Northern governments gleefully roll out the red carpets in their capitols when known corrupt African leaders come calling. In April 2007, when President Teodoro Obiang Nguema of Equatorial Guinea visited Washington, U.S. Secretary of State Condoleezza Rice welcomed the African corrupt dictator with a warm grip and grin. The secretary called the corrupt dictator a "good friend" of the United States. Not much was said about human rights abuses, about democratic reforms, or about corruption.

Such impressions render America's official demands for democracy rather comical from the world's perspective.

I wish one of the investigative newsreels would do a story on the basis for award of scholarships to foreign students by American colleges and foundations from the 1980s to now. A number of scholarships awarded to African students were based neither on merit nor need. A good many were based on, "What have your parents or uncle or grandparents or hometown done for the American company that endows this school, lately?" You have heard that cliché before I am sure, "What have you done for me lately?" It is a corrupt basis for any consideration; yet, many scholarships awarded to African students over the past two decades have been based on what the student's relative have done on behalf of a company or interest group associated with an institution of higher learning. In fact, we can safely suggest with all due respect, America is not in a strong moral position to condemn Africans for corruption, to the extent of using it as basis for holding back aid, as condemnable as corruption is.

In Indonesia, one family installed and backed by America, its military cronies and Japanese business friends control just about all the big money-making ventures. India, like China, has a number of businesses that thrive on copyrights and patents belonging to American and Europeans. In 2008 Pakistan was ranked the 46th most corrupt country in the world (lifethelove.worldpress.com). Yet, all these economies continue to progress at respectable rates, China at double digits. In fact, one can make a compelling and logical argument that corruption is the manifestation of low supply challenged by high expectations. In other words, corruption is an effect as much as it is a cause of African underdevelopment.

These few examples make my point, I hope. Regardless of the cause-and-effect relations, positive economic growth along with social progress can be attained and sustained in spite of corruption, indeed regardless of the degree and extent of corruption. Like the scourges of governance and conflict, corruption must not be used as an excuse for holding back help for Africa's recovery initiatives. Unlike developed societies, corruption in Africa is driven more by need, as a matter of survival, not so much by greed.

To some extent, responsibility for taming corruption lies with the donor community. As I see it, there is absolutely nothing that compels donors to channel investments through government or even government agencies, especially when we are also urging broad-based democratic reforms with some devolution of authority and responsibility. The donor community could devise ways and means of getting needed funds for development directly to local cooperatives and small business, since, historically, financial aid channeled through central government only delivered about 25 to

40 percent to target end users (and I am not even sure the ratio is really that high in some places). Secondly, much of the loot that is skimmed off donations and loans ends up, as we said before, in private bank accounts in donor countries.

A 2004 senate investigation discovered some $700 million of oil revenue for Equatorial Guinea in the personal account of President Obiang Nguema at the Riggs Bank in Washington, D.C. Africans used to wonder out loud why officials of donor countries like America—as concerned as they claim to be about corruption in Africa—don't do enough, if anything at all, to make it impossible for looted funds to be deposited within their spheres of influence, often right under their noses. Every African I have talked to recently seems pleased the U.S. Treasury Department fined Riggs Bank $25 million on money laundering charges for its practices in accepting such deposits (www.moneylaundering.com). According to word on the street, rogue African leaders continue to stash monies snatched from African coffers or from illicit deals; buying real estate and small businesses all over America and Europe directly but mostly through proxies.

These are not all just recent developments. When the late President Mobutu Sese Seko of Zaire, in dollar terms, the most corrupt African leader in history, visited President George H.W. Bush in the early 1980s (www.heritage.org/africa/em239.cfm), he got the red-carpet treatment . As far as we know, not a word was uttered by Mr. Bush or any member of his government about corruption during Mr. Mobutu's visit. The hundreds of millions of dollars the African leader left in trust accounts have defaulted to others, not for the benefit of Africans.

However, I am happy to announce that Africans, at all levels, have well recognized the diabolical nature of corruption. It is now largely taboo to engage in corrupt activity. The African Union has set standards with mechanisms for regular peer review of African governments that include assessments and searches for evidence of corruption. Donors, with sincere concerns for the welfare of Africa, must contribute to and cooperate with the African Union in such noble efforts.

Are Africans Ready?

The only question, though seldom asked, is the question of readiness: "Are there enough Africans ready to be rich?" Here, we must exercise caution in our definitions and assessments. Personally, I consider it a fair question simply because material acquisition, by its very nature, requires a certain desire, a certain impetus, and discipline based on the individual's temperaments as well as the collective sense of worth of society.

The African personality and African self-impressions, having been so insidiously torn down over the past 500 years, the question as to whether Africans are now mentally capable and spiritually ready to accumulate and manage material wealth is neither invalid nor unfair.

However, to debate the point at this level and in such manner assumes that every African desires or rather must desire material accumulation. As in any society, not every individual wants to be wealthy. In particular, Africans tend to be more spiritual than material. An African is likely to derive satisfaction from a good deed if even there is no material reward. That notwithstanding, the average African is much like the average American, the average European, or the average Asian. An African wants to earn enough money to take care of basic daily needs: pay his rent or mortgage, provide three meals a day for each member of the immediate and extended family, send the kids to a good school, and wear decent clothes at all times. Beyond that, perhaps own a car, take a vacation every so often, and be able to start a business without undue difficulties.

However, there is another group, though perhaps much smaller, whose expectations and desires go well beyond this level. The fact that Africans from the motherland aspire to and indeed migrate to rich countries in search of material satisfaction suggests Africans from the motherland wants to be rich. The fact that corruption in Africa remain rampant and so well entrenched might suggest the degree of desire to accumulate material wealth. The fact that an African might not hesitate to consult a diviner for guidance on how to get rich quick and the fact that an African will risk his or her life by swallowing little bags of cocaine to sell for profit are all indications that Africans have the desire to get rich, at least to be able to take care of their basic needs. Since 1980, about 80 percent of all Christian churches founded by African pastors, in America or in the motherland preach mainly prosperity gospel, with vast material rewards in return for the pastors.

If you must raise the question to a higher level, that is, are there enough Africans and African-Americans capable of managing transnational and similarly large businesses like General Electric, Exxon-Mobil, Nike, Delta Airlines, Shell, Chrysler, or Citicorp? The business savvy of Africans in America is well noted even if actively ignored and often suppressed. The business achievements of individuals like John H. Johnson, owner of Johnson Publishing Co.; Carl Ware of Coke, who contributed immensely to the expansion of the company in Africa; Russell Simmons, owner of Rush Communications and the clothing line Phat Farm; Emma Chappell of The United Bank of Philadelphia; Earl Graves, publisher of *Black Entrepreneur*; Sam Jonah, general manager of Ashanti Goldfield; Jesse Hill, former head of Atlanta Life Insurance Co.; the legendary Reginald Lewis, who so niftily acquired the Beatrice Food Company; Aliko Dangote, a Nigerian self-made billionaire; Mo Ibrahim, the Sudanese founder of Pan-African telecommunications; Jay-Z; American Express CEO and chairman, Kenneth Chenault; and of course, Madame C. J. Walker, who controlled several small businesses and managed each well.

Any differences between these and the larger global companies are probably nothing more than differences of scale. My father used to say quite often, "If you learn to manage a small establishment well, you can manage a large one to much the same degree." Indeed, the difference is largely of scale; just look at or read about the city of Atlanta and the radical expansion and modernization it has gone though over the past three decades all under the management of city mayors who are of African descent. Companies such as American Express, Time-Warner, and Shell in Nigeria have lately paraded top African CEOs and other high-level executives that occupy their boardrooms as if in part to answer this very question. For now, let us focus on the more imminent issue: how to give Africans on both side of the Sargasso Sea a jump start for a short course to a renaissance and the attainment of a robust middle class within the next 20 years.

From here on, the tricks lie mostly in the hands of Africans. The suggestions spelt out in the Lagos Plan of Action, which compels Africans on the mother continent and those in the diaspora to assume full responsibility for their future and work out actionable plans for attainment, need to be place in focus. Africans must strive to increase investments in their own productive enterprises, especially in agriculture. African institutions as well as individuals must continue to push the boundaries of markets for what Africans produce, while constantly improving the quality and methods of distribution of their products. In other words, Africans must strive to, shrewdly and prudently, negotiate greater share of world markets. Revenues, realized as such, made available to the African private and public sectors through savings and various forms of debt and equity investments.

Such revenue-based capital would help provide money to, among other things; improve and to raise the literacy rate beyond the 65 percent necessary to sustain an industrial society. Other areas such as health, social welfare, public safety, and better roads and transportation systems would all benefit. As development spirals upward, the need for supporting institutions would become increasingly pressing. Strong central banks on top of domestic retail banking systems that are privately owned, well regulated, state of the art, and capable of global offerings of shares.

To keep everyone honest a sound, fair, and vigorous judiciary, independent and capable of enforcing contracts and accountability, would be needed. Government too must be capable of policing and of policing itself; of displaying transparency, accountability, and general responsibility in ways that would inspire the citizenry toward similar conduct and thereby bolster the confidence of investors—foreign as well as African. Many of these features and structures have, in fact, already been in place in some places on the continent for decades. They only need to be broadened, strengthened, and modernized. The African Union peer review of member countries is a good example. It must be bolstered, both in its mechanism and its integrity.

As Africa's economies move forward and increasingly attract foreign companies, there is hope that some of the foreign companies will establish programs and conduct business in ways that could offer basic amenities to their employees and to the communities in which they operate. They could build schools, health care facilities, or whatever public amenities and public establishments they see as bearable and relevant to their business philosophy and convenience. Giving back some of what is taken is not mere virtue; it is in fact, prudent and good business for while such offers will neither be demanded nor expected, they will where offered, provide much-welcomed help to the community at large and to government.

Certainly, goodwill would accrue in favor of such companies for government would be able to focus on the more capital and leadership-intensive demands, such as providing inspiration and opportunities and ensuring fairness and protection. In May 2005, a large group of Nigerian youths rioted and demonstrated against the Shell oil company in the delta region of the country. Their environment and the very livelihood they derived from it had been destroyed by Shell's operation. The youths demanded more jobs from the company, but more likely, they were incensed by the fact that though much of the two and a half million barrels a day of Nigerian oil was extracted from their region and had been for decades most of the villages in the area does not yet have electricity or running water. They felt left out from the vast revenue generated from their "God-given" domain. By December 2006, these small bands of agitated youths had banded and morphed into an armed political movement.

In settings such as those that currently exist in many African countries where expectations are as high as poverty and unemployment, it is prudent and helpful for private enterprise to embrace policies that offer due consideration and sensitivity. Some companies are already making such offers: they structure work schedules to offer the most job opportunities. For example, instead of three full-time positions, they may schedule five or maybe six part-time workers for the task. Where expansion is necessary, it may be set up in other areas, especially in the rural areas, where the raw material for the product is sourced. Such offers of opportunity with flexible work hours and morale-boosting perks are most helpful to the overall African recovery efforts. Reduction in unemployment certainly reduces idleness and helps avert discontent and mischief.

Clearly, Africa's way out of its current quagmire should be based on broad economic strategies led by African consumption of what Africa produces with export of the surpluses. Africans must not treat the prospects for progress passively, leaving major determinants in the hands of non-Africans. It is up to Africans to identify the most rewarding prospects and to approach them in ways that ensure maximum benefits to Africa and Africans. America can only help if it allows itself to approach African issues with a positive and proactive posture.

A number of African countries are already well on the way with such proposals.Nigeria and South Africa, for example, maintain formidable sales forces in North America to market a wide range of products that include fruits and vegetables, film production, wines, and automobiles. South African tourism promotes African safaris and other forms of exotic tourism in South Africa (www.southafrican.net/satourism/)

More needs to be done, and it must be done in more efficient ways. A country like Ghana with its rich culture has as much to offer as it stands to benefit from its indigenous attributes. For example, Ghana's establishments, responsible for promoting production and exports, could focus on items such as kente cloth. They could develop newer uses and applications, negotiate new markets, and help develop new strains of cotton for yarn and fabrics that could give kente cloth from Ghana distinct recognition and advantage over imitations. Vigorous research could be done for newer applications and presentations of products such as shea butter and cocoa butter, in fact cocoa products in general. They could negotiate with Northern manufactures to set up secondary and tertiary operations in the shea butter and cocoa growing regions of Ghana.

If a product like potatoes can make the American states of Idaho and Maine such household names, puna (yams) can do an awful lot for the name of Ghana. If the right efforts were made to popularize puna around the world and if supply begins to approximate world demands, then, within a few short years, the positive impact on the quality of life of those who farm and market puna would begin to manifest. Sorrel is yet another product example.

With increasing likelihood that ethanol will become standard energy for operating vehicles, this may be time for Africans—public as well as private sector business leaders—to start cultivating the capacities that will enable full participation in such inevitable global enterprise. Countries like Ghana, Togo, Benin, Niger, Burkina Faso, Mali, Chad, and the Central African Republic can start producing ethanol to sell to gasohol-blending companies that are likely to establish in a number of African countries. Such companies will blend gasoline (petrol) extracted in Africa with alcohol, produced in Africa, to yield gasohol for sale on world markets. Such schemes would expand the number of African economies deriving revenue from carbon fuel. Brazil is now using well over 50 percent ethanol in its gasohol blend. The EU is nearly up there, and soon China, India, and the United States will be compelled to switch to gasohol. With all the essential factors naturally stacked in favor of Africa and Africans, such investments—if even speculative at this point— are much better than current alternatives that insultingly lends African nations to Chinese schemes to merely get more Chinese-made products into European and American markets.

Africa's regional groupings, such as ECOWAS and the Southern African Customs Union, could firmly step up closer to the plate with marketing strategies for selling African goods in global markets. In addition to other efforts, they could set up offices overseas similar to South Africa's, to promote sales of goods from member nations in global markets, with each member state enjoying the inherent benefits of pooling resources for common efforts.

Such organizations can further offer better and stronger representation for member states at any global forum, such as the WTO, World Bank, Davos, or Porto Alegre, where, for example, if the West African country of Benin must argue a case, it will have the benefit of doing so with the close collaboration and full support of the entire ECOWAS body; the entire membership would be beside and behind Benin.

Chapter Seventeen

Advantage Asia

Sometime in the 1800s, a Japanese professor presented a simple national economic development plan to the emperor. The plan proposed that Japan shut itself off from the rest of the world and depend solely on itself for all its needs. "What Japan has is for Japan alone and what Japan does not have, Japan does not need." Being an island and still largely feudal with little involvement in heavy metals, industry that is, Japan had no problem implementing such plan with great success. Among other benefits, this inward policy enabled the island nation to harness and prime its internal energies upon which it built perhaps the most formidable economy of the twentieth century. Today, Japan is counted among the top five strong economies of the world.

Some hundred years after the Japanese bold initiatives, other Asian countries have adopted similar approaches by different means. They have attempted to mold and structure their internal energies into solid foundations upon which free-market economies can thrive. China, Korea, Vietnam, India, Malaysia, and other countries have all done so. It seems a nonnegotiable prerequisite to any sustainable and meaningful development agenda. Little wonder, they are all counted among the leading developing nations. Success is not attained by chance. Such preferred inward dealings are not limited to history and certainly not to the formal sector of Asian economies. It is, in fact, a most remarkable Asian consumer behavior. At home or abroad, buying goods or services, Asians, by and large, prefer to do business with their own. An Asian might not consider it an inconvenience to trek across town past six other dry cleaners just to bring the laundry to the dry cleaners owned and operated by another Asian.

Even more remarkable is the ability of Asian businesses to collaborate among themselves. They combine resources to capitalize ventures and to grow and manage the venture collaboratively. There is the classic story of the two Vietnamese families living in America, both were on welfare. The two families shared one apartment. In fact they shared most expenses, including food. This enabled them to save and to combine their welfare monies to start and successfully grow a very profitable business. With such progressive mind- set they brought from Asia, these new American entrepreneurs are most likely to pool their resources to establish banks, insurance firms, and similar financial institutions that will serve them and the grandchildren of their great grandchildren.

At home or abroad, educated or not, with little or no English, Asian parents strive to instill in their children from an early age the values of thrift and sacrifice with hard work; these were the very themes Dr. Bill Cosby and Dr. John Rosemond tried to instill in American society at the turn of this millennium, by challenging American parents to take up greater responsibility in the development of their kids. Asians instill these values as a matter of course and in spite of obvious and hidden obstacles.

I remember back in the 1970s when I was studying pharmacy in Boston I read a lot at the MIT student center library. I often went there late at night. Of the dozen or so individuals in the library at such hours, eight or more were likely to be Asian, many of them reading with the aid of translation dictionaries. They seemed to study hard, reading all the time, even with their limited English. Indeed, I found it most remarkable—this fervent subscription to what I personally call the "Ray Charles principle"—that certain inability and refusal to see let alone recognize obstacles, natural or man-made.

Africans have not yet recognized themselves as the main, if not the only, obstacle to their progress. An African-American woman will not hesitate to spend considerable sums on manicures when she is saddled with more pressing financial obligations. An African from the motherland will easily and casually drive past two or more African-owned stores to buy African food elsewhere. He or she will not even consider the extra expense for the extra distance. Attempts to sway Africans toward the attitude of doing with self for self have often been betrayed by narrow, shortsighted, and vain self-interest (still remember our discussion on arrogance?).

Near the close of the last millennium, a West African country awarded a sizable contract to an African American owned, grain-producing company to grow and market rice in West Africa. It was a contract of great value and, in many respects, a gesture of goodwill across the sea. In America, especially to the thousands of Africans living in Washington, D.C., the word "rice" might confusingly refer to political one-upmanship between a Democratic administration and a succeeding Republican regime. Africans in Washington, however, still realize the economic and social importance of rice in the old country. In many parts of West African, the word "rice" might well be defined as "serious business." By the turn of this millennium, West Africa consumed over 3 billion dollars worth of rice a year, and nearly half of that was in the months of December and January alone. As a cash crop, it is as important as cotton is to the American South. A significant number of affluent families in West Africa acquired their wealth through dealings in rice. It is even recognized as the catalyst to a major civil war. If you remember your history, West Africans were brought to South Carolina during slavery to grow rice, which continues to provide enormous wealth to many Carolina plantation and mill owners.

Of the more than three billion dollars worth consumed annually, a significant portion is imported from Asia, mainly Pakistan, Myanmar (Burma), Thailand, Cambodia, and Vietnam. So huge is the market that, if the African American and her company had taken the prospect seriously and secured even a small slice of the market, her company could have reaped millions of dollars in profits each year. Instead, even before the "first fruit," one of the American owners (I believe she was the principal or operating owner), along with some of the African officials associated with the rice project, began to dip deep into the money from the loan. She bought luxury cars and built mansions on both sides of the Sargasso Sea. She had a lavish wedding and flauntingly gave large sums of money she had not yet earned to her church. Needless to say, the project, with its vast and dynamic prospects, collapsed before it even began. It left huge liabilities and obligations with acrimonious charges and countercharges that landed the American owner and some of the top African officials in jails in their respective countries.

The trial for the American was in Atlanta. As if by some twist of fate or some rather obscured irony, as the trial concluded, a group of African taxi drivers in Atlanta, most of them from the very country where the failed rice project had been located, won the Georgia lottery, millions of dollars! Each person in the group got over a million. This sum, at least collectively, was enough to establish a solid and dynamic financial foundation for the African community in Atlanta. It could have acquired or established a savings and loan bank, at least established some sort of financial institution, if only to underwrite insurance policies at more affordable premiums. Instead, the prospects quickly descended into squabbles that required much out-of-pocket legal expenses.

The Asian community own and operate two commercial retail banks in the Atlanta area. It provides much needed financial support for Asian business initiatives. In addition to the banks, Asian businesses also enjoy the benefits of Asian foundations that provide grants and soft loans for start-up capital. Such foundations are set up by successful Asian businessmen and financial leaders. The Aga Khan foundation is an excellent example.

Unlike Africans, and beyond the characteristics of arrogance, Asians seem better able to control their sentiments. Personal misgivings and objections do not hamper their ability to cooperate and collaborate for advantages. It is this discipline that enables Asians and Europeans, to an even greater degree, take away so much good that is otherwise destined for Africans. I have heard of many instances where an African importer would bring in a whole container load of consumer goods from Africa worth, let's say, $80 thousand maybe more. A Korean, a Chinese, an Indian, or Pakistani merchant will offer the African importer $12,000 or less to take over the entire load). Prompted by the prospect of a quick profit in spite of all his troubles importing and clearing the load through customs, the African will likely accept the measly $12 thousand profit, perhaps less. The Asian takes the load and shares it with his cooperative. With such low acquisition costs, they are able to sell African goods to African consumers at lower prices to the detriment of all African retailers. Thus African consumers, enticed by the mere difference of a few pennies, will drive past African-owned stores to buy African goods from Asian markets. This is a major contributing reason why Africans are all too often forced to close shop, in debt.

In such instances, African Americans, in spite of a far-superior financial clout, have not fared much better than the African from the mother continent. When pressed for more immediate positive cash flow, an African American who has worked hard and smart to build a business, with vast worldwide potential, might sell at least controlling interest rather than exercise a higher degree of stoicism to keep it for himself and later generations of his family. The founders of the hair-managing product line Afro-sheen could be making serious inroads into African markets by now. When the African American owners of FUBU sold the principal interest to an Asian company, most people thought they could have held on longer, at least looked for private investors. With such dismal display of stoicism, savvy and sophistication, much of the benefits and advantages that must logically favor Africans, in Africa and in the diaspora, will most certainly reorient in favor of the people of the Orient.

Whatever the guiding or misguiding principles, their effects are not limited to Africans and African Americans. The large transnational companies, even the American government, have not been able to display much stoicism or sophistication in dealing with Asian businesses. At the close of the year 2005, China alone held over $250 billion in U.S. treasury securities, giving it a solid and well-diversified base in its foreign currency reserves.

Together, with the other Asian Tigers—Japan, South Korea, and Taiwan—they hold over one trillion dollars in U.S. securities (www.salon.com). The American and Chinese bilateral trade balance has been in favor of China for many years now. At the end of 2006, America suffered a deficit of about $230 billion in trade with China; up from a deficit of US$170.7 billion the previous year (papers.ssrn.com).

The list of American companies selling high-tech software and hardware to China is long and impressive. As listed earlier, it includes AOL, Intel, Yahoo, IBM, Cisco, and others. They are constantly vying with each other to sell the Chinese the means to modernize their information management and communications systems. They are all fully aware that such help gives China the advantages it needs to dislodge the United States of America as the leading economy in the world. Wal-Mart and Target alone provide the fourth largest market for China's export of consumer goods. Already, in mid-2007, China was listed as the number one economy driving the rest of the economies in the world. It is growing at increasing rate as are many of the other Asia Tigers. China's growth rate over the past five years has been double digits, and India's about 9 percent per annum (www.chinadaily.com.cn)

Unlike most African countries, China and her Asian neighbors have no difficulty joining to form a free trade zone. Even general trends beyond such specifics give even more cause for pause and reflection. Asia as a whole is currently graduating over twenty times more engineers than America; consumption of fossil fuel, especially petrol and natural gas, has quadrupled between 1985 and 2005 and is likely to quadruple again between 2005 and 2015. Petro-China's concession for drilling for oil in the Sudan was negotiated out of dire need and is likely to be repeated elsewhere in Africa, in spite of any efforts and charades to thwart such trend. (www.eoearth.org). Even more ominous, while 90 percent of employment in China is linked to agriculture, only 10 percent of its land is arable; yet, China, as we said, maintains a robust double-digit economic growth rate and a population of over one billion that is growing at well over 1 percent a year. With such pressure for fossil fuel and agricultural supplies, not to even speak of the potential as a market, China cannot control the compulsion to develop closer ties with Africa.

Similarly, India, a largely tropical and subtropical country, has shifted its export emphasis from agriculture to manufacturing and services, a trend it is not likely to reverse. In the 1990s, while American exports to India doubled, India still managed to maintain a positive balance in its trade with America (www.ers.usda.gov/Briefing/India/Trade.htm). Its exports to

America more than doubled. Like China, India needs Africa for much of its demands for primary products and as a market.

Just imagine, China and India have a combined population of about two and a half billion and population growth rates approaching 2 percent a year. The pressure to look elsewhere for, at least, some of their needs is already compelling. It might very well be in response to such prospects that so many individual Chinese and Indians are buying land everywhere, especially or perhaps incidentally in areas with predominantly African populations; on the mother continent, in the Caribbean, and in South America and Central America. African land owners seem rather eager to sell and reinvest the proceeds, often in nonproductive, non appreciating assets.

In 2002, China established a new set of mandates, the centerpiece of which is to enable and invigorate the Chinese entrepreneur. Considering China's realities, it has no choice but to get out and look for the opportunities as well as the supplies to fulfill these new mandates. It is unprecedented, yet not surprising, therefore, that two successive Chinese heads of state (since the departure of Deng Xiao Ping) have both visited Africa, and both did so very early in their tenures (www.heritage.org). To underscore the importance with which China in particular now views Africa, Chinese President Hu Jintao made a second visit to Africa in February of 2007.

Though closer relations with Asia might be less preferable to Africans and although America might possess the means by which to discourage further Asian advances into Africa, the sheer force of African demand and desire to get out and up from under the yoke of poverty might well make any Asian overtures most attractive to them. Quotas on apparel and textiles were lifted in January 2005. Other safeguards were lifted in 2008. Such terminations could cause far-reaching reverses (www.mcclatchydc.com/2005/worldbusiness). For one thing, it could further put a temporary crunch on the textile and apparel industry in America and seal the fate of African cotton growers and textile manufacturers, shutting them out from any chances of getting a share of the American market. This will, in turn, render poor African communities that depend on cotton and related industries ever more vulnerable to the ravages of poverty. Additionally, Chinese are not known to leave much to chance; they plan years, even decades, ahead.

America has repeatedly accused the Chinese of currency manipulations, and indeed they do have their currency pegged to the American dollar such that changes in relative value are not likely to hamper China's foray into American markets with the flood of apparel and other consumer goods. Even more troubling are the implications of so much accumulation of money in the hands of China as its near and distant neighbors—India, Pakistan, Iran, and North Korea—compete to beef up their armies and armaments. China with its vast and increasing revenues and reserves (due largely to American support and patronage) can, in short order, expand and modernize its military.

In early 2007, China aimed at and struck an orbiting satellite with a surface to air missile (www.nti.org/e_research/profiles/china/missile). It was perhaps to demonstrate its capability, if not its future intent. With such military backing, China and its neighbors—the other Asian Tigers, with whom it quite likely feels more akin—will begin to build up impressive global economic and political leverage. In spite of recently thwarted Chinese attempts to acquire large tracts of land in Central America and South America; in spite of blocked Chinese attempts to deploy troops to Haiti, even under UN auspices, the Chinese could very well already be on their way to global domination, with America's unintended help.

If America and its Western allies continue to concede so much to China while they hesitate and fail to engage Africa with a more sincere and positive, proactive, and preemptive spirit backed with needed material offers, America will fail to sway Africa away from Asian overtures and advances. In midyear 2007, Malaysia signed an economic pact with the African country of Namibia in which Malaysia pledged to help Namibia develop its agriculture and build its physical infrastructure. China's communications firm, ZTE, announced a deal with Ethiopia worth hundreds of millions. The Chinese company will help Ethiopia rebuild its communications system, and the Chinese have also launched a communications satellite for Nigeria, a first in Africa. In early 2007, China wrote off forty million dollars of debt owed by the government of Cote d'Ivoire (www.bilaterals.org). All throughout Africa in small towns and large cities, you will see Asians. They are not engaged in paper maneuvers to keep Africans where they want to see them. They seem to be hands-on, engaged in building infrastructure and contributing to African progress one step after another.

It has started, and it will continue. Soon, America might well find itself competitively inhibited by a new preeminence, not only in Africa but on the world stage at large. Even the UN, the object of both credit and hate in America, will be relocated to China; hence, the Chinese and their allies, well armed and with vast numerical advantage, might feel compelled to weigh in on events anywhere in the world, especially in the Middle East.

Even more serious is the fact that both Japan and China are in deep economic trouble due to the global economic recession. Both economies are export driven. China, in particular, is worried about possible political upheavals stemming from the decline in its exports. They see Africa as a viable option for their economic and political redemption.

Forty years into this millennium when historians look back to the turn of the millennium, there will be no basis to refute the fact that Asian economic and military power have been financed by Chinese windfall material gains from America's concessions of opportunities and willful defaults, at the center of which is America's disinterest in the prospects for closer and more sincere relations with Africa. Jobs that might offer African Americans a way out of poverty, start-up capital, and job opportunities that might spark sustainable economic recovery in Africa are all going to the advantage of China and the other Asian tigers.

It is also important to keep uppermost in mind that, beyond a point, efforts to sway the cub lions of Africa away from the Asian tigers, attempts to control Africa's embrace of Asian offerings might require far more than ordinary diplomatic sway and material offerings. African acceptance of Asian offerings might be so strong even the best expressions of American goodwill, on behalf of dire human needs such as Darfur, might not be sufficient to sway and keep African Americans and Africans away from Asian courtship.

Chapter Eighteen

Sankofa

What Africans have done before, Africans can do again

A remarkable observation of the African mind-set that under-girds the exploitation of the continent and leaves Africa so weak is that, to a large extent, Africans still hold the misconceptions that enabled such exploitation and degradation. In Middle America, as in other white middle-class societies around the world, the name "Africa" still conjures up notions of gloom, doom, misery, squalor, hopelessness, and similarly sinister impressions. Sadly, these notions are as strong and as dynamic as they were some 500 years ago. I do not suggest such words are not relevant or appropriate to present conditions in Africa.

However, to the extent such impressions still influence American and European policy making and implementation, affecting Africans in America and in the motherland it provides cause for much concern and scrutiny. Even in its mildest expressions, such lingering views tend to obstruct and sometimes alienate those about whom they are expressed. Often expressed in self-fulfilling terms, even if unwittingly, they tend to limit and exclude Africans needlessly. For example, "They are intellectually inferior, not much must be spent for their education." or, "They cannot handle complex maneuvers; you need to put them in the outfields and backfields." Yet, as pernicious and pervasive as these mind-sets remain, they are more often associated with legends of Western civilization. Men like Thomas Jefferson, Cecil Rhodes, and Robert Baden-Powell. In less official circumstances, Africa is still referred to as the "dark continent," and this is not mere reference to the skin complexion of its predominant population. This reference has much deeper existential implications. To many people in Western societies, the expression connotes a vast terrain dominated by diseases, witchcraft, creepy creatures, hopelessness, and helplessness all intricately intertwined like a real version of Dante's inferno. In spite of the impact of such impressions, whenever the playing field has been leveled to include them, Africans and people of African descent have performed contrary to the conventional notions and popular expectations. Jack Johnson fought his way to and won the world heavyweight boxing title. Althea Gibson and later Arthur Ashe followed by the Williams' sisters won Wimbledon. Jesse Owens, Wilma Rudolph, Bekele Abebe, Kip Keino, Aki Bua, Michael Johnson, and Bob Beaman set Olympic track and field records, and Jackie Robinson, Roy Campanella, Willie Mays, and Hank Aaron broke barriers and established new records in baseball. They raised levels of excitement in sports, with all the social, political, and positive commercial implications.

   As in sports, Africans and African-Americans have excelled in other forms of entertainment and in life, general speaking, when the field is finally leveled. The world watched with amazed delight as Marian Anderson performed at the Metropolitan Opera, as Paul Robeson played the part of Othello, and as Sidney Poitier received due recognition for his sensational performances. Africans in America and everywhere in the world were entertained and enlightened by the literary works of Loraine Hansberry, Richard Wright, Maya Angelou, James Baldwin, Alice Walker, and Alex Haley. They broke barriers of titanic dimensions as they sold seats, records, and books to the point of disproving the preferred notions that Africans lacked appreciable capabilities that might profit themselves and others, especially others.

And so, too, it was, even in mortal national obligation. Contributions of an all-African combat force, the Buffalo Soldiers, contributed significantly to Northern victories during the American Civil War. Equally, if not more remarkable, the contributions of the famous Tuskegee Airmen, their valiant efforts that destroyed or severely damaged over 400 enemy airplanes during World War II.

However, it was the recognition of the economic clout of Africans in America that really forced the necessary concessions. It was the realization that African-Americans are increasingly turning over large sums of monies, in both the formal and informal sectors of the economy. Suddenly, even television advertising featuring Americans of African descent (seemingly forbidden) became part of the mainstream, at prime time, by the mid-1980s. I will never forget the very first time I saw a television advertisement featuring a person of African descent.

It was the summer of 1968, and I was in Worcester, Massachusetts. My roommate came in from work and headed straight to the living room and the turntable. I could hear the music, very loud, "I'm black and proud; say it loud ..." Not more than a few seconds after the music stopped, the ad came on television featuring a black man, the very first I had ever seen in America. He immersed himself and was completely submerged in the barrel of detergent water and slowly came up and announced the product, "The three Bs—bleach, borax, and brightness—the three Bs." For a minute, I was both miffed and amused or rather confused, as if I was immersed in an Alfred Hitchcock plot. I thought perhaps a sort of fifth-dimensional voice was trying to tell me I too could be bright and proud if I got washed in a barrel of bleach and borax. It did indeed sound eerily familiar, I mean in a strange sort of way.

Even more than its blockade of the fields and the stages and screens, this mind-set was certainly not inclined to consider Americans of African descent for opportunities in related management and administrative positions. There were no opportunities in the dugouts, the sidelines, the front offices, or behind the cameras. There were also no opportunities even as news reporters. However, finally, here too—by reasoning or by providence—men and women of African descent are steadily taking their fair and rightful positions as basketball coaches, baseball managers, football head coaches, and producers and reporters in print, radio, television, and the theater. It has not been all that long, just around the early 1970s, when Joe Gilliam was struggling with barriers within himself that perhaps extended from the barriers in society, to play quarterback in the professional football league. It was a position regarded by those who relished negative notions about the capabilities of Africans as too demanding for an athlete of African descent. So deeply rooted was this notion in those days that a significant number of African-American athletes could only perform to the level of society's expectations. They just could not push themselves beyond that point.

It wasn't until the turn of the 1980s when Homer Jordan of Clemson University was given a fair chance, along with encouraging expressions of confidence and high expectations in his ability to play quarterback that an African-American was positively cast in that position. Homer Jordan dominated the news headlines, weekend after weekend, with his brilliant and spectacular performances backed by his sidekick, the Nigerian-born place-kicker, Donald Igwebuike. All football-loving Americans, blacks as well as whites, were immersed in Clemson football and were impressed. Even those who might have rejected such spectacles or reports, those who clung to beliefs of inferior

African intellect and ability to perform under pressure, even such individuals were helplessly impressed. White American society was compelled to put Jordan on a pedestal. It did.

Those who insisted on dismissing his feats as mere serendipity, as a series of flukes, were quickly set straight by the even more dramatic and stunning performances of Doug Williams, who was the first truly established African American professional quarterback south of the Canadian border. He had started with Tampa Bay when Tampa Bay was an expansion team. He was later traded to Washington where, in January 1988, he led the Redskins in a stunning and spectacular defeat of John Elway and the Denver Broncos in (in the views of most football fans) indeed the most spectacular and thrilling football showdown ever, to win the 1987 season Super Bowl. By the quality of their performances, Homer Jordan and Doug Williams did not merely break down a barrier; they totally shattered a gauntlet with all its hinges, attachments, and vestiges.

Who would have dreamt that, even by the standards of the 1980s, there would ever be two African-Americans standing across each other as head coaches or managers controlling the same game? "Not in a hundred years" most people would have said back then. Now, we have it in all sports and at all levels; high school, college, and the professional ranks. Indeed, gradually the truth is asserting its rightful position in human history. As in sports whenever the playing field is leveled for Africans, in any spect of life, myths are shattered and barriers are broken by demands of the plain truth. In 1998, when the field was leveled with parity and competitors were allowed from outside the United States in the National Spelling Bee competition for high school students, Jody-Anne Maxwell, a student from Jamaica, won. So impressive and sensational, it was the last time anyone was invited from outside the United States.

As I mentioned earlier, in February 2007, both head coaches in the National Football League championship (the Super Bowl) were African-Americans, and so of course, it was also the first time a head coach of African descent won the Super Bowl. I grew up in Africa and so have learned to pay attention to certain things that might seem insignificant to most Americans. Forgive me for repeating the fact that the Colts player who scored the winning touchdown to win the AFC championship and the right to the Super Bowl was the running back with the only recognizable African (Ghanaian) name on the team: (Joseph) Addai. This fact is significant?

Those who must pay attention are increasingly realizing that African dismal achievements are virtually a function of limited opportunity. They are self-fulfilling manifestations of the mind-set and attitudes of those who control such opportunities. Do not listen to me; just look at the evidence and you too will likely conclude that African dismal performances are certainly not due to innate African qualities. Whenever opportunities have been offered, fair and even, people of Africa and of African descent have brought themselves to perform commendably well, often well beyond expectations.

Just look at examples like Dr. Charles Drew, who developed the techniques for blood banking, and Dr. Ben Carson, the head of pediatric neurosurgery at Johns Hopkins. Look at the Africans with great organizational skills like the trade union leader, A. Phillip Randolph; the Pan-Africanist, Dr. Kwame Nkrumah of Ghana; the American civil rights leader, Dr. Martin Luther King, Jr.; Nelson Mandela of South Africa; Consider entrepreneurs like; Earl Graves; Russell Simmons. Their business savvy and sophistication towers high and matches any in the world.

In January 2000, in the very final football championship game of the second millennium, the Tennessee Titans led by a quarterback of African descent squared off against the St. Louis Rams led by a quarterback of European descent. Much about the match up; the venue, the historic timing, and the outcome of the game seemed divinely designed to make a point. A team from Middle America against a team from the deep South. The South; still remembered around the world as once the bastion of white racism: the quadrant of America most associated with slavery and post-slavery atrocities against Africans in America. The venue for the game was Atlanta, which without much argument is the citadel of African American spiritual, commercial, and political revival, and perhaps the gateway for Africa into North America. This end-of-millennium Super Bowl, by most accounts, was one of the most entertaining. It provided the most exciting finish of a Super Bowl game, ever.

The Titans lost this game in Atlanta by about a yard short of a game-equalizing touchdown amid charges of poor discretionary calls by the referee that might well have yielded quite a different final score. Personally, I think the outcome was, in fact, just perfect, the script written high above. That exciting near miss was, the manifestation of a subtle yet vivid and powerful message. For one thing, it climaxed the game, the season, the millennium. Everyone who watched it raved about how exciting it was. To me, the logical metaphoric interpretation of how this end-of-the-second millennium Super Bowl game ended is simply this: in sports as in life, one does not have to win to be considered worthy of participation, recognition, and adulation. One merely need demonstrate a capacity to contribute fairly to the quality and excitement of the game. That championship game, like any other, was not merely entertaining, it also profited millions around the world in viewing rights, concessions, wagering, endorsements, memorabilia sales, and a whole lot more. Conclusion: Africans can contribute a fair share in sports, and so too in life.

In a more spiritual sense, it also suggests that opportunity must not be treated as a scheme, a commodity, or some remedy to be dispensed for political and commercial advantages. Opportunity is, more importantly, necessary to bring out the best in a society for the benefit of the society and for mankind at large. To appreciate this suggestion, just take a cursory look at the last two and a half centuries of the past millennium, and ponder for a while the extent to which humanity would have been deprived or shortchanged of the unique and progressive discoveries and achievements of certain individuals. One example is George Washington Carver, who isolated a long list of organic compounds with industrial and commercial importance from peanuts and soybeans. Benjamin Banniker, appointed by President George Washington, applied his knowledge of the higher sciences to help survey and lay out the city of Washington on grids to give the city the true scientific basis that has made it a most powerful political center in the world.

Yet even by 1960, when the name Ralph Bunche became a favorite for most Africans on both sides of the Sargasso Sea, hardly anyone imagined there would ever be Africans on the mother continent, or in the diaspora, directing and managing the affairs of the world.

Since the days of Ralph Bunche, the world continues to benefit from the leaderships of Africans, Ambassadors Andrew Young and Donald McHenry of the United States of America. Angie Brooks of Liberia, Alex Quaison-Sackey of Ghana, General Garba of Nigeria, and James Jonah of Sierra Leone all served creditably at the United Nations. Their tenure as diplomats and as secretariat officials spoke convincingly to the fact that offering Africans fair participation in world government was not just smart politics; the world would otherwise have been deprived of their dedicated and talented services.

It was therefore not at all surprising when in the very final decade of the second millennium and the turn of the third, the world saw Africans begin to take positions of even greater responsibility in world governance, secular as well as clerical: Mr. Emeka Anyuoku, Secretary General of the British Commonwealth of Nations, General Colin Powell and Dr. Condoleezza Rice as Secretaries of State of the United States of America (a position that is only third in the succession to the American presidency); Mr. Kofi Annan as Secretary General of the United Nations; Cardinal Francis Arinze; as Cardinal Deacon of St. John (Della Pigna). Indeed more "princes shall come out of Egypt" and soon. The time is now.

Available historical records from antiquity to present, suggests the remarkable ability of Africans to adapt and to persevere wherever they find themselves. No other people I know of have taken so much abuse and kept on forging ahead, with smiles.

The intellectual abilities and contributions of Africans to Western civilization are well recorded and are known to those who know. The vast collections of organized knowledge from the Mystery Schools of Luxor and other organized bodies of knowledge in ancient Egypt were pillaged and plundered by Alexander and his Greek armies. It was however knowledge that guided the development of Europe and onward to the New World, where it inspired and guided the Founding Fathers of America in the establishment of the laws of jurisprudent, ethics, morality, and the very conduct and spirit of society that were bound to make America the greatest society in the history of mankind. Indeed, many of the founding fathers were members of guilds, of masons and similar societies that drew knowledge, guidance, and inspiration from knowledge organized and harmonized by African thinkers (from the east comes en-*light*-en-ment). As I said a short while ago, the layout of America's capital, the grid system, and its orientations were established with the guidance of Benjamin Banneker, whose father had come to America from the Dogon tribe of Mali, West Africa, a society steeped in knowledge and application of the higher sciences that govern the universe.

So then, with human resources atop the list of Africa's wealth, , why does the continent and its peoples continue to wallow so much in squalor, neglect, greed, and dire need, always appearing destitute and in permanent disarray? It is perhaps a question that must be directed to a higher authority.

The Covenant

Without doubt, the most powerful document on earth is the Covenant. It is, in essence the Ten Commandments as God handed it through Moses on Mount Sinai for the salvation of mankind and to the glory of God. "The decrees of the Covenant; a contract signed and sealed with blood, demands the obedience of menkind to all Ten Commandments. Those who obey faithfully are given the inner strengths and the moral character that will unleash and direct talents and attributes toward perfect productive ends. It is by its very essence binding and nonnegotiable, yet tenable and perpetual. The covenant is housed in a metal casing referred to as the Ark. The human community that holds the Ark and abides by its decrees is blessed with fortune, strength, and favor with God." *The Sign and The Seal* by Graham Hancock.

Many Christians believe that for the past two and one half millennia, the Ark, with its powerful and dynamic content, has been in the custody of Africa. According to legend, it was removed from the Temple in Jerusalem and taken up the Nile by the faithful for safer custody in Ethiopia ("Land of Black peoples") (www.sacred-text.com), where it still rests. As we discussed earlier, the term "Ethiopia," as used by the Greeks and others in antiquity, referred to the whole of Africa. Its adjectives still often refer to all Africans and descendants of Africans. Over the years, geographic references to the term have diminished it and now such reference is reserved for the East African country that used to be called Abyssinia. If as most African Christians believe Ethiopia holds the Ark and the Covenant why does the continent continue to suffer famine, pestilence, conflicts, exploitation and manipulation?

We can debate the question and at the end we may only deduce that the dynamic power of the Covenant does not belong to and was not promised to any people in particular. That even being the earthly custodian does not absolve or excuse anyone from the demands of the terms. The power of the Covenant belongs to God and to God alone. The power might be bestowed only on those who make good faith efforts to abide by its unyielding terms.

The period of organized glory in Africa lasted for well over two millennia and is well accounted for in history. Greek, Hebrew, Arab, Roman, and other European scholars, poets, and playwrights recorded the period from Aeschylus and Pliny the Elder to the Arab historian, Ibn Battuta, and from the English playwright Shakespeare to the Spanish artist Goya. Given such an abundance of records attesting to Africa's period of glory and favor with God throughout antiquity and well beyond, it is indeed necessary to ask, "What went wrong?" What happened after the year 1499? Did the rewards of treachery, adultery, idolatry, greed, hatred, and arrogance begin to manifest and reshape the fate of Africa?

By all historical accounts of the Iberians and other Europeans who followed, it does indeed appear such qualities conspired to insidiously wear down the strengths and neutralize the glories of the African people. If even such forces merely conspired to set in motion the processes of self-destruction through indulgence in war, raids and the plunder of neighbors, indeed they allowed and helped to facilitate diabolical enterprises such as the slave trade and the dehumanizing excesses of colonialism. Through a preoccupation with the worship of idols and the practice of witchcraft, any and all of which were bound to render Africans spiritually and morally weak, Africans became complacent and satisfied with self so that the importance of humility, self–improvement, and progress were discounted and abandoned.

If, in fact, this was what happened to the African people at the turn of the sixteenth century or even if it was merely nearly so, such faults and defaults did insidiously seal the fate of Africa from that point forward. It at least contributed to make Africans vulnerable to and defenseless against external efforts to conquer, subjugate, and exploit all that God had bestowed on the continent and its people. The good news is that the power of the Covenant alone, whether it is indeed in the custody of Africa or not, is sufficient to help Africans reverse current trends and recover their true destiny.

Presently, throughout the continent, the spirits of millions of Africans, aggrieved by so callous a means of separation from kith and kin, loom large and high, and they beckon to all descendants of Africa to reconnect to the motherland for spiritual pacification and reawakening. Especially to Christians of African descent, such reconnection offers particular significance. In a classic thesis, "The African Origins of Christianity," Gerald Massey convincingly presented links between indigenous African symbols, rituals, and legends and those of Christianity; indeed, he presented the basis for many of the cardinal doctrines and references of the Christian faith. Massey's references to Africa were not to the margins. He pointed deep to the very heart of the mother continent, to the general area where also is believed to be presently sequestered, the Ark of the Covenant. This area is also the source of the Nile River, the only major river in the world that flows due north and empties into the sea at a point near the port city that inspired the conception of the Statue of Liberty. Yes, the American Statue of Liberty was conceived of on African soil, in Egypt (www.touregypt.net/portsaid.htm).

I think it is compulsory that all Africans, especially those in the diaspora, know about their glorious past. Such knowledge and awareness are nonnegotiable prerequisites to a spiritual reawaking and reconnection with the ancestral motherland. I do maintain that if African Americans knew the whole truth of their African origins, instead of the twisted logic and contorted tales designed to divide and weaken African American positive self- impressions and resolve, the inhibitions that often tend to stand in the way of African American noble intentions and achievements would be few and faint.

Africans have indeed contributed much to the greatness of America and, through America, to the world. A popular American historian, I believe it was Stephen Ambrose, once said that American fighting valor in World War II might well be attributed to the discipline America's fighting men acquired as Boy Scouts. This is without argument a tribute to Africa; for Baden-Powell, founder of the Boys Scout movement, acquired the inspiration and virtually all the principles, the techniques and skills from his campaigns in Africa. You might want to read his autobiography. He will tell you so himself.

The African diaspora now covers every continent: Asia, South America, Central America, North America, and Europe. Wherever they find themselves—in the Virgin Islands or in Virginia; in Birmingham, Alabama, or Birmingham, England; in Mandeville, Jamaica, or Brazzaville, Congo—as long as the skin is black, they know they have African ancestry; it's powerful, isn't it? This is why I have said and repeated that, the reestablishment of the torn relation between Africans at home and those abroad is vital. It is a precondition to meaningful healing and to true and lasting physical and spiritual wellness. It is a precondition to perfect and lasting wealth and for better service to mankind. This is why I applaud the "Joseph Project" in Ghana and salute all those who conceived of it and worked to establish it. There are now companies that use DNA analysis to trace ancestry to Africa. For a fee, they can tell you from which parts of Africa your ancestry originated.

You must constantly strive to know the truth about yourself for that is the only thing that will set you free: boundless to do what you must as you must for self with self and without the need for permission or apology knowing that what you seek and need to do to elevate yourself to where you once were, you have done before and therefore can do again. Indeed, it is so important for one to know oneself, one's true history of capabilities and past achievements, just like the oracle at Delphi advised. Indeed, more than anything, knowledge and awareness of self is what Africans need the most in order to seize upon their inalienable rights to do for self what is good and necessary.

Africans need to cultivate a whole new mind-set that transcends the past and transcends hope. We need a new mind-set and a new way of thinking that is inspired by faith and that manifests courage in the form of the impetus and the audacity to plan and act boldly along the lines of The Lagos Plan of Action, without stepping on any toes and without breaking any laws of man or the divine. This burden, more than any, lies solely with Africans. Yes, what Africans have done before, Africans can certainly do again, and they can do it right the first time when the right set of opportunities are in place. The first step is for Africans to know themselves again. *Sankofa*!

Chapter Nineteen

Doing the Right Things

The Way Back to Glory

A sustainable and rational African renaissance must be preceded by a period of reformation. To obtain good without breaking any laws, man's or divine, should be the basis of the new African mind-set from here onward. It sounds benign, it is in fact profound. America is vastly blessed, both materially and spiritually. By year 2000, America's strength and glory stood solid and erect on three main pillars. In private conversation, I often refer to them as the 3 Ms: money, military, and morality. I know most people refer to the same as money, might, and right. Of the three, the third, the moral strength was by far the one that was most formidable, the most dynamic, and the most rewarding to America and from America. It alone was true and sincere and engaged reciprocal love such that it attracted a certain reverence from the rest of the world.

   Such reverence afforded America a certain quiet, soft power that made people around the world stop and listen with respect when America spoke. Materially, such reverence sold American goods everywhere in Africa and in the rest of the world without much need for advertisements. People consumed American brands conspicuously simply because they were American, new or secondhand; whether it was Wrangler jeans, Coke or GE appliances. Being identifiably American was all the advertising needed, and a lot of American brands have sold in Africa since World War II - *Time* magazine, Afro Sheen, Clear Essence cosmetics, Pepsi, Miller beer, Kellogg's products, Uncle Ben's rice, Aunt Jemima pancake and syrup, H. J. Heinz, Arrow shirts, just to name a few. Neither cheaper brands from Asia nor higher-quality brands from Europe could compete with African preference for American brands.

By the end of 2003, that moral pillar had all but collapsed. Personally, I began to notice the beginnings of the collapse in the summer of 2002, when I traveled to Germany. I traveled through France both ways. In France as in Germany, the press (print as well as television) presented many expressions of public displeasure in commentaries, dialogues, public speeches and rallies, graffiti and newspaper cartoons. The level of displeasure toward America was unmistakably clear, even to me whose French and German are very limited.

In spring 2003, and again the following year, I traveled to Africa, first through Amsterdam and the second time through Frankfurt, Germany. The evidence of anti-American sentiment had worsened and was evident just about everywhere I went. It was similar, if not worse, in Africa, where there were public demonstrations, cat calls on the streets, graffiti on walls, media commentaries and discussions and in private conversations too. Until then, I never thought I'd ever see such expressions of anti-Americanism. I was in Accra the day American troops entered Baghdad. I sat at an open-air restaurant when it was announced on the television evening news with footages of jubilating Iraqis. A minute or two after the news, a waitress brought a tray of soft drinks to a table across from me.

Suddenly, there was an outburst as the patron being served repeatedly said, "Take that one back; take that one back. I don't want anything American." Even if such sentiments were only transient, America's interests were still seriously affected in many ways. Just imagine it; most American consumer-product companies make on the average less than 10 percent in profits in their overseas operations. Even if one out of every ten customers, regular or potential, boycotted American-made goods and services, it would not be long before the effects begins to be felt at home. GM, Ford, Coke, GAP, Dow, Disney in Paris, and others were already feeling the winds and seeing the shadows by year end 2005.

Africans, and I suspect people in other parts of the world, are fully aware of America's other two pillars, the strengths of money and of the military. They know America is without a shred of doubt the strongest single nation on earth today. Only China and perhaps the European Union (collectively) can offer serious challenges. In terms of money, at the end of 2004, America was still the wealthiest economy with more money than the rest of the world combined. The American economy is so strong and so expansive (GNP of about fourteen trillion dollars a year at end of fiscal year 2006—a significant portion of it is generated from outside America) that it has been the driving force behind a hefty 80 percent of all the wealth generated in the world in the past several decades. As always, the problem with such statistical representations is that it tends to hide weaknesses and flaws, committed and omitted. For one, the vast wealth the American economy helped create for others did not include Africa to any appreciable degree.

When the Soviet Union was dismantled, many Africans hoped that America, finally free of the burden of communist threats, would make intelligent provisions for the legitimate needs of those still left behind, especially those that can be described as shut out, the poor, and the destitute. It simply seemed the Christian thing to do. Such African expectations were not so much inspired by the fact that America is the most churchgoing society in the developed world. Africans expected much from America for four main reasons. First of all, most Africans, including myself, always saw

Americans as a society that abides by Christian principles. Charity inspired by the golden rule—"Love thy neighbor as thy self" (Mark 12:31 King James)—was a reasonable expectation. Secondly, Africans have always regarded Americans as a people with a certain spiritual impetus that got seemingly impossible tasks done. Thirdly, America is home to some forty million citizens of African descent. The last but certainly not the least reason is, as the saying goes, "To whom much is given, much is expected." (Luke 12:48 King James)

Regrettably, African observations fell far short of expectations. American companies and the companies of American allies were seen taking even much more from Africa and giving back little or nothing; in fact, they were showing little consideration if at all for African needs in spite of large profits and huge assets from operations on the continent. The Shell oil company, for example, has operated in Nigeria for over fifty years. It has been cited numerous times for violations of Nigeria's environmental integrity. In fact, Shell's conduct of business has devastated the livelihoods of millions of Nigerians in and around the areas of their operations. Yet, virtually nothing has been done for the people as compensation, nothing pacific and certainly nothing progressive. Such inconsideration has instigated public demonstrations, with demands for jobs for the locals and for amenities such as electricity, potable water, and schools.

To further illustrate the company's level of disregard, after so many years of operation in Nigeria, the Shell oil company only recently (July 2004 to be precise) appointed a Nigerian as president of its Nigerian operations. As it has turned out, it might very well be too little, if not too late. Recently, Shell of Nigeria has been sued on behalf of the people of the Ogoni area of Nigerian for human rights abuses and other infractions. Long before the suit, rebel groups had formed in the area, and they had threatened much disruption to the oil industry; it has encouraged and continues to foster kidnappings for ransom. This is a development that was needless and could quite easily have been averted for a tiny fraction of what it will now cost. All it required was some degree of consideration for local conditions and needs.

Another example is the case of Exxon-Mobile. The company pumps billions of dollars worth of oil each year from Equatorial Guinea, a small country in central Africa ruled by a half-educated brutal dictator with a lackey personality. Exxon-Mobil was fully aware that Equatorial Guinea lacked the capacity to negotiate a fair and equitable deal for itself. The American company, nonetheless, took full advantage of the weakness of the African country; so, when the final contract was signed, the African country's share of the deal was a measly 12 percent of the value of oil Exxon-Mobile pumps out. This does not factor in any ancillary charges Exxon-Mobile exacted beyond the 12 percent. Meanwhile, Exxon-Mobile continues to register vast profits from such operational practices.

In fiscal year 2005, Exxon-Mobile made nearly $40 billion in profits, out of which the CEO of the company got a bonus package of nearly $40 million and later retired with a severance package of almost $98 million. Business in Africa was so good that the level of profits remained the same the following year. Such bluntly inequitable exchanges might be acceptable to those who profit, but I strongly suspect Christian ethics demand something much better. Such low levels of consideration in material exchanges are perhaps the largest contributor to the rapid decline in America's soft power throughout much of Africa and elsewhere in the world. This is why I have so often rejected the half-popular suggestion that President Bush alone was to blame for America's seemingly sudden decline in popularity and respect. No, the causes of the decline, in my view, have been building up over decades.

I was born and raised in Accra, Ghana, and I became politically aware at a very early age. I can confidently chronicle the events that might have led to America's rise and fall in popularity, at least in Accra. If we may arbitrarily begin in the mid 1950s, then let us start with March 1957. It was the year of Ghana's independence from British colonial rule, and the American Vice President Richard Nixon was in town with an entourage that included Mr.

John Johnson, publisher of *Jet* and *Ebony* magazines. For weeks after the ceremonies, of the thousands of visitors that came to town, the two Americans were perhaps the most talked- about men in Accra, in the media and in private conversations. There was much talk about their warm and buoyant personalities, especially Mr. Nixon's. I heard a lot about his visit to the offices of the United States Information Services (USIS) in Accra and how he spoke to a crowd in front of the building, much to the excitement of everyone present.

Not long after, the legendary jazz trumpeter, Louis Armstrong and his band came marching in. It was pure thrill everywhere he went. From then on through the 1970s, there was a long list of American athletes and artists that came through town: Mohammed Ali (then Cassius Clay); the jazz drummer, Cozzy Cole; Wilson Pickett, Roberta Flack, and Santana.

Chubby Checker also came to show us how to twist the night away. Their appearances attracted large crowds. There were lots of ordinary Americans too that came to town. Ordinary Americans, of course, did not attract crowds but they were always easy to recognize, even from a distance - often casual looking, slim, and trim with buoyant and bubbly and sometimes jazzy self-assurance.

Africans who sojourned in America provided living proof of how America could glamorously transform anyone. I well remember the Ghanaian jazz musician, Guy Warren Akwei (The Divine Drummer). His sensational jazz album; *Africa Speaks,*

America Answers was the talk of Accra for many years. I also remember the many exciting stories told about his decade long sojourn in Chicago. We were always excited to meet an American. I remember we used to think out loud among ourselves that, these were the people who invented the airplane, electric light, the

"talking machine," and air conditioners and refrigerators, and they built very tall houses high into the skies, just below the grand palace of God. These were the "can-do" people with their

"Yankee ingenuity" and their assuring attitudes of "easy does it." They were capable of "walking and chewing gum," and, if you met one and were lucky, you were likely to get a dollar or two or more as "dash," at the very least a piece of gum or stick of cigarette.

At the state level too, America was the sentimental favorite of African governments and people, even countries like Ghana and Tanzania that had embarked on socialist programs to establish the necessary foundations upon which future free-market economies could be built. Many projects, such as the hydroelectric dam linked to an aluminum smelter in Ghana, were built with financing from America. Many in Africa, even those outside Ghana, were grateful to America for its participation in the project, even if the finance minister of Ghana who negotiated the loan was refused admission and service at a hotel in America because of his skin color (President Eisenhower corrected and compensated for the offense by inviting the African finance minister to the White House).

The trend of positive impressions and good will continued steadily through the 1970s and well into the 1980s culminating, perhaps, in the 1990s with America's reversal of policy toward the South African apartheid regime that finally helped lead to majority rule. As I said earlier, during these three decades, many American athletes and performing artists came through as ambassadors of goodwill and that did indeed help establish and maintain appreciable levels of African goodwill toward Americans.

The beginning of the erosion of the acquired goodwill lagged the buildup phase only by a few years. By the mid to late 1960s, Dr. W. E. B. Dubois and his wife, Mrs. Shirley Graham Dubois, were domiciled in Accra; an African America (Afro-American) had replaced William P. Mahoney as American ambassador to Ghana. There were many other Americans, as well, living in Accra then—Ms. Vicki Garvin, who worked with Dr. Dubois; the Ghana national track and field coach, Eugene Thomas; and Dr. Maya Angelou, who was well known and respected in the city.

Americans were exciting and inspiring, and so America was where every young African wanted to go. I remember when I finished high school; I got offers of scholarships to study medicine in Russia or dentistry in East Germany, my choice. I was not interested in either; America, the land of boundless opportunity and mobility, was where I was determined to study.

I am sure there are many retired American consular services personnel with interesting war stories about the clamor of Africans to migrate or to simply visit America. It was, to virtually all of us, a place where one could amass millions simply by working smart and hard. America was a place where one was free to speak freely and could criticize the rich and powerful, even the president, and live. America was the beacon for boundless entrepreneurial adventure, for wealth creation, and for the advocacy of democracy; in short, it was a beacon of hope and fulfillment. America was idealized and out of reach to most. Yet, Africans loved this image of America and everything even remotely connected to it.

The Decline

Indeed, the beginning of the decline (what I call the lag phase) of America's popularity began in the mid-1960s even as its popularity continued to rise. I always think back to 1965, some three years after the assassination of Congo's Prime Minister, Patrice Lumumba. Most Africans suspected American complicity in the assassination, even if only tacitly. More directly, America and its European "proxies" were seen behind the rash of coups that later raged through the continent; in the north, south, east, west, and central Africa. These coups were seen not as efforts to benefit and to improve the lot of Africans. Rather they were seen as interventions either for Western strategic positioning against further Soviet Bloc intrusions into Africa or as a push to establish the necessary internal linkages for weak, lackey governments that could easily be persuaded and manipulated by American and European negotiators seeking the maximum exploitation of Africa's resources. I think I have told you twice before to see the movies: *The Wild Geese, The Constant Gardener*, and *Critical Assignment*.

Such rash of change of regimes, often involving assassinations of heads of state or heads of governments, spread rapidly and widely - Congo, Togo, Somalia, Nigeria, Ghana, Sierra Leone, Burkina Faso (then Upper Volta), Sudan, Egypt, Libya, Mali, Ethiopia, Liberia, Algeria, Benin (then Dahomey), Uganda, and Gambia among others all experienced coup d'etat during this period. By African perceptions, any African leader who stood up to or spoke against the interests of America and Europe or simply in the interests of Africa and its people and in a manner that could hinder Western aspirations and objectives was marked for ouster, often assassinated: Tafawa Balewa of Nigeria and two of his successors; General Ironsi and two regimes later, General Murtalla

Mohammed; William Nkomo of South Africa; Eduardo Mondelane of Mozambique and his successor, Samora Machel; Sylvanus Olympio of Togo; William Tolbert of Liberia and his successor Samuel Doe; President Sankara of Burkina Faso; and Amilcar Cabral of Guinea-Bissau.

Even the deaths of African leaders that were quite likely of natural causes—as in the cases of President Agostino Neto of Angola and President Houari Boumediene of Algeria, both of whom died of blood diseases, and President Nasser of Egypt, who died suddenly of a heart attack—raised considerable suspicions among Africans, young and old, educated and not, the old men stroking bushy gray beards and looking in the direction of America. All this was against the backdrop of long-lingering suspicions that America supported the apartheid regime in South Africa; therefore, by association, America supported the atrocities committed by the death squads of UNITA in Angola and RENAMO in Mozambique.

Before we go any further, let me remind you once again that some of these were perhaps nothing more than mere suspicion and rumor, but also keep in mind that perception is what is real. It need not have a shred of truth; people act and react only by what they see, hear, and believe.

Also keep in mind that, in those days, there were myriad of subtle, but very powerful ideas that American policymakers and operatives did not and perhaps still do not quite understand—if they were at all interested in understanding such ideas. For example, America, we all know, is a society that espouses individualism. When an individual is killed, an individual is dead, just as you see in the American cowboy movie—bang! bang! fhu, fhu; the shooter rides gallantly into the sunset, end of story. From such individualist viewpoint, it might be difficult for Americans to understand why the assassination; even the ouster of one man affects the African to the extent it does. Especially when, after all, the assassinated or ousted leader was in fact a despot, his hands dripping a river of the blood of his victims.

You see, in sharp contrast to American individualism, African societies are largely communal, where each is responsible for and dependent on others in a very large and complex extended family system that sometimes consists of the entire village, sometimes a cluster of towns and villages, in which the bonds of kinship have existed for generations and remain strong. Mutual dependency is the practical order of life in such communal settings. As supply and especially opportunity are limited, a necessary welfare system thrives, based on familiarity and tradition.

In such settings and mind-sets, individuals define themselves by the community they hail from and belong to. Individuals often hold the interests of the society above their personal interests. More often than not, a job in government provides the most opportunity; thus, one person's fortune of obtaining position in government is a communal gain – it is when "the ship has come in" for an entire extended family, for a whole tribe, in some cases for a whole region of the country. When such opportunity is suddenly lost, by whatever intervention, a large number of fortunes are suddenly reversed, hopes are dashed. If something of equal or greater value is not quickly offered to compensate, at least to pacify, and apologies are not quickly and properly rendered, then disappointment, anger, and rage sets in. These are sentiments likely to be passed on to grandchildren and further on down line. While such values and systems might seem counter progressive, especially from the Western perspective, they remain a potent and dynamic basis for much of the disfavor that Africans and others have developed against the American establishment. There have been more than seventy American official interventions around the world since World War II; a good many have been in Africa, as I listed earlier.

We have a saying in West Africa, "*Monki no fine, bot ekontry peepo lakam.*" If you are familiar with pigeon English, you certainly need no translation. The interpretation is just as easy. You see, the head monkey might be ugly, wicked, and mean; as head of the pack, he is often brutal. While you might be absolutely right for your absolute hatred of him, you must also rest assured there are enough monkeys in monkeydom that like him for the very same reasons you so rightfully despise and detest him. So much so, some would not merely be willing to "take one for him," some would not hesitate to give a few, risking their lives, for him. You may qualify and characterize such attitude as you wish, but these are realities you must contend with if indeed you are interested in your own security.

There were Africans who liked and respected America so much that they had profound difficulties believing that America was in any way complicit in such atrocities as the assassination of Patrice Lumumba and the overthrow of Kwame Nkrumah. However, even those people were eventually convinced once they learned or were reminded of what was happening in America itself. They had only to be reminded of the KKK and of segregationist movements on college campuses across the South; the assassinations of President Kennedy and other progressive-minded American presidents before him; of the Birmingham, Alabama, church bombing that killed three innocent girls; and the murders of Emmett Till and Medgar Evers, Martin Luther King, Jr., Malcolm X, George Jackson, and Bobby Kennedy. The reasons for the riots in Detroit, in Watts, and in Newark were seen by most Africans as parallels to those in Accra, Algiers, Sharpeville, South Africa, and elsewhere on the continent where Africans had revolted against colonial social injustices. These observations wiped out any doubts

Africans had about America's culpability in diabolical events that eroded Africa's chances for progress. As I said before, any differences between perception and the actual facts are rather lame. Whether America was in fact complicit in any or all of these events was not as important as African perceptions, beliefs and interpretations.

Another issue that troubled Africans, one that I heard and continue to hear much about, is what Africans see as double standards in American engagements with them. Africans do not trust anyone who, they think, engages in double standards. America's push for democratic reforms as precondition for aid is noble and laudable, in my personal view. However, why is America not saying much about autocratic regimes in the Arab Gulf states? Why doesn't America say anything about Morocco; about Equatorial Guinea, where the current president grabbed power by assassinating his predecessor?

Furthermore, why doesn't America do enough about Egypt, Cameroon, and others that have not shown the slightest or sufficient incline toward democratic reforms? Will the New World Order under American leadership be this selective? All of America's allies in the Middle East, with perhaps the single exception of Israel, are run by autocracies. This is not to even mention the somersault the world witnessed when Hamas won the elections in Palestine without any dispute of the process or the results. Close to home, in March, 2004 the democratically elected president of Haiti, Jean-Bertrand Aristide was officially reported to have resigned his office and taken to Africa for his security. But President Aristide insists he was ousted in a coup carried out by American operatives.

At around the turn of this century, the U.S. State Department listed the government of Equatorial Guinea as one of the most brutal and repressive in Africa – its president have thrown many of his fellow citizens in jail on mere suspicion and conducts televised public executions. He has reportedly looted much of the country's treasury and deposited most of it in the Riggs Bank in Washington, D.C., until 2004 when Congress took action against the bank and the banking system. Yes, President Obiang Nguema has, since the year 2000, been consistently listed as a dictator. Yet, nothing has been heard from the Bush government and certainly not much from mainstream American media condemning his government let alone calling for regime change. How then does America muster moral strength to tell others to "shape up or ...?

In 1971, when the Apollo 11 spacecraft was launched, a large number of people in West Africa developed conjunctivitis, an inflammation of the eye. The popular rumor was that the American space craft had been programmed to spread certain germs over human populations in the West African region, as an exercise designed to test the pattern of spread and virulence of such germs. Not long after, in the mid to late 1970s, the International Monetary Fund and the World Bank began to urge African nations (large and small) to accept loan packages with attached demands for a wide range of reforms. The regimen was largely nonnegotiable and in most cases it included such reforms as devaluation of African currencies. Many Africans saw the entire exercise by the sister banks as nothing less than undertakings at the behest of America and its Northern allies to further weaken African economies for the advantage of the allies.

Popular media, including CNN, is now available in most parts of Africa. Even long before CNN and cable, literate Africans were always current with world news; thus, information through mainstream media, even if scant, provided enough material for Africans to put one and one together. While Africans heard and read about offers their governments "could not refuse," rumors about American intentions continued on the streets. Africans heard of attempts at currency manipulations by American banks, operating on the continent, aimed at further weakening African economies. I remember the name Meridian Bio Bank, mentioned very often. Africans continued to hear of African rogue political leaders who stole large sums of monies from African coffers and deposited the loot in American and European banks with the full knowledge of officials highly placed in the American and European governments.

What I have given you so far is but a few examples of what was being said on the streets about American negative conduct of relation with Africa, in the 1960s, 1970s, and well into 1990s. In such discussions, if there are individual culprits, in relation to the atrocity, they are merely recognized as agent of America in Africa. The offense is simply charged to –the American government. Whether such rumor was true or not, it provided the basis for the continued downward slide of African respect for America.

Why nothing sufficient was done or said to set the records straight was another issue. Such neglect does not make the issue and the impressions it creates simply blow away. Quite the contrary, it tends to feed into future incidents; it provides credence to the next round of rumors, whether that too is true or not. When charges were publicly leveled against America for complicity in the overthrow of Ghana's first president, Kwame Nkrumah, and following the assassination of Congo's first prime minister - Patrice Lumumba, nothing was heard in reply.

I remember attending a lecture at Clark University in Worcester, Massachusetts, in the winter of 1969–1970, in the company of a large number of other African students studying in New England. The speaker was none other than Ambassador Franklin Williams, who had been the U.S. Ambassador in Ghana at the time President Nkrumah was overthrown. Rumor had it throughout Africa that Ambassador Williams had lent himself and his position to the

CIA's plot against the very person who held him in such high esteem and confidence, the very person who had lobbied the U.S. government for his appointment as ambassador.

During the question-and-answer period that followed his lecture, a student raised the issue and asked the ambassador to refute or confirm and defend the charge as rumor. Mr. Williams flatly refused to give an answer, leading Africans to conclude the ambassador had taken the fifth and thus, by implication, had confirmed his role in the overthrow of Kwame Nkrumah. By sheer association all other prevailing similar rumor was deemed fact by everyone who heard about the incident in Worcester. In Africa, news of this sort travels down the street, up the highways and byways, far and fast. In 1999, the U.S. State Department declassified all related documents to the American CIA-backed plot that overthrew the Nkrumah regime. The many expletives in the declassified documents rather strengthen African suspicions about Ambassador Williams' complicity and why he needed to take the fifth in Worcester.

Even more perplexing, there was hardly any challenge to a charge that sent many in West Africa into a near frenzy. The rumor that America was preparing to ship large containers of radioactive wastes to be buried in African waters off shore. Fact or rumor, they were never addressed and remained the basis of continued negative sentiments and ill will. At the end of 2006, when a European company was found guilty of shipping hazardous waste to Cote d'Ivoire, everyone in West Africa was making references to the never-proven rumor about America that had circulated years earlier. These things do not simply blow away to please or pacify anyone. American popularity and soft power in Africa continued to wane as people began talking about America's hegemonic ambitions. Publication of "The Pentagon's New Map" by Thomas

P.M. Barnett, have only helped in ratcheting up African suspicions on this charge.

By the mid-1990s, assassination of foreign leaders had long been illegal, thanks to the U.S. Congress and the (Frank) Church commission. More positive sentiments stemming from the shift in America's position on apartheid South Africa were beginning to manifest and Africans everywhere in the world applauded America's courage and efforts in favor of change and majority rule. Africans once again seemed to have better things to say about America, especially at social gatherings. I well remember when President Clinton went on his first visit to Africa. I got calls from friends and acquaintances, everyone talking about how his mere appearance electrified crowds all over the continent.

Just when America was regaining favor with the masses of Africa, just when America's more positive attributes and contributions as the beacon of democracy and of free enterprise were beginning to take center stage once again, the appearance of impropriety in the 2000 presidential elections stepped in, then the corporate scandals: Enron, Arthur Anderson, Global Crossing, Martha Stewart, and the others on the long list. They jolted the feebly rekindled confidence of millions around the world in the American systems of justice, democracy, and free enterprise. In the view of most well-wishers of America, the beacon had begun to flicker, and badly.

America's loss of that all-important third pillar, the third rail that offered such invaluable material as well as spiritual leverage, might not be attributed to the doing and undoing of President George W. Bush alone. The baggage had, in fact, been piling up in bits and pieces on the edge of the cliff for quite some time. No one paid it particular attention. Equally important is the fact that as the pile was building up some rather trivial impressions, previously disregarded, were getting intense and taking on more serious quality – that all pervasive notion that officially, "America does not make friends but only maintains interests," and when the basis for such interest waned or shifted, America would dump you like a bunch of overripe bananas or worse. I remember the very first time I heard the expression, I was about twelve years old. It, too, has been adding weight to the pile. In my view, this notion, more than any other, contributed the most to America's decline in respect and popularity in Africa.

One thing American foreign-policy implementation managers must learn and always keep in mind is that, when people are materially poor, they tend to place premiums on their intangible and spiritual assets—assets such as pride, self-respect, dignity, and loyalty. I heard that expression about the unreliable loyalty of Americans way back in the late 1950s, and I have heard it more than a dozen times since.

If there was any chance of redemption and of early reversal of some of the negative impressions, they were all dashed with the viewing of brutal and inexplicable treatments of Africans by civil agents of the United States: the beating of Rodney King in California followed not long after, by the sodomization of Abdu Luima in New York, and then by the savage gunning down of Amadu Diallo, also in New York. In each of these cases, what seemed to disturb Africans was not so much what was done, but rather how it was done: the impunity, the bestial quality and sheer callousness. It left a frightening and indelible impression on Africans and just smothered the bit of affection and respect that remained.

Perhaps even more disturbing was the more recent impression (after 9/11) that most Americans seemed to hold the view that America have the right to assassinate leaders or overthrow regimes of other sovereign nations at will; but members of the affected societies— those who were dispossessed, bereaved, or otherwise adversely affected—have no right to seek some form of retaliation soon or later. Remember what I said earlier about communality, kinship, and familiarities in African and other societies. The bonds and obligations are intricately and tightly woven. This latest suspicion frightens Africans in the sense that, if in fact it is true that Americans think as such, such thinking nails down an impasse in the already-established cycle of American state terrorism that elicits foreign terrorism (state or privately sponsored) that in turn demands and justifies more American state terrorism.

Personally, my take on this issue is somewhat different. I have lived in America for about forty years. Generally speaking, Americans are, by nature, not a curious people. In a 2006 survey, less than half could point to Iraq on the world map in reasonable time. Even more disheartening, a similar dismal ration could not point to the American state of Louisiana several months after Katrina and its aftermath had been on the news. In another Zagby survey later that year, only one-fourth of those surveyed could name two Supreme Court judges. In a follow-up survey by ABC, none of those surveyed could name the latest Supreme Court judge (www.nitwitnation.com). Only half could name the British prime minister, in spite of his frequent visits to America and the fact that he was constantly in the news. There is a segment of the Jay Leno (NBC – Tonight show) called "Jay Walkers", watch it sometimes.

This is, in my personal view, the biggest shortcoming of America as a society—low awareness in spite of the vast availability of educational institutions, libraries, and the modern forms of news dissemination. It bothers me endlessly for more reasons than I care to list. First, we have a saying in boxing, "The punch you do not see coming or fail to recognize is the one that sends you down and out." Personally, I know Americans are as resilient and adaptable as they are formidable. Once they know the game, what is at stake, where the markers are and what is needed to bridge the gap, all they need do is put on the rally cap. More than any society I know, Americans, individually and as a society, can catch up in a hurry, even if it is the bottom of the ninth inning. This, my friends, I know to be the mark of a true Yankee. I firmly believe if Americans were aware of what has been and is still being done around the world in their name, then Americans would demand different approaches to their representations abroad so as not to be erroneously portrayed as arrogant and callous.

Another reason the level of American public awareness concerns me is that such low level causes behavior and utterances that I find unbearably embarrassing indeed being an American, if even merely by naturalization. There have been, as we said earlier, over seventy American interventions of some sort against other societies, other nations of the world: regime changes, economic sabotage, and assassinations, some covert and some overt. The point I need to make here is rather simple. It is one thing to carry out such actions around the world for so long. It is totally a different issue not to expect and anticipate that at least a few of the millions of people adversely affected by such offensive adventures will show up at the main gate demanding payment for what they fervently believe is overdue blood debt. Whether the basis for such demand is right or wrong is a third and yet separate issue. Not to anticipate and prepare for the inevitability of such reaction to our actions is, in my humble view, simply unrealistic and downright dangerous. It is even more disturbing that the American public is woefully unaware of these liabilities so they can beware and be on guard. Yes indeed, "The punch that sends you down and out is the one you do not see coming or fail to recognize"

I believe if Americans were appreciably aware, then we would certainly not hear such rather simple expressions as, "We were minding our own business when we were attacked;"

"They hate us because of our lifestyle"; "... is to form a Caliphate ... and nothing else". In addition to breeding so much scorn, it is such utterances that lead people around the world to think Americans illogically believe the people they hurt abroad have no right to retaliate. As far as the idea that President Bush and his administration were responsible for all of that, my answer is a flat no. From all that I know, I will only go as far as to say, the Vulcan of Company W merely drove the 2,000-ton armored truck that shoved the pile over the edge of the cliff. Hang on! The good news is yet to come.

When we talk of the loss of esteem and respect (the moral) of America, it is not mere losses in politics; in fact it is more in economics. As I said earlier, American-made goods sold very well in Africa with little or no advertising. They sold well simply because of what the label said, "Made in America." or what consumers knew for sure was American – H.J. Heinz; Coca-Cola, Carolina Rice, Arrow shirt, Wrangler Jeans

You also remember the incident I witnessed in Accra, Ghana, on the day American troops entered Baghdad, when a patron at an open-air restaurant refused a beverage because it was American. That incident, in fact, was more ominous than it seemed; it was a microcosm of what was to become a global backlash. Most of the leading American consumer brands on the world market have begun to report decline in sales and profits (knowledge@emory.edu). A significant ratio of the American GNP is earned overseas. On the average, American consumer sales overseas earn less than 10 percent profit; therefore, if even only one out of every ten consumers of American-made goods decides to boycott—out of sheer disgust from American intrusions and misadventures, for example—soon the effects will hit home and hit hard on Main Street and Wall Street. This is what most Africans mean when they say America will not win the war in Iraq. They are not talking about the military outcome; they are talking about the broader moral, political, and economic losses that will surely fall out from popular disgust and disappointment around the world, and that, in my view, far outweighs and overshadows any military victory.

Chapter Twenty

Doing the Right Things the Right Way

Return to Respect and Favor

If I have listened well and if I have heard Africans correctly, then their fears and displeasures are neither bound by nor based on the war in Iraq per se. The war and the way and manner it has been conducted merely confirm lingering suspicions about America's planned approach to globalization. As Africans and perhaps much of the world sees it, there is an unreserved and unapologetic leviathan approach that says to everyone who dares to challenge or to question America, "We will do what we wish, as we very well please, as long as no one can do anything about it, and damn whoever it may displease." Some of the historic events we discussed earlier merely explain the increasing worldwide resentments toward such attitudes.

The added perceptions of hubris, plus America's assertion of exceptionalism, for example, its refusal to sign the Kyoto Accord on global warming when 140 of the other more-advanced countries of the world have done so, simply added to building resentments. Even more threatening to most people in Africa is America's refusal to commit troops to United Nations command and a show of preference to remain above the discretions of the World Court. Since September of 2001, certain defensive remarks have also tended to awe and amuse many non-Americans, those living in the America and those living outside.

The example I referred to earlier, "They hate us because of our lifestyle," plus "You are either with us or against us." One is seen as an attempt to hide and the other as simply a mark of simplicity. Truly speaking, there is no hate without cause. No one hates another because of their lifestyle. They might be envious perhaps, but envy is not hate. People hate only when they feel deeply aggrieved or betrayed. What seems to bother most people about such statements is not so much the fact it lacks logic, but rather its tendency to keep hidden from the American public what the rest of the world knows and knows all too well.

As I said before I, like most Africans, strongly believe that if Americans were generally more aware of what has been done around the world since the late 1940s in their name and the causal relations of such events with global terror, American public influence would cause both domestic and international policies to be formulated differently. American main stream media can help with better focus on world events. Such awareness and the public influences that may stem from it would likely make American foreign policy less coercive and perhaps more diplomatic, persuasive, and friendly.

An African professor, an acquaintance of mine, expressed great disappointment on this particular issue in a telephone conversation we had recently. He had heard his favorite political commentator make that very assertion, "They hate us because of our lifestyle." His observations and comments were similar to mine. "It somehow sounds rehearsed, like an orchestrated feeble effort to rationalize," he said. In a more damaging way, it subjects the face of America to impressions of simplicity and to scorn and ridicule around the world.

If America's future relations with Africa must proceed smoothly, then several misperceptions must be corrected. For example, the prevailing African fears that America still nurtures ambitions to take over and control by force, to the exclusion of Africans, all the good that remains for the peoples of the continent, must be quelled. Beyond what might be vain African fears and suspicions, all that might be required are sets of simpler remedies; perhaps nothing more than the simple expression, "I am sorry."

Such apologies, I might add, will not in any way take away or diminish the quality of good deeds that America, on the other hand, is all too well recognized, appreciated and respected for. Africans, like others around the world, are sophisticated enough to discern the difference between America's enormous good deeds and the not so good adventures; between the spirits of Liberal Internationalism and the diametrically opposite Vital Interest approach to its international dealings. At the turn of this millennium, the Belgians apologized for their part in the assassination of Patrice Lumumba. It calmed a lot of inflamed nerves in Africa.

As I have said before, there is a feature film on the subject. The title is *Lumumba*. It chronicles the events that led to Mr. Lumumba's assassination and the eventual installation of Mobutu Sese Seko, whose autocratic rule lasted over thirty years and benefited America and other Northern economies immensely. The film strongly suggested that the long-held African belief was correct; the belief that President Kennedy wanted Lumumba out and that American officials on the ground were, at least, well informed of all that went on in relation to the progressive Congolese premier's demise. Up until now, I have not heard any expression of regret, let alone a formal apology on behalf of America. It might be cool domestically but in Africa, I know it could very well be suppressing sales and profits of many American consumer product companies.

Official American reluctance or inability to render an apology, even where it is obviously due, might be in response to the

American popular attitude about apologies. However, we must always bear in mind that what might seem prudent in its applications in America might not be so in Africa and elsewhere. When former President Bill Clinton went to Africa, he did apologize for America's involvement in slavery and the slave trade. It resonated very well on both sides of the Sargasso Sea, and it calmed nerves and softened many hardened hearts. Those words have true magical powers; when they are well timed and sincerely rendered, they can turn back a whole armada loaded down with weapons of mass destruction. The need to strive to do the right thing, the right way, at all times cannot be overstated especially at this rather tricky juncture of transitions into globalization.

If America should fail to turn its fortunes around, back onto a favorable course, it will indeed be most regrettable. First of all, I firmly believe that most people in Africa yearn for better relations with America once again. You can hear it in their voices, in what they say, and how they say it. They like to be able to wear Wrangler Jeans, to drink Coke and Pepsi and Budweiser freely, and to patronize what is identifiably American, without sneers from neighbors and friends. So, it is my personal belief that the need for reversal of America's current disfavor with the world at large is indeed significant.

Secondly, America has everything necessary to make it happen and to make it happen smoothly. There are individuals whose very presence and approach to issues and to people exudes and demands respect and enables forgiveness. Examples of such individuals are former Presidents Jimmy Carter and Bill Clinton. I see them as individuals with remarkable insights whose mere approach to others elicits and enables forgiveness and commands respect. I think of other individuals like Senator Chuck Hegel of Nebraska, Senator Joe Biden of Delaware, Senator Barack Obama, Reverend

Jesse Jackson, former secretary of state - General Colin Powell, and and perhaps a few others.

When historians begin to write objective accounts about the turn of the twenty-first century, a topic that will quite likely cover the subject is, "How America squandered countless golden opportunities to win over and lead the world for a thousand more years." As I said earlier, progress tends to be cyclical and so, in my view, America's present disfavor in the rest of the world is merely a downturn, a low point in its social rhythm. Favor can and will be regained, even better than before if greater care is exercised in future approaches and advances. How and by whom America is represented must always be of serious consideration. I remember the early part of the 1990s when the Clinton administration took office; it was perhaps a year to a year and a half into its tenure, when I began to hear the name of a high-ranking state department official. Often, mention of her name was followed with less-than-complimentary remarks about her attitude toward African officials: words like arrogant, condescending, obnoxious, disrespectful and similar adjectives.

I did not really pay that much attention, but I began to see pictures of her in the press around 1997 and met her for a minute or two in the fall of 1998. She did not impress me in anyway like my preconceived impressions of her. Yes, when she spoke, it confirmed she had Ivy League education. She is, as they said of her, well connected and perhaps for such reasons she had exaggerated impressions of herself. Yet, I believe she could very easily have avoided all the negative impressions she accrued in the name of America, on her rounds in Africa. The ability to maintain a presence of mind and to exercise, at least, a modicum of sensitivity must be a requirement for all diplomats during this transition period of globalization, especially for a roving diplomat or one to the United Nations.

We could go deeper and deeper, but let me end by simply saying this: about 60 to 80 percent of the people in the world regard themselves poor (those who live on less than the equivalent of US$10 a day). When people are poor, especially when they are also highly aware, they tend to hold on dearly to their spirituality. That spirituality includes pride in all forms and at all levels: personal, ethnic, national, racial, and sectarian. In such settings, even a mere unguarded expression of condescension, or the challenge of an elder (even if reasonable) might offend a whole community. It could be misconstrued, amplified, and recorded in posterity. They will forgive when asked to, but they certainly will never forget, and that may cost you dearly in many and various subtle ways. This is precisely why diplomacy has its own cultivated language and protocols.

This is why I have said repeatedly, in my personal view, that Senator Barack Obama may well be a blessing to America for coming into public life at this point in history. As president, as vice president, as secretary of state or as US ambassador to the UN, Mr. Obama, more than anyone I see in America, possesses the right set of qualities and experience—accidental and acquired, and in just the right proportions—to help bring the world back to America. In addition to his laudable acquired credentials, he has been there, heard it, seen it, and knows it. He comports himself well, he is intelligent yet humble and affable with youthful exuberance. He has just the combination Africans tend to respect. Whenever I see and hear him speak, several individuals who have made significant contributions through the conduct of foreign affairs come to mind: General George Marshall, John Foster Dulles, Ralph Bunche, Henry Cabot Lodge, and Andrew Young.

America is no longer the leader of the free world. America is the leader of the world until China, Russia, and India catch up; hopefully, this will not happen for a few decades. The fact that others hesitate or simply refuse to follow should prompt those in charge of American foreign policy and its conduct to take a step back and reassess the existing basis and rationale for foreign policies. More logical options might be quite obvious, and, by all means, sentimental intelligence must not be allowed in any reformulation. In my personal opinion, America is the most logical leader in this transitional and globalizing period. America, in my personal view, is God's best model yet of an ideal society (with all its imperfections and shortcomings). In fact, I suspect the imperfections are there to tell mankind that a society need not be perfect to be good and glorious. That is why all well-meaning people in the world, the hundreds of millions of them, care about the well-being of America even if they passionately hate the conduct of American foreign policy. America's two remaining pillars of supremacy, financial and military, though sufficiently formidable, are both inherently limited.

For one thing, money does not buy respect, love, or loyalty. At best, money can buy the pretenses of respect, love, and loyalty. Military power is perhaps even more limited. The dreadful, debilitating effects of shock and awe with expected fight or flight response wears off with exposure. In this day and age of information, people in all corners of the world are familiar with every mode of fire power, at least by virtual reality. They have seen it on cable or on the Internet or at the arcade and have mentally processed its worst possible effects.

When American troops landed on the shores of Mogadishu, Somalia, in the last days of President George H. W. Bush's administration, it was in fact the American troops that seemed awed by the presence of women and children on the cliffs of the beach, so nonchalantly inspecting the gun-toting foreign soldiers wading onto their shores. Somalia women and children did not flee as marines are accustomed to. Even the more frightening question, how do you pick out and deter or punish a person demonstrably willing and seemingly eager to commit suicide for his or her course, not to mention possible proliferation of such notion in spite of our best efforts against it?

In spite of our thinking and expectations, aggression inherently breeds retaliation, and it might go back and forth with no guarantee that one side or the other will retain the upper hand forever. I do not mean to suggest that America, the world's superpower, should go around carrying a big stick just for show, even if it is more comforting to imagine so. Most Africans also recognize the fact that the stick must be swung every now and then to keep a fellow or two sane and honest. Indeed, every African I know personally wants the perpetrators of terror eliminated or at least rendered ineffective, but discretion is always the better part of valor. What troubles most Africans is not what could be done, but how it might be done.

They are concerned about the style and approach and what response such styles and approaches might elicit. Most worrisome of all are the consequential retaliations that we somehow prefer to think are illogical. If America's declared war on terror were to be waged against the conventional forces of Iraq, for example then a conventional style, out of the pages of the textbooks and from the chalkboards of West Point, would be perfect. Take the fight to the enemy squarely, much like a macho matador facing a bull that has well-defined features and has predictable moves and behavior.

The problem here is that this enemy does not lend itself to rigid definitions. The challenge we have labeled "terror," appropriately or not, is essentially more abstract than physical. In my personal view, what America in particular and the West in general are faced with is a global undercurrent, an idea that spans much of the world's poor and under privileged communities. It might be found nestled in every borough and every shantytown with dissatisfied, disillusioned, and disgruntled youths. Low on supply, high in awareness, a troublesome combination that often produces restlessness and tendencies toward mischief. Formal unemployment in many such communities approaches 40 percent. Most of the employed, especially in the informal sector, earn less than 2 dollars a day.

Metaphorically, the terror we face is more like a snake. Its natural habitat is under the grass. Even its outward manifestations, like those of the Shining Path, Al-Qaeda or Ansar al-Islamia, lack rigid and predictable forms and behavior, certainly not well defined like a bull. Perhaps, more accurately, it is like a snake with the genetic endowment of a planarian worm. When it is slashed into four pieces, it only multiplies into four new serpents. Its point of growth is at the tail. It is not easy to aim at, because it is nimble, nebulous, and wiggles backward, forward, and sideways. The way an African will logically deal with such threat is certainly not by a head-on, macho-matador style but rather by a more nifty engagement from behind.

You see, like currents on the surface of the earth, ideas and reason also change direction when they cross the equator. Rent and watch the movie, *The Gods Must Be Crazy*. Watch carefully, and you will observe how the Bushman of the Kalahari Desert engages an ill-defined threat. Don't be fooled by his style of dressing, with humility and efficiency, he eliminates the threat with one grab and swing - neat.

Meanwhile, back on the ranch, President Bush vowed to continue the fight against terror in a style most Africans would deem suitable only against a threat with a well-defined form and predictable moves. "We cannot negotiate with these people," he said at a Midwestern political campaign rally in midsummer of 2004, much to the pleasure of the large audience and, I suspect, to many within his constituency. I am very happy to note what appears to be a shift in approach of Mr. Bush's administration. In March 2007, Mr. Bush's appointed president of the World Bank, Paul Wolfowitz's implicitly recognized the Bushman's wisdom of tackling the problem from behind. Mr. Wolfowitz visited poor communities in Africa to gain firsthand impression of why so many African youths are dissatisfied, disillusioned, and disgruntled.

After the cheers and the kudos, we can only hope that out of Mr. Wolfowitz's firsthand observations, a logical and more realistic framework for approaching the war on terror through a war on poverty might emerge. Regrettably, Mr. Wolfowitz did not stay in office much longer after this noble fact-finding and photo-op tour of Africa. But really, such photo ops with the poor and destitute of the world are not necessary. What African countries are asking for is quite simple: fair trade deals with parity so Africans can take care of their own issues. Africans don't need charity or any form of paternal patronage. Mr. Wolfowitz and all other officials have open invitation to visit Africa anytime for fun and frolic with photo ops.

Greater demands for care and for the truth are a challenge for leaders all over the world for the new paradigm in communication that include satellite and cable, e-mail, faxes, and cell phones in addition to the old, but still effective modalities of print media as well as barroom and street corner conversations. Synergistically they have taken the acquisition and dissemination of information to dizzying new heights. Failure to recognize and respect such new reality might cause officials to commit blunders that may subject a whole nation to the scorns and ridicules of the rest of the world.

When I was in Africa in April 2004, I read a magazine article about misapplication of the Global Fund. The Global Fund as you know is set up by the rich Western nations led by the United States to combat the three diseases most threatening to the world's populations.

The three main pandemics are - tuberculosis, malaria, and AIDS. The article presented a comparative epidemiology of the three diseases. It concluded that deaths as well as the inability to work due to malaria and other waterborne diseases far exceed those of AIDS and related diseases. Around the Lakes Region of East Africa and Central Africa, for example, about one child in five under the age of six is likely to die of malaria. Globally, three to five million people die each year of malaria, gangue fever, and other waterborne diseases. This has Africans all over wondering out loud why there is such dogged insistence on aid for AIDS rather than more aid to fight the more deadly and debilitating waterborne diseases and to improve general health with good nutrition that will also help maintain robust systemic resistance.

Death by AIDS, malaria, or any other cause is tragic and while the very idea of a global fund is indeed thoughtful, noble and praiseworthy, the ways and means of applying it have turned it into as much a problem as the very maladies it was set up to fight. The Bush administration threatened to withdraw its contributions to the fund, but then later, at the end of 2006, it (conditionally) awarded Ghana some $500 million to fight malaria. The money was to be given piecemeal. It was a noble offer, but memories of similar offers and the reason for the threats to withhold it caused many throughout Africa and America to ask if indeed such donations are sincerely for the benefit of Africa or convenient vehicles to funnel monies into the pockets of Western pharmaceutical companies.

It is such appearance and the suspicions they breed that raise the more troubling questions about the true origins of AIDS. It provides impetus for rumors on the streets that advances conspiracy theories. It is no wonder that African youths all over now refer tongue-in-cheek to the Centers for Disease Control and Prevention (CDC-P) in Atlanta as the "Centers for Disease Creation and Proliferation." Such scornful references affect the image of a whole nation, not just its administration, institutions, and agencies. One person even repeated out loud with sarcasm and in my face when I was introduced and she was told that I lived in Atlanta. Most regrettably, it is needless and avoidable.

The forces of globalization are imminent. If America will lead, as indeed it must, then all traces of perceived arrogance in its approaches and dealings must be addressed and rectified. Africans and the world community at large are fully aware of the weaknesses and dangers of what seem an increasingly arrogant society, especially one that is also seen as inward.

What they are truly afraid of is the prospect of being led down into the abyss, spiritually and materially, and from which there might be little or no chance for escape.

Chapter Twenty One

Where Does the Elephant Sleep?

The Leviathan Trap

Where does the elephant sleep? You are right; it is rhetoric. Africans often talk in metaphors when talking about sensitive issues. The following metaphor is to illustrate an important point.

In the African jungle, the elephant reigns supreme. It is, in fact, the true king of the jungle, big and strong. All the other animals—even the lion, the leopard, the cheetah, the hyena, and the crocodile—all run for cover when the elephant approaches. There is no challenge to its power. Thus, the elephant roams the jungle with utter impunity. With its enormous power, it knocks down trees, it invades farms to helps itself to as much as it pleases, and, when afterward it must lie down to sleep it all off, it alone decides where to lie. No one dare to protest or challenge its decisions and choices.

One afternoon, the elephant with its typical disregard, laid down on a small anthill, unintentionally squashing the colony and unleashing the entire queendom of worker and soldier ants. Before long, the ants were all over the mammoth creature, striving to reach deep into the nostrils with its abundance of purulent, but nutritious discharges. Voraciously, they fed their way up the trails of mucus. Soon, there was not enough mucus to satisfy the hordes of ants. Desperate for more, they began to pull on the inner membrane of the trunk. So discomforting the sensation, the elephant made every attempt to dislodge and dispel the insects, but nothing worked.

Finally, the elephant went to the closest tree and began to strike its trunk, with increasing desperation, against the tree. Before long, the animal broke a few capillaries in its nose, and, in the African mid-afternoon heat, it bled copiously. The bleeding continued as the elephant, with unrelenting vigor, got locked in a battle of wills with the ants and with the tree.

The following morning, having bled so heavily, the elephant was noticeably weak and staggering. The other animals sensed a chance to kill the jungle giant. They all began to draw closer. One after another, they made dry runs from safe distances and when finally they were certain the giant was indeed too weak to charge back, they pounced, one after another. The lion, the leopard, the hyena, the crocodile, and the vultures all had their fill leaving what they must for the insects, maggots, and lesser creatures.

Just imagine the fickle little ant killed the giant elephant, how odd? This otherwise insignificant semi-demy, tiny, puny, diminutive version of a creepy creature was able to make the most ferocious of all land animals bring itself down and out, the victim of its own arrogance and impunity - sleeping wherever it damn well pleased.

I grew up in the city, and, frankly, I do not know whether this story is based on true jungle dynamics; however, I have heard it told many times. It always sounded good, and it makes an important point. Africans worry that if America continues with the type of military adventures it has become so well known for, it will someday soon get caught in an unsuspected and inescapable vortex that will drain off American resources, men and materials much needed for critical areas of its domestic obligations of health, education, and affordable energy. Such diversions and resulting deprivations are likely to weaken and render America vulnerable to anyone who, for whatever reasons, wishes to do harm to Americans; to the state and any of its parts.

There have been seventy or so such adventures since the Second World War. The more recent include Vietnam, the Congo (operation Dragon Rouge), the Dominican Republic (to oust President Juan Bosch), Grenada, Lebanon, Panama (to oust President Manuel Noriega), Somalia (after President Farrah Aidid), and Haiti (to oust President Aristide). The ambitious "The Pentagon's New Map" suggests what has already happened are, perhaps, mere rehearsals.

Why should Africans care what happens to America? The answer is neither short nor all that simple. Consider, at least, the following: America's wealth and power radiates outward. Even what America does internally often has far-reaching effects. As I said earlier, about a good 80 percent of all the wealth created in the last three decades of the past millennium was created by the force of the American economy. Asia, the Caribbean, South America, "Old Europe," "New Europe," and Australasia have all benefited. Only Africa has not benefited, at least not yet. Africans desperately want America to remain strong, and that is why most tend to advocate an American pullout from Iraq before it really "hits the fan."

Africans express such desire and the hope that lessons have been learned—lessons that stand to serve all mankind as we go forward in the processes toward globalization. The lesson that going after a leader in a sovereign nation or any defined community, for that matter, is not quite the same as sending a posse after a notorious mean-spirited cattle rustler. Going after a leader of a communal community carries dire consequences that are likely to reach far, both in time and in space. Another lesson hopefully learned is that in communal societies, folkways and norms are so intricately woven they are not changed merely by coercion or by command, certainly not by mere suggestion.

Personally, for these very reasons, I disagree with the African suggestion for a pullout from Iraq. I rather side squarely with former President Bush. Granted, as I just remarked, going after the leader of a sovereign nation, regardless of how abominable such leader is, is not quite the same as sending a posse after a notorious, mean-spirited cattle rustler. However, we must also recognize that two wrongs do not equal one right. A certain impression about the American fighting ability has been building quietly over the decades; this might be a "last straw." If the world should even remotely get the impression that in fact America was "run out of Dodge City," the consequences would be ugly. The insurgency, which has thus far been low key and declining, would suddenly gain immeasurable impetus. It would flare up and swell and like a squadron of tornados run amok, it would swirl around the Middle East toppling governments, especially those friendly to America. All strategic institutions and installations in the region would be rearranged to the disadvantage of America and America's allies. These would likely include the Suez Canal and all American bases in the region. Russia and China would likely not be on the side of America, and India would likely "turn coat." America would suddenly find itself facing China and Russia and, to their rear, India, Pakistan, and Turkey. They all sit atop the very oil basin in contention. America has helped make China and India rich and powerful. They will use that wealth when and how they please. However, all this, really, is not so central to the worries of most Africans.

For as we speak, there are dozens of political rebel groups, large and small, throughout the continent of Africa on both sides of mainstream, each waiting for the most opportune time to express its wishes and impose its will. If the impression should spread through the continent that, after all, America is but a paper elephant, then much of the goodwill America has contributed toward the establishment of democracy and the building of democratic institutions on the continent; in South Africa, in Nigeria and other places, and most recently in Liberia would all be at great risk. Yes, many Africans fear the impression given by a cut and run from Dodge City would inspire a rash of coups and countercoups throughout the continent that would reduce America's recent noble accomplishments and offers to nothing more than mere brilliant flashes in the pan.

Equally important is the fact that the reorganization of the world into a new order requires capable and inspiring leadership. There are about three, certainly not more than five, countries and institutions capable of organizing the rest of the nations of the world into a broad-based new system: of doing things and living with each other on this earth. Such select countries will lead with culture, style of government, and economic system. Most Africans, in spite of disappointments and suspicions and similar misgivings, prefer such leadership to be, at least to be largely, provided by America. Africans still have fond memories of the old American personality: buoyant, friendly, caring, and intensely helpful and above all, sincere. Africans still see the American people as capable, at least in times of good leadership, and of doing much good with sincere kindness.

Most importantly, the African knows that of all the nations and non state organizations capable of such leadership i.e. The European Union, China, Russia, India, and the United Nations, America is the one that is home to about forty million descendants of Africa; this is a fact that holds significant and important prospects for the coming African renaissance. There is rational evidence to support such expectation. Just look at Ireland. When sons and daughters of Ireland, those at home as well as those abroad, gained prominence on the world stage of politics, economics, and the arts: Connor Cruise O'Brien, John F. Kennedy,

Ronald Reagan, Brian Mulroney, Mary Robinson, C. S. Lewis, Daniel Patrick Moynihan, John Brutton, and George Bernard Shaw, Yeats, to mention but a few; their prominence benefited the Irish motherland as much as it did Irish communities in North America and elsewhere in the world. It certainly helped the Irish motherland with its renaissance so that even the

"troubles" responded with a noble bow. Africans recognize these parallels and thus feel justified to worry about "where the elephant sleeps."

Chapter Twenty Two

The Debt Forgiveness

If we assume that America's interest in global expansion would be for the material security of the American people, we would also expect to see America, led by its government, rushing back and forth to Africa and helping to implement a well-thought-out, planned recovery agenda. America would readily commit time, effort, and resources for such course, not necessarily for goodness sake and not even for the sake of Africa as such. America would expect to help Africans rebuild and establish strong, thriving middle-class societies capable of consuming significantly large amounts of American-made goods and services, which, in turn, would keep American producers and service providers busy and happy.

Many reasons have been offered to explain why America seems so disinterested in such prospect. The most frequent explanation is that those who lead America, especially from behind—"the movers and shakers" in commerce and civil society—do not see a clear, concise, and decent return on the risks of American resources on Africa. To that I say, fair enough. However, tell such individuals that stocks and mutual funds in African markets are yielding double digit return on investments. European and Asian companies are selling prepaid phone cards, operating fast-food franchises, and raking in millions of dollars a year in profits. In fact, according to the American government's Overseas Private Investment Corporation (OPIC) reports, Africa, at year end 2004, offered attractive returns on foreign direct investment. The IMF reported in 2007 that some sectors of African economies are growing at an aggregate rate of about 9 percent a year. We can only forgive such negative thinking, not everyone is blessed with the ability to recognize diamonds in the rough.

Another popular explanation is that America prefers to deal with Europe. Of course, former President George Bush so eloquently expressed this preference in one of the debates for the 2000 presidential elections, and, when you go to Europe today, you see the manifestation of it. There are logos of American companies all around; the Golden Arches, CNN, Coca-Cola, Northwest Airlines, Pepsi, FEDEX, and a whole host of American company insignia. However, to a similar extent, European companies have set up in America: Daimler owned Chrysler. Volvo, BMW, Porsche, and Volkswagen have all set up shop in one form or another. Indeed, on a dollar basis, European cars enjoy a significant share of the American market as well as European gasoline retailers, including BP, Shell, and Total; they command a significant presence on the American highways and byways. So too the European air carriers; KLM/Air France, Lufthansa, Alitalia, Swiss International Airlines, Aer Lingus, Olympic Airlines, Scandinavian Airlines, British Airways, Virgin Atlantic Airways, and Icelandic Airlines. The Europeans practically dominate international air travel in and out of America in spite of the numerous code shares. European defense contractor able to win American defense contract over American counterpart. The home furnishing retailer, Ikea is eating everybody's lunch.

My point is that for every American gain of European market share of consumer goods and services, there seems a reciprocal European gain in the American market. While some American companies in Europe enjoy immediate and significant gains, other American companies at home face the threat of shrinking fortunes due to the European presence in the American market. It is taking a long time but America might someday soon realize that Europeans (the new as well as the old) have not yet quite embraced the plebian character of American consumer offering and behavior, a fact that renders American consumer goods and services subject to scoffs and quiet, polite boycotts thus limiting market potentials. Don't get me wrong; the volume of business between America and Europe is vast, much of it is in securities trade. The cardinal questions are how long can securities trade sustain itself without a firm domestic manufacturing and consumer base? How many Americans know about, let alone know how to profit in securities trading?

A third explanation I've often heard as to why Africa is not getting needed attention from America is Asia. It has been said that Asia offers greater prospects than Africa. Indeed, it does. Asia's economies are much further advanced than those of Africa, thanks in large part to America's offer of both capital and patronage. Each of the Asian economies offers tremendous prospects. China, Japan, Hong Kong, Korea, Taiwan, Indonesia, Malaysia, India, and Pakistan together offer a market of about three billion people with prospects for a large middle class by the year 2020. The problem with Asia, especially China and India, is that they are all so well advanced, and they also have the capacity to produce just about any consumer goods they need. They do not need to continue to import such goods or services from Western economies. Just ask yourself why they are producing so many engineers (about twenty times more than America), according to some estimates. Beyond such prospects, both India and especially China are well known for their flagrant violations of intellectual property rights, violations which cost legitimate owners in the West billions of dollars each year.

If American leaders remain unperturbed by such disadvantages in their preferred commercial relations with Europe and Asia, then it might very well explain the more popular notions held at the lower levels of African societies, at the street level. While some might sound simple or superstitious, much of it sounds rational and logical.

- a) Sheer white American racism: There is a fear by some white Americans that developed African societies will open the gates for "miscegenation," which, by the power of the one-eighth rule, is bound to turn this into a black man's world much sooner than the white man is willing to concede.
- b) Curse of doom on Africa (Canaan and his descendants): No one can help Africa.
- c) African ancestral spirits want no offers from white America because of the slave trade, slavery, and colonial exploitations.
- d) America has become stingy.
- e) America wants Africa to remain nothing more than a source for raw materials and perhaps its market later on.
- f) Just as Africans in America have always gone on to dominate when the playing field is finally leveled, the powers that be in America are afraid that able Africans will quickly challenge Americans for global opportunities and might soon go on to dominate and control much of the material world.
- g) Africans, when powerful enough, will develop a systematic regimen for retaliation for slavery and colonialism.

This last notion, if true, cannot be anything more than the projection of European thinking, for Africans are the most forgiving people I know of on this planet. It seems many non Africans see the forgiving nature of Africans as a weakness. Only

Africans themselves recognize their forgiving nature as the source of their great resilience and boundless inner strengths.

There are still a few other explanations, most of which I really do not care to discuss, except perhaps for one.

I once read in, *America: Cradle For The Second Coming Of The Christ* by Helen Wright in which she recounted Wesley Bradshaw's *George Washington's Vision* (published in the *National Tribune*, Vol.4, No.12 December 1880) about three perils that faced the nation of America. It was, in fact, a vision that America's first president, George Washington, had.

Most interpreters agree the first vision was about the American Revolution. The second was as clear as the first. It was about the American Civil War. The third, the only one relevant to this discussion, has been widely and variedly interpreted.

The content of President Washington's third vision might be recounted as follows:

"Then, my eyes beheld a fearful scene. From each of these countries (Europe, Asia, Africa) arose thick black clouds which were soon joined into one. And throughout this mass there gleamed a dark red light by which I saw hordes of armed men who, moving with the cloud, marched by land and sailed by sea to America, which country was enveloped in the volume of cloud. I dimly saw these vast armies devastate the whole country and burn villages, towns and cities that I had beheld springing up."

As you might expect and as I said earlier, there are several interpretations, in whole or in part, of George Washington's vision; some are quite relevant to this discussion. Could this also be a premonition? What might happen if the poor of the world, especially of Asia and Africa where they abound and of Europe where idealism and "enlightenment" still quietly flourishes with champions always looking for courses and venues for expression, are not offered sufficient opportunity for positive self fulfillment?

Now that the Soviet Union has been dismantled and world communism is under revision, America has the "all clear" sign from above to extend itself over the earth, " to go on, increasing in power and goodness, until her borders shall end only in the remotest corners of the earth, and the whole earth shall, beneath her sheltering wing, become a universal Republic. Let her, in her prosperity however, remember the Lord her God, let her trust be always in Him, and she shall never be confounded" (Revelations 13:20).

Friends, I will not bore you with any attempts at interpretation. I wouldn't even know how to begin, but at least I do recognize the fact that this blessing, expressed through Revelations, is conditional. The provisions are spelled out in the first half of the last sentence,

"Let her in her prosperity, however, remember the Lord her God, ..." America will dominate the world and in a positive way; there is no doubt about that. What I have difficulty imagining is how the globalizing efforts led by America might be smooth and peaceful when there are hundreds of millions of people with high and increasing expectations, but cannot make ends meet even within their relatively primitive local economies. How can a world made up largely of well-informed masses with high expectations be held down for so long?

I still strongly believe that many of us, especially people in high positions of authority, have not quite grasped the full implications of the magnitude of change in information dissemination; the new dynamics created by the augmentations and expansions in information technology. Visit a small African village, and talk with the locals—the Masai in East Africa; the Bushman of the Kalahari Desert (the Koikoi and the San); or people in Ghana, Nigeria, or anywhere on the continent—and you will be stunned by their level of awareness. People you happen to talk to might be only seventeen, perhaps not more than twenty-one, and none of them might have ever traveled more than sixty miles beyond their village; yet, some of them know what goes on in Hollywood, in Las Vegas, on Madison Avenue, and on Wall Street.

Their knowledge might be more current than yours and mine.

They are beginning to wonder why they are left so far behind when they also know that not very long ago, there was some good that was to serve as the foundation for a fair and decent life for them and future generations of their lineage. Young Africans are already asking such questions. It is good to extend some good to them before they begin to organize destructive actions in place of such questions.

This is why Africans worry about what they see is America's half-hearted offers of help to Africa and the baseless fear that a developed Africa will enable Africans to compete with Americans for global goods and opportunities.

Extending American resources and the spirit of goodness, for which its people are still well known, is not mere altruism; it is in a larger sense an acknowledgement of God and of all the blessings that flows from above. It also fulfills the terms of the provisional blessing. The illumination of George Washington's vision by a dark red light might just be ominous warnings about possible sinister events that might befall America if poverty is allowed to continue to flourish in the midst of plenty and in an atmosphere of rising awareness and expectations. There is still time to heed the warning. Regrettably, while light comes from the east, its illuminating benefits are reserved for only those who can see. When the American embassies were bombed in East Africa followed with the bombing of the *USS Cole*, they were to serve as warnings, to alert us with plenty of time to preempt and reorganize our defenses.

We failed to recognize it, perhaps because after all, it happened in Africa. Dr. Paul Wolfowitz's round of visits to Africa in early 2007 was too little if not too late. It was nonetheless a beginning, assuring, at least to some extent. What will be most helpful at this point is a well-titrated help regimen that will certainly push Africa's development efforts well beyond the threshold.

If the blessings and anointing of America as world leader should be taken away, directly by God or through the intervention of man, what will make it most unfortunate, truly tragic, is that it could all have been prevented and with a mere tiny fraction of what is now spent against truly built-up and exaggerated fears. The more effective and efficient way to eliminate the true threat we now face is not by direct confrontation, but as demonstrated by the Bushman of the Kalahari, by such neat and nifty engagement from behind. My grandmother used to say, "I go to bed and wake up with a free mind. I have no fears, because I have no enemies." America still has a latent, hidden morale capital to reduce its list of enemies to near zero.

This, I suspect, is what prompted former U.S. Treasury Secretary Paul O'Neill's philosophy and efforts on the issue of global poverty reduction. His ideas, well represented with documented plans, continue to inspire the millennium challenge; it is a philosophy and position rapidly gaining popularity and whose champions include former British Prime Minister Tony Blair, former American Secretary of State Colin Powell, talk show hostess Oprah Winfrey; the popular Irish rock band U2 leader, Bono; and Nobel Prize winner Dr.

Muhammad Yunus, among others.

On July 2, 2005, a group in London organized a "Live 8" concert that featured a long list of artists in ten cities on four continents simultaneously. Bono, Bjork, Will Smith, and Stevie Wonder were joined by a host of African artists, who donated their time and talents just to draw the world's attention to the need for true and meaningful help for Africa beginning with, at least, a sincere pledge of some twenty-five billion dollars worth of additional help from the G8 Gleneagles 2005 that was scheduled to meet in Scotland the following week.

Microsoft's Bill Gates and former South African President Nelson Mandela also participated in the campaign. The effort achieved its main goal. In very short order, the world's attention, including that of ordinary Americans, was focused on Africa.

Much has been said, with concern, that soon official America will gain world recognition for its marginal offers to Africa. Tony Blair and his co-champions for Africa are fully aware that American full participation is significant for any meaningful regimen for change in Africa. George Washington's vision needs to further alert us with a few frightening facts. By the year 1919 (less than a hundred years ago), the world had hardly heard of a communist state. Before the early 1970s, when a young Italian idealist made a bold attempt, no one had ever heard of airplane hijacking, and, before 1990, no rational mind could imagine suicide bombing. The need to always strive to do the right thing and do the right thing the right way the first time is important.

Sometime at the end of the 2002 professional football season, I was on a subway train when I overheard a group of five or six guys talking about the steady rise of African- Americans in politics, commerce, and sports management. They were not saying anything new; I was fully aware of all they were talking about, but I listened if only because it confirmed my own personal thoughts on the subject. Historically, when Americans of African descent have been excluded from particular sports, particular positions or events, they have not merely smashed records when finally allowed in, they have also gone on to dominate the sport, the position, event, and, more often than not, have done so in short order.

One of the guys on the train recounted a story that sounded familiar. I too remember that incident; during preparations for the Mexico City Olympic track and field. The U.S. team was training in South Lake Tahoe in late spring 1968. One of the long-distance runners for the United States (a white athlete) was asked in a network interview what he thought was the reason why Africans and African descendants only did well in the sprints and not in the long-distance track events. His answer was something to the effect that Africans and their descendants are lazy and were therefore essentially limited to the short sprints.

In the Olympic "metric mile" (1,500 meters), later that summer, Kip Keino of Kenya won the 1,500 meters race (1 mile) beating the American and world record holder, Jim Ryun who took the silver. The fellow who gave that racist answer did not even show in his long- distance event. To boot, an African, Mamo Wolde of Ethiopia, won the most grueling of all distance races, the twenty-six-mile marathon, just as his compatriot Bikila Abebe had won it race the previous two Olympics (Rome 1960, and Tokyo 1964). Africans have dominated the long-distance events since 1968. They continue to come in first, second, and third place in the "metric mile" and other long-distance races, including the recent Olympic "metric mile" in Athens, Greece (2004).

The group on the train was engaged in a very lively discussion of the history of African-Americans in athletics as the train pulled into Peachtree Street Station, where I was to get off. At that point, they were on the subject of African-Americans playing the position of quarterback in the game of football, a subject that had always interested me. Ask anyone who was born during or before the mid-1960s, and they will tell you. Up until about the mid to late1970s, when Doug Williams started for Tampa Bay and Homer Jordan was at Clemson, an African-American quarterback in the college or pro ranks was virtually unheard of and not really expected.

Athletes of African descent were conventionally deemed not intelligent enough to master and direct the intricate maneuvers of the position. Since Jordan and Williams established compelling reasons to level the playing field, African-American quarterbacks at all levels of the game are on a steep and steady rise, a fact that speaks directly to the issue at hand. You give people opportunity on a level playing field, and they might do more than you expect. If I am repeating some things I have said before, please allow me.

Some of these facts bear repetition.

And so, in February 2007 (Black History Month, incidentally) when the Super Bowl game that determines the National Football League championship featured two African- American head coaches, it conclusively confirmed the dynamics, the need and the wisdom for offering opportunity to all and on a level playing field. In the season, the guys on the train were talking about (2002), ten of the thirty-two or so starting quarterbacks in the professional football league were of African descent; it was a ratio of about 30 percent, attained in less than fifteen years since Doug Williams led the Washington Redskins in their spectacular and historic Super Bowl win; yes indeed, success breeds success. It seems to be the pattern in sports as in life.

Jesse Owens did not merely break track and field records at the Berlin Olympics in 1936, he also shattered a myth that caused Adolph Hitler to scram out of the stadium; Dr. Ben Carson, head of pediatric neurosurgery at the prestigious Johns Hopkins University Center, did not only break a barrier; he turned a whole stereotype upside down. Remember the young lady from Jamaica I mentioned earlier, the one that was invited to the American spelling bee contest: she stunned the contest organizers and fans. The organizers immediately put an end to foreign participation. Indeed, in all walks of life, African-Americans are rising to positions of responsibility and respectability, directing and managing with remarkable skill and style in the game of life as in sports.

When you and I see men who happen to be of African descent displaying talent and hard work for entertainment—whether it's Pele, Okocha, Ronaldinho, or George Weir in soccer; Warrick Dunn, Michael Vick, Samkon Gado, Joseph Addai, or Donavan McNabb in football; Vejay Singh and Tiger Woods in golf; or Iverson, Euel Deng, Lebron James, Michael Jordan, or Ervin Johnson in basketball, you and I are amused and entertained.

Interestingly, others see the same game, the same athletes, and instead they sublimely see ethnic anomalies that are entertaining yet threatening. They see black men who are capable of working magic with big, brown bouncy balls on level playing fields. Even when the field is not level, they see black men with dark sticks capable of hitting small white balls into little black round holes. They sublimely interpret their impressions in phallic allegoric terms and draw parallels to real life. Seemingly, their fears are that the extension of opportunities to Africans will essentially diminish their own, perhaps diminish even their very manhood and thus remove or prevent them from their "rightful stations in life " and influence in society, domestic as well as global. Such sublime aberrations manifest in policy, attitudes, and actions.

Chapter Twenty Three

Reparation

I use the word "reparation" in its singular form in reference to the prevailing movement to demand material compensation for every man, woman, and child of African descent in America for all that the African race lost as a result of slavery. If it has thus far failed to garner appreciable support, then it might, at least, partly be because its terms often seem poorly defined.

Beyond the rather benevolent demands and concessions of leveling the playing field, the issue of debt forgiveness for Africa and reparation for African-Americans still looms large. By the end of year 2004, you and I had heard several arguments on the merits of reparation with references to Japanese Americans who were interned during World War II and Jews who had suffered at the hands of the Nazis. The expressions of demand for Africans in America seem mainly confined to the African American communities. This is a subject on which my personal views are markedly different from the popular. Let me explain mine. If African Americans should accept packages of material compensations for the effects of the slave trade, slavery and segregation, Africans in America might well have shortchanged themselves. First of all, how do you put material value on the lives of over ten million human beings, not counting those who died in the process of capture or in transit? Stop and think about it for a minute.

To forcibly remove human beings from their kith and kin causes deep emotional pain to those taken away as to those left behind. When people had to end their own lives or run and hide deep in the jungles of the Caribbean and South America just to escape the humiliation, subjugation, exploitation, and dehumanizing effects of slavery, how does anyone put material value on such human losses? Any material awards against such suffering are not even pacific; at most, they are merely symbolic admission of a diabolic epoch in history.

The facts are irrefutable; without African higher knowledge and African labor and contribution of culture, America would not manifest such blessings of power and glory as it enjoys today. One would therefore expect present generations of Americans, with grace, gratitude and perhaps some magnanimity, to extend a fair measure of restorative or pacific good to the other generations whose blood, sweat, and tears—those who sacrificed their God-given lives and the future security of their offspring to lay the foundations and erect the framework for building the power and glory that is the United States of America.

In short, here is what I would propose: considering our patterns and habits of consumption, instead of giving every African American $100 thousand in cash, grant free tuition to any state or federally funded college. Let such a program run for a definite period of twelve to twenty years. That, to me would be far more meaningful. It would benefit the recipients and help strengthen African American societies in particular and America as a whole. While China, Russia, and India are investing so heavily in their youth, turning out engineers of all sorts to participate in the global marketplace, African American youths languish in jail in disproportionate numbers. Many such "delinquents" have the acumen and talents that could be cultivated and harnessed to help America maintain its edge in technological innovations by developing alternative sources for energy and improving existing ones.

Some might be trained and employed as construction technician and managers or as structural designers and inspectors. Indeed, America has millions of young minds who could offer boundless innovations in consumer technology. In late 2006, a number of American universities and colleges offered free and discounted tuitions, mostly online, for degree programs. This is just what America needs to help it stay ahead with offers particularly extended to African Americans, for reparation. Beyond reparation, it offers opportunity for accomplishments, possible Nobel Prize winners, both of which are better than two minutes of shame on a Fox Television show.

Across the water, most African countries had, by the end of year 2004, long paid off most of the interest on the original loans advanced by the IMF and the World Bank. In fact, by year 2002, Africa had paid back $550 billion of the principal plus interest of the original principal amount of $540 billion borrowed between 1970 and 2002. The balance remaining at the end of 2004 was just about $200 billion, nearly all of it interest. If only these countries could be free of such debt burdens, then they would be better able to use the monies they save for more basic and pressing needs. Needs that include education, health-care, and infrastructure developments? In addition to the monies that might be available due to debt relief, Africa needs about twenty-five billion dollars a year in further aid to meet these basic demands.

On June 7, 2005, British Prime Minister Tony Blair flew to Washington to convince President George Bush to join the efforts in monetary aid to Africa. The American president refused to contribute a fair share, citing African corruption as a reason to hold back any significant contribution as such.

As a token, Mr. Bush pledged about $670 million in a cash advance to help Africa with its basic needs; perhaps, it was a step in the right direction but far too short of what was needed. Things have changed; yet, things remain much the same. We failed to recognize the jubilee year that passed (year 2000). For true Christians, it meant a year for forgiveness, to allow new beginning (Matthew 25:31_46).

However, on June 13, 2005, less than a week after Mr. Blair's visit and lobbying, Mr.

Bush announced the forgiveness of forty billion dollars of debt to eighteen of the poorest indebted nation in the world, heavily indebted poor countries (HIPIC), fourteen of which are in Africa. Here again, it was a noble gesture and in the right direction, but, again, it was insufficient to provide the needed critical mass for a meaningful and sustainable recovery effect. This cancelled debt only erased a mere 15 percent of the outstanding external debt. While a number of Africans deemed the very idea of HIPIC considerate, at least in principle, many more saw it as demeaning and offensive, casting a select group of African nations as destitute.

Some Africans see HIPIC forgiveness as a trap. Much of what is forgiven is, in fact, the little bit that remains of the interest. The lenders have long made their profits. Secondly, the write-off will most certainly, soon or later, be used as leverage to negotiate favorable trade terms in the donor's favor. Most Africans I have spoken to believe, much as I do, that a more considerate trade relation, favorable to Africa as a whole and attached to nonselective debt cancellation would be more helpful and respectful. In short, what Africa needs is trade with parity and consideration, not charity. Democratic reforms and serious efforts toward progress are certainly not unfair demands. However, such demand also raises many questions. For example, how do we define "democratic reforms?" Are these conditions one size fits all? Do we apply the same set of demands for every country? To what extent will that work? What are the pitfalls? Anyhow, these are questions better reserved for a whole separate discussion.

Many Africans also express hope that such conditionality does not evolve into a basis for exercising the unwritten policy of "convenient selectivity," where supposed conditions are used as pretext and as means of facilitating favors. Even more important is the fact that, at this point in history, most Africans, especially the poor and uneducated, regard Western-style democracy as a luxury they can afford to park in the back of the garage. They do not readily see the link between democratic reforms and immediate improvements in their harsh living conditions; the alleviation of poverty: provision of decent housing, health care, schools for their kids, and small capital to start a business. A benevolent dictator can provide all this and more as far as they know.

The educated also seem to have, at least, some misgivings with the push for democratic reforms. For one thing, many of them feel confused. They see the definition for democracy demonstrably shifting at the whims of those who advocate it. I don't blame them. After all, they are human, and humans, like all primates, do what they see, not what they are told to.

They also express concerns for the necessary supporting conditions and institutions such as freedom of speech and of the press; about free, efficient, and effective judiciary. These are, understandably, prerequisites necessary to support the ideals of democracy.

Of even greater concern to me, regarding both reparations to African Americans and debt forgiveness for Africa is the position of the average individual American on the subject. Enough Americans must understand the need for reparation to avoid any sort of moral and other liabilities to its beneficiaries in the near and distant future. I recently overheard white, educated professionals in Atlanta, Georgia express their objections to the very idea of reparation. I have even heard objections to entitlement programs that extend ordinary, everyday benefits to African-Americans, saying "... not with my tax money." Even though such expressions might be mere reflection of a regional ethos, they do suggest the need for efforts to educate the public on the merits of reparations to Africans in America and debt cancellation to African nations. The average American is highly capable of making fair and just decisions when given the opportunity with accurate information.

In order not to be taken totally by surprise, one must always bear in mind that "the one who gives can also take away." While it is true that by 2005, African Americans had climbed to levels high up on the socioeconomic ladder, it is also true that in relative terms, African Americans have attained similar levels in the past and lost much or all of it after only a few decades. In the early days of slavery, there were free Africans who owned land and had their own farms and other forms of property. During reconstruction, a significant African-American middle class flourished, and, by the early twentieth century, the middle class expanded into urban communities. Some areas in the South had African American legislators in both chambers of the U.S. Congress. Then came a time when such gains began to be reversed, undermined, at least partly from within or plowed under by others.

The African-American middle class began to shrink and, before long, African- Americans could not even vote in many areas of the South. As recently as the 1930s, a whole section of Tulsa, Oklahoma, popularly known as the "Black Wall Street," a district lined with thriving commercial enterprise and professional offices, was totally demolished by U.S. marshals for official reasons that did not match the degree of offence. At about the same time, the movement founded and headed by Marcus Garvey, trying to organize Africans to do positively for themselves, was undermined and betrayed; its members were castigated, the movement finally disbanded, and later all vestiges of it were wiped out. Africans always need to be vigilant and resolute. "Forward ever, backward never." A useful and perhaps necessary mantra

Chapter Twenty Four

Beyond Reparation and Debt Cancellation

The obligations and opportunities for Africa's renaissance straddle the Sargasso Sea. Although Africa ultimately and logically bears the brunt of the responsibilities and obligations, America which stands to gain materially and spiritually, must share the burden. I believe it was America's second president John Adams, who once said something to the effect that the American Constitution was made for a just and moral society and that it might seem inadequate only to a society that is not just and moral. That statement was made over 200 years ago, and it has proven itself a profound truth. A society is particularly moral when its people live by the golden rule, "Love thy neighbor as thyself (Mathew 19:19)." As simple as it is, this scriptural creed does impose demands. To love another as oneself, one must first love oneself. One must recognize neighbor as deserving as oneself. Above all, one must believe in and love the Lord with all their heart, mind, and soul. For, if the community of man must go through the processes of globalization in peace and forever maintain the peace, then these are the laws that must guide and govern all human activity.

In the push toward globalization and particularly in forging new, more rational and meaningful relations between Africa and America, whole sets of new demands are necessary. Fulfillment of such demands must begin with the most basic: It must begin with a new mindset, a new way of thinking about Africa and Africans. Notions of the "Congo syndrome" need to be radically revised.

The "no news is good news" basis of reporting on Africa must change. There are, at any given time, stacks of good and happy stories out of Africa. A more positive mind-set will ferret out good news, if indeed good news out of Africa is so hard to find. African societies must no longer be treated with the old "one size fits all" approach and style of reporting and policy making.

The prevailing "Africa on the cheap" style and method of management whereby ventures, even those in America's vital interest, are expected to yield high returns with minimal input. These are no longer viable approaches. The violent demonstration in the Delta area of Nigeria in May 2005, which continues, is an example that speaks loudly to this demand.

The old notion that all gains and acquisitions need be zero-sum will no longer tread water. Africans are beginning to demand greater parity in exchange for what they concede. African governments are reviewing and revising terms of contracts. Other notions such as, "Africa is a lost cause" must not continue to mean that Africans are proving too difficult to negotiate with and to control.

It means "expert on Africa" must no longer be a reference to one who can recommend ways and means to exact concessions from Africans for maximum gain and limited liability. Above all, the advocacy of the *Pentagon's New Map* must be abandoned for more peaceful and friendly alternatives.

Perhaps most important, America, for material or strategic advantages, must not irrationally be selective in ways that might harm African states and their people. America's engagement against the Sudanese atrocities is laudable, but what about those suffering in the Delta region of Nigeria, are they less important? Are the millions of victims in the yet-to-be- recognized civil war in the Central Africa Republic and in Congo DR not important too?

Some observers rank these atrocities as worse than multiples of the worst tsunami in recent memory. UN Commissioner for Refugees Antonio Guterez stated that the number of people who die every three months in the civil war in the Congo is equal to about the number of victims of one tsunami. Another UN high-ranking official, Jan Eglund, has repeated the alarm. By the end of 2005, about four million people had died in the Congo compared to two million in Darfur, "why such selectivity?" Africans ask.

While such changes in attitude will be helpful, the material help necessary to hold down the long list of obstacles to rapid growth will be just as important. God being so good, at least the European Union has recognized this fact. In a May 2005 article entitled, "EU Proposes Economic Master Plan' for Africa," the author described, in glowing terms, the European Union's economic strategy aimed at helping Africa develop extensive networks of road, rail, and communications infrastructure throughout the continent. Investments are necessary to facilitate a serious developmental agenda. Leaders of the EU also believed that implementation of such developments might not work so well without full participation of America. That was why former British Prime Minister Tony Blair rushed to Washington to coax President Bush to hop aboard the train across the Sargasso Bridge to Africa.

Mr. Bush refused to commit fully, citing among other reasons (fear of) corruption.

Most people readily aptly tagged President Bush's "fear of corruption in Africa" as mere a lame excuse. For one thing, highly corrupt regimes such as those of Nigeria's Sanni Abacha and Zaire's Mobutu are long gone. Mobutu, in fact, had friends in very high places in America during his three-decade tenure.

The most notable of the current corrupt regimes is that of President Nguema Obiang, of Equatorial Guinea. It is where the Houston, Texas, based petroleum company Exxon-Mobile pumps large quantities with only a tiny fraction of the proceeds going to the government of Equatorial Guinea. That tiny fraction is mostly transferred out and stashed in the private bank account of the president (in Western banks of all places), while the people of Equatorial Guinea wallowed in abject poverty.

Thirdly, Africans have, of late, recognized the retardant effects of corruption on progress. The African Union's own recent research report suggested that Africa loses about $148 billion a year through corruption; this is money that should have been available for development and for everyday needs for which African governments go around begging. The African Union has set up its own peer review system with which to check, among other factors, corruption within African governments.

Finally, it takes two to tango. A significant number of scholarships awarded to African students over the past twenty years or so have been given on the basis of favors, not on merit.

"What have your parents, your uncle, your sugar daddy done for my favorite company, my corporate sponsor operating in Africa, lately?" Mr. Bush's reservations might seem fair. Corruption is bad anywhere and in any form. Yes, Africans have a notorious track record with corruption, but Africans do not hold a monopoly on corruption, as I pointed out earlier. The scope and level of corruption are no more and no worse than it is in many developed and developing countries, most of which are past or present allies of the United States. In the United States itself, look at the not-so-distant history, the administrations of Rutherford B. Hayes and President Grant and President Arthur. The recent practices of Enron, the military, Halliburton's no bid / no price ceiling contracts, American contractors in Iraq in jail, and seasoned U.S. congressmen in jail or on trial, Ponzi schemes galore. Most recent PBS's *FRONTLINE* revelations about a scheme that involved

American president George W. Bush; Prime Minister, Tony Blair and the British royal family; and the Saudi royal family.

Reportedly they all received benefits from contracts for Saudi Arabian procurements from British Aerospace Engineering Systems (www.pbs.org/frontlineworld/stories/bribe/). While concerns over the propensity for corruption are in order, they should not be used as reasons for holding back aid, rather the contrary. Much of Africa's corruption is fueled by dire need. The chasm between need and supply is vast. Corruption is a problem when it manifests as a function of greed.

However, when corruption is a function of need, it ought to compel hasty help that might alleviate the sufferings that fuels the corruption. I have always held the suspicion that people who have never been poor tend to think that the poor, those on the lower end of the socioeconomic scale, necessarily have low expectations in life. Nothing I know of is further from the truth.

Where there is sufficient will, there is certainly a way. The trick to helping Africa and avoiding the myriad pitfalls that include corruption is to be willing to sit down with African leaders, including leaders of the African Union, and diligently craft rational, prudent, and pragmatic means for a way out, not just doing the right things but striving to do the right things the right way. There are a number of possibilities that offer rational solutions to the challenge of corruption in Africa.

One that I have often suggested is to begin by using some of the means already at hand. The African Union may be a suitable entity to handle certain challenges that may include health issues, the development and management of cross-border infrastructure such as railways and highways. It is already handling conflict resolutions and peer reviews, which require capacity and resources. Multilateral agencies might help strengthen the African Union by channeling specific offers of aid to individual African states through the auspices of the African Union.

Non-governmental organizations such as CARE, the Carter Center, the Red Cross, and the Peace Corps would also be useful in providing materials and services. The Peace Corps is over sixty years old now and needs new challenges and new mandates. Why not beef it up and unleash its goodness for the sake of America and the world? In my mind, I can see newly created departments for management and accountability within a new and improved Peace Corps whose sole task would be to write checks and help local stakeholders manage American-financed projects overseas, including, of course, Africa.

Other possible departments within a new and improved Peace Corps might be in the areas of community planning and development, public and primary (basic) health, and building schools. The Peace Corps could manage USAID-dependent and similar American- financed projects responsibly and efficiently. There are lots of unemployed and underemployed young or retired Americans with skills as accountants, project managers, and technical experts who would love just such an experience. I personally know many underemployed but well-qualified Africans living in the United States who could help with such arrangements. All NGOs can be restructured and reorganized under one directorate to help maximize efficiency, minimize redundancies and in ways that will contribute to overall development efforts of host nation.

In fact, I have also suggested and often, that the Peace Corps might as well be charged with the task of helping to spread Americana (the American culture) with the expressed purpose of regaining the hearts and minds of old friends and well-wishers America has lost in recent times and in making new ones where they have not existed before. If you take Africa, for example, the

Peace Corps might select and incubate this idea in just eight of the regional core states—Egypt, Morocco, Senegal, Nigeria, Congo DR, Tanzania, Mozambique, and South Africa. In each, let the Peace Corps establish, at high school and college levels, intramural and interschool (varsity) sports competitions in the three American classic sports: basketball, football, and baseball.

Every year, there could be national championships at both levels, followed with intra- African championships. For instance, the champions of Nigerian college football would play their South African counterparts. Make such championship games fun, a showpiece of American culture, with liberal supply of anything and everything Americana—for example, hot dogs, barbecue, pretzels, sherbets and ice cream on cones, Coke and Pepsi, Miller, Bud and Blue Ribbon, and Uncle Ben's rice—all at locally affordable prices. Rent and watch the movie, *The Air Up There* starring Kevin Bacon. Start small, and expand with the Peace Corp managing and directing. Provide the coaches and train locals to manage and officiate games.

We can make it all profitable for American companies. Yearly contracts to build schools, sports complexes, and lots of stadiums and sports complexes even in remote areas of the world could be reserved for American companies like Bechtel, Halliburton, Parsons, Vappi and Asphaldi. Gap and Nike and Footlocker could supply all the sportswear, if even the exotic design that makes the athlete look like an intergalactic warrior. Let there be lots of T-shirts and baseball caps. All the foods for such festive gala events must be supplied by Tyson Foods, General Foods, Oscar-Myers, Cargill, and ADM. Let Halliburton provide the catering, and bill any shortfall in its expected profits to the Millennium Challenge Account, the State Department, or the Defense Department.

My friends, what I am saying is let us put the pursuit of world peace on a rational national agenda with high priority. Funding for its implementations might be drawn out of the Millennium Challenge Account, duly authorized and appropriated by congress. Other Northern economies, in Europe and Asia, can chip in. The budget for such approach will replace, at least reduce, the budget for armaments but will certainly, most certainly not replace the established beneficiaries of defense contracts. In other words, instead of supplying for war, the same companies will supply even larger volumes of orders for winning and maintaining peace. This way, the military industrial complex can easily transform to the peace industrial complex, with prospects for even higher profits and offers of greater job opportunities for millions around the world, not just China. Dispensing goodwill around the world and helping to reduce, perhaps eliminate, poverty from this planet does not need to be a zero-sum game.

Such acts of goodwill will likely yield profound and far-reaching benefits for America and Americans—not just spiritual goodwill, but material as well. I recently heard the story of an American who went to Saudi Arabia in the 1920s. He lived among Wahabi Muslims and noticed the lack of good medical facilities. He mobilized the necessary resources and built a hospital for the community. Years later, when oil was struck in the area and several foreign concerns were vying for concessions King Saud remembered the altruism of the American and awarded the largest concession to the company he represented, in return. That is why I say that winning back the favor of the world is not just to gratify ego; it has profound and far- reaching economic implications.

In addition to the introduction of American popular sports and popular culinary culture and similar offers of goodwill, a reinstatement of the United States Information Services (USIS) would be useful. It must not merely be online. A reestablished USIS must provide an opportunity to showcase the old American personality that was so admired and loved in the 1950s and 1960s through the mid-1990s. Periodically, perhaps once every three months or so, the USIS could purchase time and space in the local media to clearly explain America's plans and policy positions that affect the region in particular and the continent as a whole. And how about the Harlem Globetrotters, did they not make significant contributions toward America's popularity around the world? Bring them back. Also, start organizing trade shows again and lots of them. In short, we do need those old people-to-people, face-to-face-oriented establishments, organizations, and activities in this globalization processes.

If any of these make sense, then they might also be financed out of the same Millennium Challenge Account. Make sure all the contracts for organizing and managing such new orders are awarded to former defense contractors, such as The Carlyle Group, Lockheed-Martin, and the others. When the tobacco giant R. J. Reynolds was compelled to cut back productions of tobacco, it made the adjustment smoothly by diversifying into production of condiments—RJR-Nabisco.

Efforts such as I have suggested offer great potential for the expression of America's will, while they eliminate conditions that might nurture hornets' nests within African communities from which disgruntled and misguided youth, by any simple label or description, might be recruited for diabolical causes. It would better serve local politics, diplomatic relations, business, and security. It would work wonders for world peace and for the sake of peace, we could make peace profitable. We could replace the military industrial complex with a *Peace Industrial Complex*, a switch that could very well reduce spending on destruction and increase spending on constructive, more civilized ventures around the world. Who needs all the tensions and animosities that accompany the violence?

America currently spends almost hundreds of billions a year on defense-related demands, a figure bound to go up if the war in the Middle East drags on. America has already spent about four and a half trillion dollars as of yearend 2006 on that war. That is less than four years of fighting. Weekly expenditure on the war is over three billion dollars, and the cost in human lives is beyond any monetary value. My point is that, instead of wars and conflicts, increases in human-centered, quality-of-life expenditures by a mere fifty billion dollars a year—well channeled under, let us say, the Peace Corps' administration with most or all of it, flowing back to American companies—would cut current and escalating levels of military expenditure. and win back friends, make new friends, and disarm potential enemies.

The idea propounded by Dr. Nicholas Negroponte of MIT to supply all children of the world with low-cost laptops is truly brilliant and deserving of consideration for a Nobel Prize. Give Lockheed-Martin and Boeing contracts, under the Millennium Challenge Account, to build winged Zeppelins, derringers that might cart food from areas of high supply to areas of high demand. The time has come when we can beat our swords into ploughshares. Indeed, the Peace Corps as managers of the Peace Industrial Complex could do a whole lot more for America than the Marine Corps and the Special Forces that wield the sword.

Chapter Twenty Five

A Second Chance

Thousands of Africans come to America each year in search of opportunities for a better life. Many are professionals willing to give up nobler occupations for menial ones just because they find life in America "a wonderful life." You might meet them anywhere and, indeed, everywhere in America, in cities and towns large and small, working long hours in a wide variety of low-paying jobs; as taxi driver, janitors, stock clerks and cahiers. There are also many Africans in high-paying occupations; as health care professionals, college professors, engineers, bankers and lawyers. Unlike Africans who came to America 200 to 500 years ago, these recently arrived Africans came voluntarily. They all hope and pray that America continues to be a beacon of hope, an encouragement for peace and fairness, and an opportunity for anyone who wants to try for a good and decent life. They are right; it is a good and rewarding life indeed, a wonderful life.

Like any Frank Capra story, this discussion is about second chances. Africans still feel disappointed and frustrated that (right or wrong) America carefully measures the extension of the helping hand extended toward its needs. Its pressing need to embark on an al African renaissance. America, always appearing helpful yet giving what is in fact far short of a necessary minimum to elicit adequate, dynamic and sustainable recovery responses.

Conversely and ironically, such African frustrations and disappointments are similar to those expressed by Middle America, the moral majority of the 1970s and 1980s. All factors considered: Africa's resources plus Africa's historical links to America, compared to what other regions of the world have to offer America; it is Africa that offers America the most opportunity for a second chance at a full-fledged industrialization. It could thus be a second chance for the revival of old glories that included love and respect for Americans for no other reason than the fact that they are American.

The near sudden down turn in the US economy have demonstrated that America's economic well-being must remain well-grounded on productivity - strong agriculture and manufacturing sectors. Dealings in securities with Europe and outsourcing manufacturing to Asia are at least counter-productive. What America really need for its own recovery is Africa, as a viable trading partner.

To begin the process, to help Africa to that point, America only needs to focus, at least for a short while, on the problems of Africa among whose populations are the poorest in the world. Africa's huddled masses and assertive professionals need not move to America to find sustenance, opportunity, and fulfillment. America can merely reach out with adequate offers of help. The Bush administration's refusal to give what would be helpful, offering instead some $670 million (a mere penny in the cup considering Africa's many and pressing challenges) must not be repeated by any succeeding government.

American help for Africa might, after all, come from the American people, possibly from the other "moral majority" that is now virtually silent. The other moral majority should take heed of the context of President John Adams's remarks, ever mindful of the fact that indeed "a just and moral society" is one capable of showing love for neighbor as for self. They should be equally mindful of the fact that China, India, the European Union, and other economies at similar levels of development already have their sights set on Africa's resource potential. The time for

America to act is now, with a positive, proactive, and preemptive posture that will recreate, rebuild, and redirect African popular interest toward America and at the same time keep the African poor, the more than half a billion people, at least hopeful and away from less-than-noble influences.

As I have said over and again, some in high places have seen the light and heard the call. Former Senator Bill Frits of Tennessee goes to Africa every year to help support efforts against AIDS and other diseases. He later joined forces with former Senator Tom Daschle to push forward an agenda to help reduce, if possible, eradicate world poverty. This is noble indeed, and the rest of the world is also watching, to learn and perhaps join in.

The Redemption

As Babylon was the agent of punishment for the sins and arrogance of Judah, could the houses of Ephraim and Manasseh be the agents of punishment for the sins and arrogance of Africa? If we accept this supposition, we might also make a logical claim that as God held a glorious future for Judah, God also holds a glorious future for Africa. Believers often say that God punishes those he loves in order to bring them closer to him. When Manasseh, son of Hezekiah, was king of Judah, he was judged the most wicked of kings. He had turned Israel into an idolatrous society, prompting the faithful to remove the Ark of the Covenant to Africa for safekeeping.

In spite of Manasseh's wickedness and decadence, he was not punished for long. So, if the ten plagues of Egypt were not enough, is the addition of half a millennia of slavery, colonialism, and neocolonialism still not enough punishment for Africa? Is one and a half millennium of Noah's curse on Canaan and his descendants not too long or are we rather to recognize that God loves Africa so much that its punishment must continue a while longer?

Personally, I find it hard to believe that Africa's shortcomings and transgressions warrant such lengthy punishment. Even my own personal conviction that Africans display a wide variety of arrogance does not allow me to accept the suggestion that Africans must suffer so much and so long for it. After all, others on this earth display arrogance too, if even in different ways and forms. It was, after all, European rationalizations born of arrogance that enabled the slave trade, slavery, colonialism, and the prevailing regimes of neocolonialism.

As C. S. Lewis cautions in his book, *Mere Christianity*, much of the rationale that has provided impetus for racist behavior and attitudes has been based on the misrepresentations that failed to acknowledge African achievements and capabilities as recognized in biblical literature.

When you find the answer as to why Africans must suffer so much for so long, please let me know. Until then, I will hold onto my belief that God certainly does not want Africa to suffer so much for so long. God has already shed his blessings on Africa. It only remains theirs to recognize so as to realize it. Africans have not yet learned to do by themselves, with themselves, and for themselves. Others notice such weakness and simply take advantage of it, depriving Africans of their God-given good while exposing them to all sorts of needless exploitations.

I do not know if any more laws are necessary. The first ten amendments already guarantee the African in America individual freedoms to be able to apply talent in pursuit of enterprise that might strengthen the individual, the society, and the nation.

Like the leopard, the African cannot change the color of its skin. With fervent prayers to the God of second chances, everyone with interest in Africa must pray for a second chance for the continent, prayers backed by deeds that are well intended and well planned. Like the Phoenix, Africa will rise again from its ashes. We must plan and jump on the new bandwagon for the crusade of moral rearmament that includes a search for the truth that will allow the right kinds of restorations. Even before any organized attempts to search for truth, Africans must recognize the need to forgive each other not only for the commissions of sins against self and other, but also for having failed so far to do enough good for self and for each other.

The Scriptures are full of verses with which to pray for ourselves and for those who have wronged us. One that I enjoy to recite is, "For all races and nations, may repentance for past injustices lead to mutual forgiveness." For smooth sailing and the utmost benefit, the African renaissance must be preceded by an African reformation. Africans cannot merely remain familiar with the Scriptures. Africans on both sides of the Sargasso Sea must strive to understand and embrace the scriptural prophesies of the redemption and salvation of Africans:

"From beyond the rivers of Ethiopia my suppliants, even the daughter of my dispersed shall bring mine offspring." (Zephaniah 3:10)

In this prophesy, Zephaniah expresses God's willingness to forgive Africa for her transgressions and to provide ample opportunity for her peoples at home and abroad to reconnect with hope for salvation and restoration. The first ten amendments of the American constitution are laws of man, and they are easy to manipulate. The Ten Commandments, however, are immutable. They guarantee the right degree of inner strength and moral character necessary to unleash and direct talent toward perfect productive ends.

Africa's bright future in God's grand design is further recognized in the Book of Psalms (68: 29–34 King James) the

Psalmist celebrates the supreme, the one and only ruler of the universe. Implicit in these verses is God's regard for and expectations of Africa in his design of a world empire to be established here on earth. Most poignant and prophetic of this Psalm is verse thirty-one: "Princes shall come out of Egypt; Ethiopia shall soon stretch forth her hands unto God."

Here, it is interesting to note that both nations chosen to represent mankind's universal acknowledgement of God's supremacy with material offerings and refined human qualities are African. This possibly suggests the quality of manpower and the material wealth that Africa is deemed capable of contributing to a new world order.

Perhaps equally interesting, we must note that the children of Jacob (Israel) died and were buried in Africa; that like the children of Israel, Africans in the diaspora started preparations for future glories as slaves and as much as the children of Jacob and his son Joseph were subjugated and subjected to harsh treatments as slaves because, "There arose up a new king over Egypt, which knew not Joseph." (Exedus 1:8) Africans in the diaspora also have been subjected to unspeakable treatments as slaves, because the children of Israel (Ephraim and Menasha) had forgotten the many positive contributions Africans had made to their own history in particular and to the history of mankind in general.

As we have discussed earlier, in the summer of 2007, the country of Ghana launched The Joseph Project. The goal of the Joseph Project is to encourage sons and daughters of Africa to reconnect with the African motherland symbolically, spiritually, and substantially. It is indeed a profound and cheerful recognition of the need for all from one to return and at least reconnect, all to one.

The demand for new thinking and a new attitude is compelled by the fact that past and prevailing attitudes in human relations, especially in relation to Africa, have stemmed from conjectural assertions based on subjective interpretations that are tenuous at best and self- serving at least, and which is potentially a basis for future controversy.

Take, for instance, the claim that the children of Ephraim are today's Britons and those of Manasseh are the people of America. Convincing as it is, one might also note that the people in the prophecy have evolved. Today, more than half the nations of the British Commonwealth (the children of Ephraim) are in Africa and the Caribbean where populations are largely African.

To a similar extent, the United States of America (the children of Manasseh) has a significantly large African population on the verge of ascending to its proper position in American and global society, politics, and economics. New realities have produced modern- day prophets, heretics for the most part maybe, but with diverse interpretations that only give rise to cycles of charges and countercharges. Even old and steadfast truths (for instance, the fact that God gave the Covenant to man through the son of a slave) present parallels that might support and strengthen a wide range of interpretations.

During the Israeli–Hezbollah war in the summer of 2006, the two main negotiators for a cease fire and for peace were Africans: Kofi Annan of the motherland and Condoleezza Rice of the diaspora. The two convened and presided over negotiations in Rome, Italy, to work out a cease-fire agreement. Most Africans as well as others around the world saw this as a sign of positive things to come.

In his book, *The United States and Britain in Prophecy*, Herbert W. Armstrong supported his contention that America is descended from the house of Manasseh with a simple conjecture. In his postulate, he concluded that the fact that the house of Manasseh is the thirteenth tribe of Israel and America was founded with thirteen colonies is concrete proof that America is indeed the house of Manasseh. Such postulates cannot be supported with simple conjecture, for, sooner or later, they fall into their contradictions and dangerously betray their weaknesses.

As I remember the story, Jacob received the birthright from his father by deception, by tricking his father into believing that he was his brother Esau. When Jacob passed on the birthright to his grandsons (Joseph's two sons), he gave the first birthright to Ephraim, the younger grandson, instead of giving it to Manasseh, the older grandson. What further inferences must we make from such trickery and reversal? Yes, Britain (house of Ephraim) abolished slavery some thirty years before America (house of Manasseh). However, slavery in America was abolished with the Thirteenth Amendment. How does this fact square with the claim that the house of Manasseh, the thirteenth tribe of Israel and the start of America with the thirteen colonies, prove that indeed America is descended from the house of Manasseh? Can we extend the logic to mean the beneficiaries of the thirteenth amendment will ultimately inherit the house of Manasseh?

Beyond a point, some of these arguments even become self-propagating and only end in provocations and further divisions. For example, Jeremiah 51:55 talks of the God of recompense. This provides scriptural support to those who demand reparation for the deprivation and sufferings of Africans Americans and Africans, who suffered social and economic regressions due to the slave trade and slavery.

Humanity will be better served and salvation for all mankind will be readily attained if we make efforts, painful though they might be, to discard refutable and self-serving notions and claims. Instead, we must spend our energies and resources seeking the truth and replacing hatred and spite with love and compassion. We must repair and restore where there have been hurt, callous exploitations, deprivation, and neglect. I hope you remember the prayer we recited earlier, "For all races and nations, may repentance for past injustices lead to mutual forgiveness." The year 2000 was a jubilee year, but seemingly we failed to seize upon its meaning and power; we failed to make it a threshold, the Ash Wednesday for a new beginning and a moral rearmament for a better and brighter world for all mankind.

For two millennia, the human race has woefully betrayed itself with war, treachery, exploitation, and neglect and has gotten away with it all. I am not so sure of a third millennium. The three-strike rule might well be in effect. Man must replace tendencies for arrogant imperialistic inclinations on one hand and the urge for despise and vengeance on the other. Instead, we must all strive for parity, consideration, compassion, and love; love is the most compelling and dynamic force on earth. Maintaining relationships on this basis affords us more productive and civilized modalities with which to conduct our affairs. They offer greater salvation for us all, more than those we have chosen and continue to use (decadent qualities of exaction, exploitation, and exclusion that only breed distrust, hatred, vengeance, and fear), a truly vicious circle.

We must particularly seek for Africa a sincere and meaningful regimen for restoration; we should seek restoration whereby Africa is no longer a weak-link in the upward trend of global society. Restoration should be done to the point whereby Africa, once again, serves as a yardstick for self-assessment by other regions of the world.

Yes, though some may argue the fact, most Africans fervently believe the Ark with its contents, the Covenant, is still in Africa. It needs no new seal by blood, not even the blood of substitute from sacrifices. The blood of Christ is already on the cross and provides the necessary seal till eternity. All Christians in Africa need is to accept the terms and begin to honor their end of the divine contract: to abide by every word of the Ten Commandments. It is a way of life that can only embolden and encourage productivity with quality. Indeed, God has for Africans at large, redemption, elevation, and exaltation. What Africans must give back is humility (in place of arrogance), diligent, relentless efforts to elevate self, and, certainly not the least, clean and righteous living.

Chapter Twenty Six

Beyond Redemption

To the more enlightened, the history of the slave trade and of slavery holds deep existential significance. Such beliefs tend to argue that the mere demand for reparation implies that someone else has possession of what is owed, to be given back to those from whom it has been taken. Whether it is given forth or given back, whoever gives gets to also hold the keys to the future of those to whom it is given. One thing I know is that all good comes from God and from God alone. Man can only serve as an instrument, a channel, or a conduit in the transfer of good. I also believe the argument that those from whom Africans ask for reparation have already served the purpose of God by helping to set up Africans to receive boundless material and spiritual blessings. What more do Africans need to ask of them?

Even more important is the fact that Africans already hold in their hands the staff with which to part the waters to establish the necessary path across and reconnect the diaspora with the motherland for their common good. The forbearers of European Americans, with calculated profit motives, organized and conducted the African slave trade with trickery, treachery, coercion, and some collaboration. Yet, present-day descendants of eighteenth- and nineteenth-century slave profiteers, with ease, are able to transfer blame to the descendants of those who were victims, those who were forcibly taken away from home and those left to suffer grief and deprivation of their loved ones. The hidden fact is that the resulting separation holds within it a divine design intended only for the two sides that suffered it.

The very exercise of the slave trade, as diabolical as it is to the human mind, also established a divine dipole (two forces at opposite ends pulling toward each other with latent force). The power in this dipole that might be harnessed for good is tremendous. This power, more than any other, is what Africans on both side of the Sargasso Sea need to learn to recognize fully so they can draw up relevant and prudent plans for all the good it holds for them. The sinister character of the slave trade and slavery is so obvious that, if there is the will and enough material compensation from others, it will be offered with no demands, none whatsoever.

A case in point, in early July 2005, a group of popular musicians led by Bono, leader of the Irish rock band U-2, staged a worldwide, nine-city concert. The effort was to draw the world's attention to Africa. It was well timed, just a few days before the annual summit of the eight most industrialized nations began in Glenn Eagle, Scotland, where British Prime Minister Tony Blair was expected to ask the rich nations to dip deep into their pockets for a kitty of some fifty billion dollars, to assist Africa in embarking on its much awaited renaissance.

Shortly after the summit got under way, before Mr. Blair had even had a chance to make a formal appeal on behalf of Africa, four fatal explosions in the London transit system (underground and above ground) derailed this noble crusade. Perpetrators of the hideous act could not be punished. Instead, it descended into further tragedy. Days later, an innocent young man, who had left his home across the Atlantic to seek a better life in Britain, was mistakenly shot and killed by British police.

To most African minds, the message in this tragedy, this irony, is profound. There seems to be a voice above it all that speaks to both sides. To the British and other Western societies, the message underscores the very idea that inspired the Big Eight concert and urged Tony Blair's intended apologetic or benevolent consideration. It is a message that says, in no uncertain terms, that "terrorists" are people with grievance, bitter and disillusioned and certainly foolish, criminal in fact. They are, however, human. They inflict terror upon us either because of something they believe we have done or something we have failed to do, and the way to conquer such terror is not by the head-on approaches we so doggedly insist on. This approach caused British police to, most regrettably, chase down and kill an innocent poor Brazilian who was only seeking economic refuge and opportunity for salvation. This tragic irony prompts us to seek more rational and effective ways of engagements—most advisedly, perhaps, from behind, just as the Bushman of the Kalahari would handle it.

It calls on us to strive to identify and address the very basis of discontent and fury, in ways that will eliminate all possible reasons for terrorism with offers of opportunity, equity, education, health care, adequate supplies, and a fair access to modernity. There are several tragedies to speak of regarding July 2005, in London and elsewhere in the world. To me, the one that lies at the core is that which I just mentioned: the killing of an innocent Brazilian trying to acquire the means to help himself and his family back in Brazil. A most regrettable mistake, with potential dire consequences.

Brazilian society is largely in the mainstream of the growing global undercurrent; it is an undercurrent that people in high places, the older generation of movers and shaker in economics, politics and society across the world, have yet to recognize, let alone understand. While we may be able to pacify the victim's family with material offers, such reparation might not be acceptable to sympathetic Brazilians at large. Poverty, along with the ills and dangers it breeds, must be recognized and addressed wherever it exists. The poor should not need to send their children abroad to better developed societies just for material salvation.

To me, the more compelling advice from the voice above is directed at Africans, those at home and those abroad. Instead of expecting reparations, bailouts and handouts so vigorously and in ways that might further subjugate Africans and prolong exploitation along with scorn and stigma, I suggest Africans ask for divine inspiration and guidance so as to recognize the dynamics of the staff they already hold so firmly in hand, much like the story of Moses who held the staff with which to part the sea in his hand all along, not aware of its significance and importance.

Africa is without argument the richest continent in the world, in terms of natural and human resources. Across the Sargasso Sea at the other end of the dipole is America, where African Americans have attained considerable wealth and influence. Indeed, African-Americans are one of the wealthiest and most influential groups of people on earth today, with an estimated annual spending power of about one trillion dollars a year. That alone is tremendous power. All that monetary power, couched in a capacity to create and to manage. That's double dipole, my friend, double power. It might seem double trouble only for others, certainly not to Africans on either side of the Sargasso Sea.

The Africans in America also have one additional big advantage over the Africans on the mother continent. Africans in America have certain disaffection, an innocent disconnect to ethnic identity, differences and affection. Such disaffection will be most useful in rebuilding African institutions and societies.

I do not suggest that all African Americans should move from America to settle in the ancestral homeland. Extending a helping hand to Africa and going back and forth must forever remain the pleasure and privilege of every American, especially those in whom there still is affection of kinship with Africa.

Unprecedented and catastrophic events since 2000 are leading mankind away from material to more spiritual lifestyles. There is already a resurgence of morality in America and in Africa too; it is a morality that speaks to a new set of issues facing mankind, issues such as poverty and homelessness, environmental concerns, a new light on patriotism, and new definitions that espouse and extend the principles that used to be the basis for so much love for America and for Americans. Perhaps at the top of the list is freedom, God's gift to every man and woman on earth, including Africans: the freedom to worship, the freedom to engage in enterprise, the freedom to pursue happiness, and the freedom to share some of that happiness with others.

As things stood at the close of 2005, there still linger in Africa a certain quiet fear, spurred by what may well be sheer rumor. Rumor that the Pentagon had plans to take over all that is good in Africa for the benefit of a few American families and to the exclusion of Africans. Most Africans fear this might actually be carried out simply because it seems to derive from the cryptic rationale of "Manifest Destiny." These rumors and fears are encouraged by the book - *The Pentagon's New Map*. Then, there are others around the world, including many Africans, who believe that rather, *The Pentagon's new map* merely sets the stage for a swan-song. This is, by no means vain fear. Indeed, American global adventures, since 2000 have drastically eliminated any rational basis, spiritual and material, for logical and favorable international relations. Africans expect reasonable Americans, the other moral majority, to extend a different set of hands that will help them make the upward changes.

Chapter Twenty Seven

The Need for Midcourse Correction

(Put on your rally cap.)

Like an individual, a nation can be punished. The alienating effects of pursuits "in the interest of America" compel the nation to spend resources unwisely, such that they deprive basic needs to segments of society. Often measures intended as palliatives turn out to be too feeble to elicit any meaningful result. An example is one I gave earlier, President Bush's $670 million offer to Africa and as I said then, it was gracious, but so little for such an extensive set of challenges. In 2004, congress voted over seventy-six billion dollars for American manufacturers, corporate farmers, and oil companies in the form of tax breaks on the profits repatriated to America. It, however, failed to include demands that would press these companies to reinvest in the American economy, monies they thus realize.

That brings up an even more interesting issue. If they do reinvest such gains in the American economy, how will the excess productions be consumed to yield appreciable profits that may sustain the viability of such investment? How many refrigerators can one American family buy a year? How many diapers can Wal-Mart sell a month at the current birth rate?

Immigration liberalization that might help swell internal consumer markets has become a political hot potato. The only immediate option favorable to the American production economy is to look for viable external markets.

The prayer of Abraham advises us that the misdeeds of a few will not cause the destruction of a whole society, "If I find in Sodom fifty righteous within the city, then I will spare all the place for their sakes" (Genesis 18:26) Often, in our material pursuits, our preoccupations compels us to reduce life to only the relevant considerations of material security, overlooking or marginalizing the moral aspects. The main plot of the movie, *The Day After Tomorrow* depicts that suggestion. From both a moral and material standpoint American society certainly has within it far more than enough of the righteous to, among other virtues, recognize the folly and indeed the sin of ignoring or marginalizing Africa.

If Africa had a strong middle class capable of significant consumption, then African businessmen and women would be flying American and American code-share carriers back and forth to shop for merchandise to turn into profits back in Africa. I am not talking about the few thousands who come to New York's Fourteenth Street two or three times a year to load up twenty to fifty suitcases of marked-down women's and children's apparel they carry back to sell at the various "bend-down boutiques" throughout Africa. In fact, that trade with New York has virtually died out. Now, such African petty traders prefer Shanghai, in China or nearby Dubai in the United Arab Emirates.

I am not talking about that level of business; I am talking more about businessmen and businesswomen with greater capacities who can travel to negotiate with Black & Decker, Blue Bird Bus company, Carpets of Dalton, John Deere, GM, and GE to order large units of electronics, fabric, farm equipment, planes, trains, trolleys, and, of course, automobiles for sale and use in Africa. Any rational analysis would suggest that up until at least the end of the first century of this new millennium, it was the "dark continent" that offered America the most opportunity to begin to write the bottom line of its budget and trade balance in black.

A slight tilt in America's foreign trade and economic policies will go a long way to yield enormous returns and contribute greatly to make its global image and reputation less tainted. If you ask me why I am so optimistic and so hopeful about a positive turnaround in American popular attitude toward Africa, I could give you a long list of answers. To save you the drudgery of a long explanation, allow me to simply say that the average American I know is, regardless of race, gender or religion, a caring person capable of any level of compassion. It is one of the more discernable characteristics in the nature of Americans.

America, as a society, gave the most material donations to the Pacific Rim tsunami victims. American popular generosity, in cash and in kind, keeps going toward the Katrina victims of New Orleans. The offers of Angelina Jolie and Brad Pitt's (Jolie/Pitt foundation) are well known. The offers of Oprah Winfrey, Madonna, Michael Jackson's family, Michael Jordan's mother, Isaac Hayes, the Metro-Atlanta Neurosurgery Foundation, and organizations such as the Peachtree Baptist Church in Atlanta, among thousands of others, are also well known.

When Americans recognize genuine need, nothing stands in the way of their benevolence.. Secondly, and perhaps a reason for the first, Americans are the most churchgoing society I know of. There is a church or two or more at just about every corner, in the cities and the countryside, free standing and in the malls, not to mention the millions of home-based prayer meetings that go on every day.

It is, I suspect, this faith-driven attitude of church going and daily prayers that make Americans also courageous, always willing, never afraid to make efforts to forge ahead, to correct, and to rally, even against seemingly heavy odds. You remember the story about a race horse called, Sea Biscuit; in a way, it symbolizes that American quality.

An event that left an indelible impression on me when I first came to America was a rowing event at the 1968 Mexico City Olympics. The Harvard team represented the United States and was trailing much of the race; it almost seemed The Americans were out of the running. Then, seemingly from nowhere, they rallied and just nixed the front runner at the finish line to take gold. This is how I have always pictured America and Americans when it comes to trying moments; they are capable of swinging from one extreme to the other once they are convinced they must change course.

To the extent the moral majority swayed Middle America away from a prevailing popular mind-set in the 1970s and 1980s, the other moral majority, including the Liberal Evangelicals, will, at the right time, sway all of America toward an even more noble and productive way of seeing themselves in the world. That uncanny ability to shift when stared down by the truth is indeed the mark of great leaders and of great societies throughout history. The Roman emperor Hadrian erected a stalwart wall to keep out the Caledonians of Scotland from intruding into England or vice versa. Before long, Hadrian himself ordered the wall down, not because he was coerced to do so, but because he finally realized his empire was better off with the Caledonians rather than without them. The Berlin Wall was erected and was guarded with deadly force by the Soviet-backed regime of East Germany. In the end, that very same regime ordered the wall down, because it realized it was blocked from the good of the rest of world, and so it has continued; the wall of apartheid was dismantled by the apartheid regime.

All the walls that remain, high and low, will also be dismantled; the wall on the Mason-Dixie line, the wall on the North and South divide. In the end, these walls will be torn down by the very same who erected and guarded them so passionately and only because they finally realize they are better served without them.

Equality in the corporate boardrooms of America and the developed world is the civil rights push that is now gaining center stage. You have probably heard of Debra Lee, chairperson of Black Entertainment Television (BET); Shell oil of Nigeria is now run by a native Nigerian. There are many more such Africans and direct descendants of Africans, from second to twentieth generation, working hard to earn a place in the boardrooms of corporate America and boardrooms elsewhere in the world.

The need for greater equity in material deals must not take second place to any other. The push to narrow the wealth gap between the North (developed world), and the South (underdeveloped world) has taken seed in Davos and in Porto Alegre. At the latter, it is pushed by the World Socialist Forum, a formal version of the global undercurrent. It is rapidly gaining strength as part of the undercurrent moving through parts of Latin America, Asia, and Africa. It makes one think back to General George Washington's vision.

As often as I say it, I don't believe I can say enough that America is a land of vast opportunities, and Americans (individuals and as a society) are respected all over the world for that uncanny ability to recognize opportunity and to create new ones. When Blanche Rickie signed Jackie Robinson into major league baseball, he recognized, among other potentials, the opportunity to create wealth and income for many others: owners, scouts, journalist, groundskeepers, and vendors. It has helped broaden the consumer base of American society in many subtle ways also. The first time I ate popcorn was at the Fenway Park in Boston, during the Black Liberation Movement of the late sixties. I went to the game to see George Scott and Reggie Smith of the Boston Red Sox play against Frank Robinson and Paul Blair of the

Baltimore Orioles. My whole family and I have been regular consumers of popcorn ever since.

When enough Americans learn enough about the true potential of African contributions to America's redemption and America's role as the cradle of the second coming, as suggested by some, Americans will certainly begin to do the right things toward Africa, small at first (watch the movie *About Schmidt* starring Jack Nicholson). As the facts and merits become increasingly obvious, Americans will increase their efforts to help, with more meaningful offers.

Former British Prime Minister Tony Blair's vision and offers to champion such a cause were probably inspired by Britain's missed opportunities nearly a hundred year ago when the sun did not set on the empire. Then, if Britain had realized it and earnestly pursued programs such as those suggested by the foresighted English merchant John Holt, to develop the societies of her colonies, then the descendants of Ephraim could have basked in the sun a while longer, perhaps much, much longer. It is just smart business. Instead, those who controlled and managed the affairs of the empire were obviously more interested in short-term fantastic gains, the same age old practice of "Africa on the cheap." They failed or rather, refused, to "make hay while the sun was shining" on their empire.

America has lost a lot of jobs over the past two decades. America has the ability to create new ones, bigger and better, at home and abroad, on renewable energy sources that include wind farms and the manufacture of solar panels and bio-fuels. Indeed, Africa offers vast supplies of the raw materials, the logistics, and every factor necessary for large-scale production of ethanol and biodiesel; in creating greater opportunities for shipping and freight forwarding; and a whole lot more. If America is to feature in Africa's recovery efforts, it must begin with debt cancellations for all of Africa, not just a select few countries and certainly not in such ways that seem so demeaning and manipulative. Some of the countries favored by such selective criteria, lack all that is needed to optimize the benefits offered by such cancellation.

It must also include investments in private sector enterprises. Yes, stocks and other forms of direct personal investments in Africa are yielding fantastic returns. Those in the know are quietly reaping fortunes. Most importantly, allow real African-made goods into American markets with more liberal import regimes. The cryptic practices of allowing disguised Asian and European goods that are passed as African in order to bypass American import quotas must be honestly recognized for what they are; they corrupt African productive efforts, plain and simple.

Only such offers and vigilance will help grow a middle class capable of consuming American made goods in significant amounts. We are talking about a market potential of about half a billion people: that is the populations of the United States, Canada, and Mexico all combined. Just think about it for a while my friends; the best is yet to come.

Chapter Twenty Eight

Back to Africa

Reconnect with the Motherland.

Since Christopher Columbus acquainted Europeans with the lands that lie to their west, across the Atlantic Ocean, Africans have been forced to labor for the material benefit and comfort of Europeans. Africans, those that were taken away and those left behind, suffered. Able bodies and minds were lost to societies that, like any other, must maintain life-sustaining systems: farmers, traders, craftsmen and women, defensive armies, and simply the men and women who must grow and maintain African societies.

While Africans cannot and are not expected to change the past, future prospects remain in the hands of Africans. Everything has its karma, its spirit of destiny. Have you ever wondered why an enterprise as diabolic as the slave trade and slavery carried on, the victims helpless to the point they often gave help and support to their captors and exploiters? The captors and exploiters were otherwise men of God. Some were even pastors, priests, and preachers of the Word. Yet, they helped to rationalize the practices of the slave trade and slavery. Think about it sometimes.

The slave trade and slavery could not have been so extensive in scope, time, and intensity without the conspiracies of its own karma, its own internal spirits. Any value placed on the experience cannot exclude the end result. So the question to ask is this: What has the experience produced for those who endured it for 500 years? It resulted in the additional shedding of blood, sweat, and tears for dehumanization and humiliation instead of gratitude. If Africans and African Americans must take up the mantle and begin to design the schemes and strategies by which to benefit from the power inherent in the experience of forced separation from kith and kin and of slavery, then they must allow themselves the angles of light and the plane from which to gain and maintain a more accurate perspective. Such perspective need not include what is popular, vain, or sentimental. Old thinking must yield to new ideas, insights and perceptions. There are already signs that thinking is changing with new realization.

In a recent conversation on the *Charlie Rose Show*, a group of African American popular artists from the 1960 and 1970s talked about how they had climbed up to fame and glory and about their trials and tribulations and outright humiliations on their way up. I cannot remember exactly who was on the panel (forgive me if I am wrong). I think it included Carla Thomas, Rufus Thomas, Sam Moore (of Sam and Dave fame), Mary Wilson, and Wilson Pickett. Anyway, who was or was not on the panel is really not as important as what was said.

During all those years when they were performing on "The Chitlin Circuit" and constantly being harassed by white policemen; being forced to enter restaurants and hotels, even where they performed, by the side or back door and to sleep in fifth-rate hotels, little did they realize they were also being prepared for the glory they enjoy today. The negative experiences had disciplined and toughened them internally; otherwise, they all concluded, some of them might not have been able to handle their level of success. In other words, that level of fame and fortune can actually have been destructive to some, not only by what they do to self, but also by what they fail to do for self. Instead, that period of rough and humiliating treatments gave them a certain internal fortitude, a better perspective on life, and greater zeal to do what is good with their God-given talents. Moses was eighty years old when God appointed him to lead the Jew out of bondage. He fulfilled the task so well, because he had lots of experience from tending sheep for his father-in-law for forty years. 'When you are chosen, you are prepared'. African suffering is not in vain.

In spite of the hardships and dangers, they persevered. They did not sit and wait till 1964–1965 for the civil rights and voting rights acts. They remained determined, always striving to do the right things the right way regardless of the mistreatments, harassments, and embarrassments. That quiet, determined attitude and that refusal to see, let alone recognize hardships and obstacles are precisely what I often refer to as "The Ray Charles Doctrine." Five hundred years of African sufferings, of the slave trade, slavery, and colonialism has produced a tough and resilient people stretched between opposite socioeconomic poles; they are a people who need only the recognition and the will to harness the good in store for them within the latent dynamics of their long separation and sufferings, and they are a people who realize that it does not have to come easy; that it must only be good. They are a people who have long realized that God does not promise a comfortable journey, only a safe landing.

The former world heavyweight boxing champion Muhammad Ali fought the then- reigning champion George Foreman in Zaire (the Congo) to regain his title. Ali, who had always crusaded for Africa and for African American causes outside the ring, took a lot of body-killing blows from the heavy-handed Foreman throughout much of the fight. Yet, Ali was able to turn Foreman and the fight around, putting the champion down for a final count to thunderous cheers all over Africa and America. To really bring out the significance of that fight, I'd have to write another book.

Everything about that fight was ironic and significant: the timing vis a vis that point in African/African-American history, the venue - in the very heart of Africa from where so much good have flowed out to Northern and Western societies and where also lies the Ark of the Covenant. This is the area where mankind originated, according to scientific findings and it is the area of origin of much of Christian symbolisms and Christian rituals, according to those who have studied the subject.

The characters too, Ali the victor, was widely regarded as a champion and symbolic leader of social and economic underdogs, of most Africans around the world (especially in Africa and in America). I can establish a long list without even expounding on any of the points.

I also remember the Larry Holmes and Jerry Cooney fight. Cooney was reputed to throw the sharpest left hook in the business at the time. One of those left hooks landed right where it hurts the most. Holmes absorbed it gallantly and went on to win the fight.

As in sports so it is in real life. Until about the mid-1960s, many universities and colleges in America were fighting vehemently, in full view of the rest of the world, to exclude African Americans. By the last jubilee year (2000), the trend was in reverse. Enrollment of African American students in colleges and universities has climbed upward significantly. So too has the ratio of African American faculty and staff. African Americans have served as president of Princeton University and Harvard and Brown Universities (Ivy League schools). We have college athletic directors. There are countless other examples: as academic deans, as researchers, as comptrollers etc. African-Americans and Africans are taking positions of responsibility in colleges as in other areas of administration and governance, all over the world. Such positions for people of African descent on such scale were unthinkable even as recent as the mid-1980s.

Also today, in fashion, as in other areas of the popular culture, African-Americans are the most emulated in the world. African-

American creations are the most sought after, the most popular. Asian and European youths are dancing to African beat through African- American productions—from hip-hop to soul and jazz to the movies and sports; FUBU, Phat Farm, Tina Turner, Denzel Washington, Halle Berry, Serena and Venus Williams, LeBron James and Tiger Woods. What African-Americans produce and display is what everybody in the world admires and wants. Often, my fear is that without long-term plans to harness such gains and attributes, they might well remain just that, short term gains and attributes. Like African societies, African-Americans need no permission to take up full responsibility to plan for progress having already, "crossed burning sands before and again." Indeed, in administrations, African Americans have occupied positions that are high up in the chain of succession to the American presidency.

In spite of the fact that the American economy remains the strongest in the world, America and Americans are increasingly in debt. The national budget and the trade balance have been in deficit for a sometime. Consumer debt is still on the rise. Total national debt is estimated to be over a billion a day by yearend 2005. Between years 2000 and 2005, congress raised the national debt ceiling three times, a record. Perhaps only manufacturers and distributors of red ink have been having good Christmases of late.

American job prospects are also shrinking and shrinking fast, much of it outsourced to time and to other countries with no obvious plans or expressed vision to replace them. As recently as February 2007, significant layoffs with plant closings were announced in Atlanta and Detroit. The national debt as a ratio of GDP is very high and climbing fast. Such losses threaten the very integrity of American society. It fosters those very same diabolical values that stand in the way of a second covenant. Prostitution and street corner drug deals are on the rise and are no longer confound to the inner cities of America. Dogfights and cockfights are now in the inner cities, no longer secret operations in the rural backwoods. This is not what is expected of a covenant society. This is not what the social conservatives, the moral majority, wanted or expected. How low must we go before we begin to demand measures that might turn around the downward slide?

Two points we made earlier merit repeating. To improve job opportunities for all Americans and to sustain progress, American producers will have to be able to export more than America imports, especially those goods that require lots of hands and hours to manufacture such as refrigerators, television sets, and power tools. For this to happen, there must be a lot of people at the other end with need and enough money to buy such American exports.

The African renaissance, by necessity, will include large-scale urban renewal, much like the urban and neighborhood renewals we witnessed throughout America in the 1980s and 1990s and continue with multiuse developments as centerpieces. The centers of most African urban communities are over 200 years old and are begging for all sorts of renewals and expansion. Many sit on prime real estate, with equity that can be prudently leveraged to acquire debt for needed expansion, modernization, and revitalization.

Just imagine the enormity of scale and scope. There could be opportunities for building professionals and technicians, for financiers on both sides of the Sargasso Bridge, and certainly opportunities for African stakeholders to collect decent rents and still hold title to more livable neighborhoods, they can certainly have their stake and eat it too. Gain on one side does not have to equal loss on the other. Indeed, no part of the African renaissance needs to be a zero-sum proposal. All can be structured to produce win, win, win dividends.

The African renaissance will, by even greater necessity, include rural developments with the aim of improving the lot, the consumption capacity, and the standard of living of the African masses, so they too might participate in the global economy and society. As I also said earlier, the responsibilities for an African renaissance and the necessary second chance for restoring America's role as the cradle for the second coming lie between America and Africa. It has been the hope of many Africans that America would see it as such and seize the opportunity to revise old policies and attitudes, adding new ones to initiate and facilitate needed relations in more rational and prudent terms. Such manner of help is what is needed to initiate and restore Africa to its proper place in the community of man and America to its place as the beacon of hope to all humanity.

These policies and attitudes will include ways and means to overcome and compensate for Africa's prevailing weaknesses. Such weaknesses must not continue to be employed as excuses to limit help to levels well below any necessary thresholds. All plans and attempts to restore Africa and America to the right level of favor with God require inspiration and guidance from above. It is a task that cannot be reserved for government alone; not for the United States, not for the UN, EU, or AU These super states, sovereign or otherwise, in spite of noble intentions, are all too often heavily saddled with and hindered by their political, economic, and social considerations much of which are not intended for the benefit of Africa.

All humans are prone to arrogance. Africans must take heart and continue to strive to strengthen demands on themselves. Africans must take greater responsibility and make the necessary sacrifices for the future, and they must learn to recognize manifestations of negative arrogance, such as flaunting of position or possessions and other forms of vanity and reject them. They must instead strive for more positive forms of arrogance that include pride in responsibility, in achievements and in cooperation.

Africans must maintain hope as they get together to plan the future, knowing at all times that the Father of all loves each of his creations equally and his abundance is all inclusive. We can receive as much of it as we are ready to accept, God giving all and man having all that God gives. This is man's inalienable right, and it includes Africans, those at home as well as those abroad. Inspiration and guidance from above might be better expressed through the peoples on both sides of the Sargasso and for good reason.

I am not aware if there is any Christian society on earth that takes its relations with God more seriously than the people of America. I think I've said that before, and I am saying it again. Such people are always aware of the fact that good relations with others, extending care and love for neighbor as to self, facilitates stronger and better relations with God. Much the same can be said for Africans who have had the opportunity to know God.

Both Americans and Africans are spiritual. Catastrophes, since the jubilee year of 2000, seem to have shifted attitudes even more toward spirituality. Spirituality enables an individual to offer and appreciate good deeds just for goodness sake. A new American attitude might lend itself to the delivery of promises to improve conditions in Africa to the degree expected. In sacrificing, Americans will not be disappointed, knowing with satisfaction, that good has been done for humanity (1 Thessalonians 4:13–17 and Matthew 25:31–46).

Americans are always full of goodwill, often upbeat and willing to share when well informed of someone else's need. The one question often raised with regard to the issue of making Africans able to meet, at least, their daily needs and responsibilities is whether Africans are indeed ready to be rich. I discussed this earlier, but let us revisit that question with the same answers. Africans have high awareness and even higher and ever-rising levels of expectations and aspirations while opportunity, is woefully low. As I said earlier, this is why there is so much corruption; this is why traditional diviners continue to thrive; this is why an estimated 80 percent of all churches under pastoral leadership of African or African-American clergy preach the prosperity gospel and are all doing remarkably well with the collection plate. This is why Africans are willing to risk their lives to swallow little balloons and condoms filled with cocaine knowing fully well that if even one should bust, it's the end, no remedy, finito! Think about these last two examples for a moment. If you do not condemn hastily, then you will begin to get the extent of African readiness. Indeed Africans have been "fired up and ready to go".

For the most part, most Africans are not interested in riches, at least not at this point. They merely want to survive and to be able to have their basic, Machiavellian needs; a roof over their heads; a square meal or two a day for each member of the family; and at least a fair access to education and modernity. As African societies develop, those who, by the new success of the society, move into the ranks of the middle class will of course be capable of higher levels of consumption. Such consumption will undoubtedly include American imports of all descriptions. It will no doubt be fulfilling to America, economically and in other ways.

That is why I remain so confident that once the people of America become better informed of the dynamics of what is at stake for Africa and for the rebound effect on America, Americans will no doubt begin to show even more dramatic shifts in response to and changes in attitude toward Africa. If you have not already seen the movie that I suggested earlier, *About Schmidt*, then rent it during your spare time. Also, see if you can get *Ryan's Well*. PBS offered it sometime ago. It is about a young Canadian who sent money to an Africa village specifically for the people to dig a well for water supply. On the American side of the big river, similar stories abound in spite of all the murkiness that dominates the history of American social relations.

I recently read about Julius Rosenfeld who, with similar spirit and intent as John Holt and Gordon Guggisberg in Africa, helped opened thousands of schools in rural America for underprivileged African American children. He did this while he served as president of the Sears and Roebuck Company. There is also the story of Lucy Rockefeller who donated funds for building Spelman College for African American women. There are enough Americans who will certainly not harden their hearts to the African poor. They will, if asked, open their hands, with purpose.

It is nearly half a century now since the bulk of African countries gained independence and since the civil and voting rights acts were passed. I am not aware of any courageous, comprehensive, actionable plan designed to transform hope into long-term economic and political gains for Africans, at home or abroad. Yes, I am aware of plans currently on the table—the Lagos Plan of Action is still viable, the Lome Convention, and NEPAD; however, invariably, each lacks the action potential and the critical final push that might rally and assure the people. Planning is always necessary for any meaningful and sustainable success. It must be well thought out, pragmatic and well done.

When the Reverend Jesse Jackson broke the barrier and contested the Democratic nomination for the 1984 presidential elections, he failed; yet, the mere attempt was political capital that could have been built upon. Without a well worked-out contingency plan for just such eventuality, not much was gained from his efforts. When apartheid was abolished in South Africa, Africans at home and abroad who had prayed and pushed for majority rule also hoped the new South Africa would be able to forge a workable confederation of surrounding states; perhaps, a stronger, more cohesive version of the SADC, a small union that might develop into a larger continental government. Here, too, there seemed to be no preplanning even when gain seemed assured, much to the benefits and glee of those who prefer to deal with a fragmented and weaker Africa.

Nonetheless, "princes shall come out of Egypt, and Ethiopia shall soon stretch forth her hands unto God". In fact, and symbolically, princes and princesses are coming out of Egypt.

Former UN Secretary General Boutros Boutros-Galli is from Egypt, and his successor at the UN, Kofi Annan, started out his fabulous carrier with the U.N. in Egypt. U.S. Secretary of State Condoleezza Rice and former Secretary of State Colin Powell, Oprah Winfrey, Michael Jackson, Nobel Peace Prize winner Wangari Maathai, Roman Catholic Archbishop Wilton Gregory of Atlanta, and the many, many more I simply cannot list here.

There are enough good-natured Africans on both sides of the Sargasso Sea to win favor with God and for his grace to forgive and restore Africa and Africans, and the call is already out. Listen to the call of - It's Your Time Lyrics by Luther Barnes - "For your faithfulness, prepare yourself for your blessings; it is your time." Africans on the Western side of the Sargasso must expect the sun that will shine over them to soon rise in the eastern sky. Both the spiritual and material connections with Africa are crucial for realizing the promised blessings.

It is, indeed, time for Africans in America to be free of the old mind-set that has bound and stifled productive expressions and to recognize that liberty and freedom, though not guaranteed, are nonetheless gifts from God; they are hard-won achievements with the blessings of God. Surely, God knows that for 500 years, one long epoch, Africans have toiled and sacrificed more for others than for themselves, 400 years of it in America as in Africa. Africans in America have 'made bricks without straws', and it is now time to start doing, at least some, for themselves, not so much out of self-interest but more in fulfillment of a higher expectation, a higher calling as positive contributors to Gods kingdom on earth. Africans now know, at least, that divine providence did not bring a whole people to America just to be subjugated, exploited, and left by the wayside. This may be basic training for a higher calling. 'When you are chosen, you are prepared'.

Within the struggles, the trials and tribulation, there is a message of instruction and expectation; there is a regimen to prepare a people for greater responsibility over God's dominion, a calling for greater good and glory. At age sixteen, Saint Patrick, patron saint of Ireland, was captured and sold into slavery. The six years he spent in slavery prepared him for his apostolate to deliver the good news of redemption that would ultimately win the favor of God to liberate the Irish people and unleash many Irish men and women, at home and abroad, for greater good and service to mankind. The list, as we said before is long. Their many and various contributions have greatly benefited Ireland and people of Irish descent everywhere.

Inspired by the Irish and certainly the Israeli demonstration of the positive dynamics of the diaspora, the Africa Union declared the African diaspora the sixth region of Africa. In July 2007, the Joseph Project was also launched in Ghana. With these overtures, Africa seeks to formally call back to the motherland her peoples in the diaspora. Under the banner of the Joseph Project, diasporic Africans will be able to acquire land for development with greater ease. There may be provisions for tax concession and tax deduction for businesses. There might be provisions for visa-free entry to African countries. There should be programs to encourage and facilitate dual citizenship.

Most of us are familiar with the biblical story of Joseph who was sold into slavery by his brothers. In fact, God had chosen him to prepare the way for his entire people, for all the children of Jacob (Israel) to follow. African Americans too have raised the mantle of all peoples of recent African descent for glorious times ahead. African societies and African politicians have recognized this fact and have been preparing for this idea and its inevitable manifestations since the mid-1950s when Ghana's first president Dr. Kwame Nkrumah invited all Africans in the diaspora to reconnect with the motherland.

Even in those early days, there were impressive responses. I remember Ghana's national track coach, Eugene Thomas, and a fellow from Philadelphia who bought and ran a night club, the Tip-Toe, in Accra. We simply called him Mr. Paige. There was Robert E. Lee. No, this is not the legendary Confederate general. Dr. Lee is a dentist who brought his entire family in the 1950s and became domiciled in Accra. He served as advisor to the president before settling to practice dentistry years later. He is now in his eighties, and he was still in Accra when I visited in February 2007. Dr. Maya Angelou and Dr. W. E. B. DuBois also responded early, and so too did several others. This formidable idea has been raised to higher levels by successive governments in Ghana since it was initiated in the 1950s by Dr. Nkrumah.

It finally reached the threshold to be launched for takeoff. In July 2007, launching of the Joseph Project kicked off in Accra, Ghana. The launch marked the formal recognition of the inevitability of Africans in America to reconnect with the motherland. We must all applaud the government and people of Ghana, indeed of all of Africa for giving form and full recognition to this noble, necessary and dynamic idea. It refashions "the door of no return" to the golden revolving door through which Africans from the Americas and from elsewhere in the diaspora might come and stay or to visit, to reconnect spiritually and physically. It shatters the wedge and gives Africans on all sides of the Sargasso

Sea the opportunity to recognize and begin to devise ways to harness the good hidden within their separation.

Particular praise is due former cabinet minister, Hon. Jake Nii Okanta Obetsebi-Lamptey who shuttled tirelessly, back and forth, across the Sargasso Bridge to drum up the noble idea of the Joseph Project and to prepare for its formal launch.

To realize "your blessings," Africans in the Americas must earnestly begin to prepare themselves and acquire an even greater array of skills. Africans in the Americas must strive to learn African languages in addition to European languages with which they are aculturated: Swahili, Amharic, Hausa, Wolof, Arabic, Zulu, Akan, Ga, Mende, Lingala, Ewe, Yuroba, Fon, any of the Mandingo dialects, Sutu, or whichever other one prefers. No, I do not mean you as an individual must learn all these languages. I mean Americans as a people; each individual might learn one or two or more languages or dialects spoken in Africa besides English, Spanish, French, Dutch and their Patuah . Yes, it can be done, my mother spoke about five of them. Africans, on both sides, must take greater interest in far-reaching enterprises such as trade, finance, freight forwarding, international marketing, international banking and finance, information management, film production specializing in African topics, communications, and transportation of all forms and at all levels.

However, do not overlook the simpler things that may help forge closer relations. Get better acquainted with your co-workers, church members, and neighbors who hail from the other side of the Sargasso Sea. Invite one or more every so often, especially when you have social events, a family reunion for example. Join one or more of the new organizations reaching out to Africa and the world. The ONE campaign is a good one www.one.org, the O Ambassadors is another www.oambassadors.org. Cultivate a more liberal and vibrant mind-set, energized and boundless to live and to do things by yourselves, with yourselves, and for yourselves. Use the kind of God-given power that manifests in Tiger Woods, the Williams sisters, Bernard Hopkins, Michael Vick, Jack Johnson, Muhammad Ali, Sugar Ray Robinson, and Althea Gibson; be a men or women who can throw, hit with the fist or hit a bal: round or not, large or small, of any color—on any given day, whether the playing field is level or rolling and undulating.

There is no need to ask permission, and there is no need to apologize. Know that God indeed has created boundless opportunities for the good of all mankind, including Africans. During the 2006 Winter Olympic Games in Turin, Italy, the world saw two formidable American athletes of African descent who performed gallantly and represented America so gracefully in their respective events. Neither had an easy time preparing for the glory they received. However, each knew deep within that it did not have to be easy. Thus, as "Uncle Ray" Charles would have done, they each failed to see any of the many obstacles in their paths to the limelight.

Africans at large only need to be informed, perhaps reminded, that the days of subjugation on both sides of the Sargasso Sea are really over, at least officially. Africans must be advised that the past can once again become the future only if Africans fail to follow the call from above to get together to plan the basis upon which to establish future glories for self and for mankind at large. Indeed, the power with which to connect that boundless bounty, the power to part the path across The Sargasso Sea and reconnect Africans on both sides for their common good, is already firmly in hand.

And so, launching the Joseph Project, with all its noble and glorious implications and offers, merely recognized the need and inevitability of the reunion. It remains up to Africans to also recognize the dynamic sets of powers within and to plan upon it for the manifestations of common glories. Changing conditions and events in the not-too-distant future will also encourage, indeed compel, non-Africans to join in building and maintaining a bridge across the Sargasso Sea. Such development will include the need, as I said earlier, to make the new long-range, super jumbo jets with their vast capacities to seat 500 passengers or more, economically viable. Guided by satellite global positioning systems, these giant luxury flying machines will drastically reduce transit time and thus encourage more direct flights across the Sargasso Sea.

With enough earnings, Africans will fly constantly and help make investments in such air transportation profitable. The owners, on their part, must be considerate in the conduct of business. In 1999, Delta Airlines announced the start of a code-share plan by which South African Airlines would fly passengers directly from Atlanta to Africa. However, here is how it was supposed to work: passengers would fly from Atlanta to South Africa from where they would be distributed to various destinations in Africa.

I prefer not to comment on such arrangements. Just look on the map, and I am sure you too will make the obvious observations. This, I suspect, might well have been based on the old thinking that Africans will blindly and helplessly accept anything thrown at them. There are other African-operated airlines that could have been offered similar code-share privileges if sincerely the goal was to increase business to Africa and for Delta Airlines. Ethiopian Airways is one of the most efficiently run airlines I that know of, at least it was at the time. Ironically, it was an African-American, Colonel Julian of Harlem, who, at least indirectly, helped start Ethiopia Airlines.

The Delta Airlines I spoke of was of course the old Delta Airlines, before the company filed for bankruptcy. In December 2006, as Delta neared the end of its bankruptcy protection, it initiated direct flights between New York and Accra, Ghana. Two months later, in February 2007, it announced direct flights between New York and Lagos, Nigeria. It will continue to expand as such I am sure, to other African cities in the long run.

If Africans are expected to support such enterprises, then Africans must first be helped out of the current poverty traps, starting now. Begin with total debt forgiveness. Contribute what you can to help improve farms in areas of your choosing, build a school, or help equip and modernize a clinic or a hospital. Build an orphanage or donate some computers, new or old; help a village market what it produces. Adopt a medical school, and help expand and modernize it. Helen Keller who was born blind, deaf and mute said it most cogently, "I am only one, but still I am one. I cannot do everything, but I can do something; and because I cannot do everything, I will not refuse to do something that I can do." Let's take heed of her laudable, bright and sound advice. Send what you can. Be like Ryan, be like Schmidt.

Chapter Twenty Nine

Beginning of the African Renaissance

(What is the necessary minimum)

We have a saying in Africa, "When the mother has so openly expressed her total opinion of you, nothing any of her children do to you or refuses to do for you need surprise you." You are responsible for your God-given destiny. The choices are arranged before you.

Happily a number of Americans have recognized this idea. The level of awareness and offers is still low, as perhaps it should be at this point and especially considering the current economic climate. But Americans, being Americans are already giving. Individuals and small institutions are offering help, making a difference, and making significant impact. We all know the enormous good Oprah Winfrey have done so far, not just in Africa but on the other side of the Sargasso Sea as well. In Atlanta, a group of physicians and surgeons at the Metro Atlanta Neurosurgery Foundation have set up a program, Adopt a Village, through which they propose to provide Western medical services to poor communities in Africa. A number of church groups have done similarly. I mentioned earlier, the Peachtree Baptist Church in Atlanta. They visit a village they have adopted in Ghana every year and bring eye care supplies for an eye infirmary in the village. They also support a vocational school for girls in that village.

There are untold sacrifices in addition to the material donations. At the end of the 2005 football season, during the Super Bowl game, Cathy Holmgren, the wife of the head coach of the Seattle Seas Hawks, Mike Holmgren, was in Central Africa where their daughter was offering medical help to needy Africans. There are charitable organizations such as Med- Shares in Decatur, Georgia; Mapp in Brunswick, Georgia; and others large and small organizations, including Coca-Cola, Sprint, and Western Union that all continue to donate to African causes, with Christian-inspired charity, "He that giveth unto the poor shall not lack:" (Proverbs 28:27) We have already mentioned the ONE Campaign and the O Ambassadors.

The list of donors is long, yet it falls far short of the necessary threshold to lift Africa up. Africa is big and complex, weakened by centuries of pillage and plunder. We need people like you and me to join in too with cash but especially in kind, directly or indirectly.

You too can get with some of your friends to get something like that, large or small, going. Ryan was only a school boy when he was sending monies to the African village to dig a well for water; Schmidt was living on pension.

There are Africans born on the mother continent and now living in America who have joined the crusade to help: Dekembe Motambo and Luol Deng both of the NBA. Yes, much has been done. Yet, because of the sheer size of Africa and the enormity and scope of its needs and challenges, much more remains to be done to get it to the takeoff point for its renaissance. What remains, all that remains really, is our engagement, yours and mine. Can you encourage your church, school, or hospital to adopt a church, a school, or a hospital in Africa that you might communicate with? You could visit as often as possible and appreciate their progress purely for your satisfaction, knowing that you could be a judge for what is right and what is good in the eyes of God and though you may only be one, you too can make a difference.

Above all, can you lobby your congressman for legislations that will genuinely increase the quota for African-made goods into American markets? Asian producers seem to have the whole

American market; allow Africans to have a piece of it, at least in exchange for what they have already given. You will appreciate the difference before long. British Prime Minister Tony Blair remained undaunted; he urged the G-8 to increase their aid pledges for Africa to about sixty billion dollars. It is a lot, and that is how it is with doing the right thing the right way. The right way in this case is to determine the baseline; just how much is needed for what is determined necessary to get the job done and get it done well. There are experts who can do this most effectively.

What concerns me and many Africans is whether African governments and institutions at all levels will be able to accept and infuse all the good that has begun to trickle in. Diligence that will help distribute and multiply the goods such that before long African societies are truly able to provide all they need for themselves by themselves and are no longer dependent or expectant of handouts and bailouts. Such responsibility must be expected from African leaders at all levels, not excluding the African Union.

What also worries many Africans is that even at this point in the history of the North– South relationship, Africans continue to find themselves at the short end of policies and measures that seem particularly designed to further exploit them. A case in point I heard discussed recently is the imposition of transit visas by European countries for Africans on their way to America through Europe. Just ask yourself why Africans, who are already poor and hurting, must pay indirect taxes to Europe just to travel to America. African travelers must pay the equivalent of about thirty-five dollars to the consulate or visa office of the European country that is home to the air carrier by which the African has chosen to travel to America. It might not seem like much to you, but thirty-five dollars is the equivalent of the monthly salary of the average teacher in most parts of Africa.

The African traveler must pay for this visa whether they plan to enter the European country or not. How can the African poor ever get out of the poverty trap when there are such sly traps wherever they turn? Before they have even received any good from Mr. Blair's advocated sixty billion dollars, the devices to get most of it back from them are already in place. Some Africans laugh, saying that the trap is actually set by America for European carriers to lure African travelers away from European carriers to American carriers that plan to fly directly between America and Africa. In this case, Delta Airlines' introduction of direct flights is a most-welcomed intervention.

The back-to-Africa movement is not new. Many captured slaves who jumped from the slave ships into the waters wanted to swim and get back home even if the chances were ever so slim. In more rational and organized fashion, it has been in practice for some 200 years. Most of you might remember the movie, *Amistad*. Some of you might also be familiar with the history of the American Colonization Society and its efforts in the resettlement of freed slaves in Africa. The spirit of the movement has not stopped since that time. Out of the initial stages of that movement the sister states of Liberia and Sierra Leone were founded.

Groups as well as individuals have moved from the Americas and from Europe to settle back in Africa. Some lived in Africa for considerable lengths of time and returned to Europe or to America. Some just went to visit and to acquaint themselves with the land of their ancestors, on a spiritual pilgrimage of sorts. An example is Colonel Julian of Harlem who built the Ethiopian Air Force, and there are the examples of Eugene Thomas and Lee Evans who coached track and field in Africa.

Indeed, the once "door of no return" is now the golden revolving door; you may go and come at will. Dr. W. E. B. Dubois lived his final years in Ghana where he worked to establish the framework for an encyclopedia on Africa. Dr. Lee, a dentist, was an advisor to Ghana's first president. The (Marcus) Garvey Movement in the 1920s encouraged and inspired hundreds of thousands of Africans in America to move to the motherland. Richard Wright visited and stayed for a while in the late 1950s, perhaps to scout and report his findings. Many made the necessary preparations to move; it continues to this day. I still remember vividly in the very early 1960s, an American from New York traced his ancestry to the town of Prampram, near Accra in Ghana. If I remember his name and the spelling of it correctly, it was Leo Stevenson. In May 2007, a delegation of elders from that very same town, Prampram, traveled to Atlanta to formally appoint and install a native of Michigan, as chief of community development for Prampram. Mr. Badi Murphy as he is known in private life now assumes the title of Nii Martey Kwao. He will hence reside, at least half of the time, in Ghana.

In the 1970s, America began to open new doors for its citizens of African descent and to express popular interest in Africa. Shirley Chisholm of New York was elected the first African-American congresswoman to the U.S. House of Representatives.

Across the Sargasso Sea, Mrs. Shirley Graham Dubois was offering contributions in Africa, especially in Algeria and Ghana, and Shirley Temple was America's ambassador in Ghana. Ghana is the leading cocao producer in Africa - but her mission was not to dance on the chocolate bar. Ambassador Temple-Black embraced the flamboyant Ghanaian culture and presented it to official circles in the West. The trend has continued.

Some Africans on the motherland have expressed fear about Americans coming to settle in Africa in such large numbers, even if they are of African descent. It often sounds like echo from both sides of the Sargasso Sea. Given the history of Africans, in the motherland as well as in America, it is quite understandable why

Africans would be hesitant to embrace even sincere and passionate offers of help.

The slave trade was conducted with much trickery and treachery and Africans contributed to the process, unwittingly for the most part. The period of reconstruction was much the same, Africans in America unwittingly contributed to the degradation of their gains. The dominion of South Africa was carved out of African lands rustled with trickery and treachery. The peoples of the Gold Coast lost their independence when a group of their chiefs asked the British garrisons stationed at nearby forts and castles to help them fend off the aggressions of tribes from the Ashanti forest. Gradually, British protection of the coastal tribes turned into friendly domination, then into serious subjugation, and, before long, outright colonization with fully assumed mandate to exploit the peoples.

Friends and acquaintances of mine have referred to events such as Operation Dragon Rouge, in which an all African-American detachment of the 82nd Airborne Division from Fort Bragg, North Carolina, was sent on a covert mission to the Congo in 1964. The platoon was so selected to confuse the Congolese rebel soldiers as to who was friend and who was not. Watch the movie *Dark of the Sun*, starring Jim Brown, Rod Taylor, and Yvette Mimmieux. You may also read about it on line (www.historynet.com/congo-crisis-operation-dragon-rouge.htm)

I have already referred to the relationship between Ghana's first president, Kwame Nkrumah, and African-American ambassador, Franklin Williams. We discussed that earlier. Africans on both sides of the Sargasso obviously have rational reasons to see a Trojan horse behind every offer of help, even those that seem most brotherly.

Personally, I look at it at different levels and perhaps from a different perspective. The assumption that Africans can easily fall prey to the ploy and manipulations of others is not as valid as it was a generation or two ago. Africans, especially the youth, are quite sophisticated. Pulling the banana leaves over the head of an African these days does not guarantee he or she will see only the green. More than likely, he or she will also see what the green is made of. They will see through the tiny pores of the leaves.

What I worry about is whether African leaders at every level are awake, astute, and responsible enough to devise the ways and means to harness and infuse all the offers of help that have started to come in for long-term benefits of their societies. I was in Ghana for the celebrations of the fiftieth anniversary of independence from Britain. From what I read and was told, the equivalent of tens of millions of dollars was spent for the celebrations. To me, the amount spent was really not so important. The only question I asked was what exactly are we celebrating? Was it a mere idea of being tossed back what someone stole from you? It would have been truly noble if the occasion also celebrated a milestone of sort in Ghana's economic and industrial achievements; if for example, bauxite mined in Ghana is being worked into consumer products like aluminum cooking pots, pans, window frames and aircraft body parts to supply, at least, the whole of West Africa. Sadly, there was no such component to the celebration. An occasion that required the expenditure of such vast sums of money demands celebration of deeper and far-reaching substantial achievements in addition to the mere ceremonial reflections.

I do not worry, for the ordinary peoples of Africa, as I know them to be far more astute and much smarter than they are often given credit for. If Africans are allowed to elect leaders they know to have the right levels of acumen, sensitivity and inner sophistication, then Africans will have little or no reason to worry about ploys, trickeries, and treacheries. A whole division-sized cavalry of Trojan horses can march through the length and breadth of the continent. The most it will do is eat grass and help fertilize the fields and pastures of Africa.

Thousands of Africans in the diaspora have lived or visited the motherland. Others will continue the trend. My family, that is my father and his entire family, left Trinidad in the late 1920s. They lived in Panama and then in London for a few years, and finally settled in West Africa where I was born, in Ghana (then the Gold Coast). I will not tell you the year.

Chapter Thirty

Back Home at Last

Opportunity deferred is not opportunity denied. Deferment, sometimes, might even have ironic implications. In 1957, Dr. W. E. B. DuBois was invited to attend the independence celebrations of Ghana. Dr. DuBois could not obtain permission from the American government to honor Ghana's invitation. Years later, he moved to Ghana where he directed the development of the *Encyclopedia Africana.*

On the other hand, the Reverend Martin Luther King and his wife were able to attend Ghana's independence celebrations in 1957. The celebration left the couple with profound impressions of what Africans out of bondage and servitude can do. In 1960, when Dr. King once again received an invitation to visit Africa, he was almost immediately summoned by the authorities in Georgia and was summarily tried and jailed. The incident so enraged Americans of African descent that they voted for the Kennedy/Johnson presidential ticket, ironically setting the stage for the signing of the civil rights and voting rights bills. Some forty years later, the invitation has multiplied forty million times, and the means to go back and forth at will have multiplied millions of times. African-Americans now have far greater means to honor the invitation extended through Dr. Martin Luther King at the middle of the last century of the second millennium.

Recently, since the 1990s, the trend has taken on even greater fervor. Large gatherings, such as the biannual PANAFEST held in Ghana in late summer, bring together large numbers of African-Americans with Africans and with the ancestral homeland and its indigenous cultures and unifying history. There is also the annual films festival, FESPACO, in Ouagadougou, Burkina Faso. It draws many from all over Africa and from the diaspora. The biannual Africa/African-American summit was another. As I said earlier, celebrated personalities—including the Reverend Jesse Jackson; Isaac Hayes (Nii Ocansey), who built a school for his adopted town of Ada in West Africa; Chris Tucker; Stevie Wonder; Karen Senbene; Oprah Winfrey; Dionne Warwick; Dr. Leonard Jefferies; and the Reverend T. D. Jakes—and many, many others have all gone to Africa to visit. Millions of ordinary Americans just like you and me could also go at will.

To say that Africans have visited America in similar terms is an understatement. Since the department of immigration began to keep records, millions of Africans have migrated and taken up residence in America. Millions more travel for short or long visits each year. Upward trends of such visits will be, in many ways, good for African spiritual and material strength, especially for the airline industry in America and hospitality industries in Africa.

At this point, we can only hope with positive expectations that African leaders—those who hesitate out of confusion and vague, baseless misgivings—will soon realize the need and merit for reunification, reconciliation, pacification, and restoration of the greater African community. As I have said once or twice earlier, such recognition will encourage and enable the right degree of embracing the idea of African reunion. And just as I have said numerous times before, the launching of the Joseph Project in Ghana in 2007 formally recognizes the idea. The degree to which the latent good within the pains of the separation will manifest for the benefit of Africans on the two sides of the Sargasso Sea depends largely on you and me.

A lot depends on how well Africans and the descendants of Africa recognize the inherent hidden blessings and the practicality of the plans the two side together are willing to design to unlock it all for human good and glory. It has been about half a century since the "I have a dream" speech by Dr. King. Relatively speaking, not much has yet been achieved in the form of material gains for the masses of the subject of his expressed vision. It remains a challenge to Africans and the descendants of Africa to demonstrate that they are not dreamers. Efforts to set down this challenge must begin with the removal of all partitions. It also demands the bridging of social, physical, and economic gaps. One thing I have always advocated is for Africans on both sides of the bridge to get together and organize some other type of focal point in addition to the biannual summit, the biannual PANAFEST in Ghana, and the annual Black Arts Festivals in Chicago, Atlanta, and elsewhere. They are all great ideas. More would be greater. How about a Pan-African Games every four years that will include the diaspora, with Africans playing with each other, against each other, like a family that wants to get together and stay together?

"We all come from Africa." That is what the scientists have told us of late. While no one need be excluded from going back to a restored Africa, conventional wisdom will suggest those who came out of Africa recently and are still connected, at least by affection, must lead the way back as in all other examples in America's bridges with the old worlds. Asians in America form the cultural, and, to a large extent, commercial bridge between America and the various parts of Asia.

When America needed to reestablish positive relations with Russia, during the dismantling of the Soviet Union, prominent Russians contributed to the necessary public relations. The late Dr. Armand Hammer, then chairman of Occidental Petroleum; the famous journalist Vladimir Posner; and even the comedian Yakov Smirnoff were drafted for the course. As Americans stretch forth across the span of the bridge with overtures and offers to Africa,

African-Americans must not just be the middle, certainly not the tail. African- Americans must be the head, facing the rising sun of a new day just dawning as they reunite with long-lost kin. African-Americans will then be able to click their heels, jump for joy and say, "We have arrived and are also back in Africa." Africans will then have gone full circle: "All from one, all to one."

At the formal level, America's new attitude to Africa must be driven by America's imperative interests. Those who direct policy must bear in mind that, considering America's present needs and expectations, the liberal internationalist approach is the policy that will ultimately hold up and guarantee America's vital interests. American policy makers and managers must bear in mind that America's quests need not be based on the old, false, and troublesome assumptions of zero-sum games. America's gain need not be a loss to anyone else, certainly not to Africa.

There is no force greater than an idea whose time has come. "Ethiopia shall rise" (Psalm 68:31) is a divine idea, and that alone makes it an indomitable force. Any efforts to suppress it might yield results more than bargained for. America has a choice in this scripturally inspired coming event. America might choose to be considered a friend of Africa so the two might waltz together or choose not to be a friend and one day find itself compelled to march against Africa. In the bleak mid spring of 2007, on a day celebrating Africa, President Bush was seen by the world doing a Washington rendition of the Watusi. By all accounts, it was as disarming and as assuring as it was spectacular; it was so assuring the New York Stock market applauded with a record-setting surge. When I spoke to friends in Africa, they all admitted the president's non choreographed, nifty moves on television were indeed stunningly amusing and disarming.

I can only imagine the thousands of people such a simple, friendly gesture affected positively. America holds both the baton and the strings for the overture to open up its markets to more African products and convince America's allies around the world to do the same. America's forgiveness of the balance on the loans under the HIPIC program is well noted with much appreciation. However, Africa cannot develop on bailouts and handouts. Those are only of short-term benefit. What Africa needs at this stage of post-HIPIC benevolence is trade, not more aid.

Trade with parity: company A from country X is raking in handsome profits and repatriating millions of dollars a year from Kenya to country X. This must serve as leverage for Kenya to negotiate similar value of exports of non-traditional commodities to country X. There must be something people in country X need that can be produced in Kenya, if even by contract. Example II: "One man's poison is another man's meat." This is not as trivial as it sounds. Within Africa, within any of the regions, consumer products prohibited in one community might be just what another community need or like. More structured and aggressive marketing might be helpful. Every African government must have trade ambassadors, i.e. a cadre of well-organized, highly formidable and hard-nose trade negotiators, at cabinet or sub cabinet level. These must also be individuals whose vision and insights are not limited to the obvious. In other words these must be effectively, public sector sales and marketing executives, highly capable of selling for the country.

Everything I have just told you so far has been directed at the government of America. My faith in the success of any campaign for Africa lies more with the American people, ordinary folks like you and me. Just think back at the very dramatic response the American public and government showed when told of the Indian Ocean Tsunami. Hundreds of millions of dollars were raised within a few days. Recently, when there was extensive damage after a hurricane hit an Atlanta suburb, a group of young students drove a bus for twelve hours from Texas to offer help to the victims. That is how Americans are known around the world.

If, however, official America, with short-term self-interests or hidden sentiments and existential compulsions, continue to hide behind weak excuses to suppress the truth regarding the prospects and needs of Africa, then African-Americans, with unbridled affection for both America and for Africa will be obliged to take up the mantle and to use their God- given power in hand to part a clear path across the Sargasso Sea and connect the two communities. Sit back and muse on it for a minute.

With direct super jumbo jet flights from Atlanta and New York to most parts of Africa taking eight hours or less, just imagine what the connection would be like by the year 2020.

Poverty in Africa would be cut in half all because America and its allies and the multilateral aid agencies will have written off the balance on the loans they advanced to Africa some forty to fifty years earlier.

America and her allies and friends around the world will have allowed into their markets increased amounts of made-in-Africa goods such as farm produce, cut flowers, decorative and utility artifacts, and value-added forest products all in addition to the petroleum and minerals currently exported out of Africa.

In addition, American companies like United Fruit, General Mills, Arkansas Rice, Tyson Foods, Goya, Birdseye, Coca-Cola, Beatrice, Wal-Mart, and General Foods are giving contracts to farmers and packers throughout Africa to grow and pack for North American markets much like Chile, Ecuador, Argentina, and Central American republics do now, so that African farmers and rural dwellers are earning substantially more. Many Africans have money to spend on their personal basic needs with some left over to buy luxury items, much of it imported from America. American companies, large and small, and franchises and chains like Dunkin

Donuts, Days Inn, Sheratons, Pascal's Restaurant, Yasin Seafood, Six Flags, UPS, FedEx, Harley-Davidson will have recognized a new market and likely respond to it. Some, like Money Gram, Western Union, and Coca-Cola are already in.

Yes, you can very well say that it has already started. One of the more popular night spots in Accra today is Jazz Tones. It is owned and operated by an American lady, from Louisiana. It is fast growing in popularity. Such enterprise offers prospects for a franchise. Imagine a jazz club in every large African city. Imagine the opportunity it might create for American and African jazz musicians? Not to even mention the ripple benefits, both material and spiritual.

Even sports franchises—especially football, basketball, and baseball—might find the African market attractive. American franchise owners might buy and operate (whole or partnered) sports franchises in Africa with great returns on investments, as long as they do not fear that the African teams will outperform the American teams anytime soon (as in life, so in sports). I was telling an American friend just the other day that if Africans had half as much spending money as Europeans, football and basketball leagues in Africa would certainly be viable now, and with more patronage than Europe, quite likely.

However, just as I have said before, the right thing must be done the right way. Since about 2005, I have been talking to friends and acquaintances about the idea of starting American sports franchises in Africa in the not-too-distant future. It must, of course, begin with the necessary grooming and priming. I often thought of approaching someone like the late legendary Eddie Robinson at Grambling University to possibly help set up the grooming and priming processes with a few classic games in Africa. You can very well imagine "The Coke African Classics". Africa, of course is one of Coke's more vibrant markets; more Coke Cola beverages are sold in Nigeria than in New York.

Anyway, in November 2006, I mentioned this idea to a friend of mine who played football at Grambling under Coach Robinson. In February 2007, it was announced on the news that Mr. Robinson's grandson was attempting to organize just such an event in Nigeria. Regrettably, it turned out a fiasco. The failure was simply blamed on corruption in Nigeria. While I will not argue that corruption might have played a part, I am sure there were other equally important contributions to the failure.

Such unfortunate turn of events needs to remind us of what I discussed earlier: the need to do not just the right thing, but to strive always to do the right thing the right way, the first time. It is quite important. To express it in simple terms, Americans naturally exude a certain impetus, a great deal of zeal in whatever they do. Americans like everything done fast; what is for tomorrow must be done yesterday. Americans even like their food prepared fast.

Africans, on the other hand, have significant built-in inertia in their dealings and activities. Time has much less quantitative value, certainly not the same as it is in Western societies. In addition to low material regard for time and the prevalence of corruption, I can also list factors like differences in protocol, differences in the basis for prioritization, factors like poor capacity. Poor capacity is, in fact, at the base or rather at the core of most if not all the difficulties in African transactions. It is also the most difficult to intelligently and adequately explain to an American.

In America, electricity is constantly working, and the traffic lights seldom fail. In public, when you go to the toilet, there is a roll of paper right where you must find it, with extras perched somewhere above or below. There is even fragrant soap and ornate paper towels and napkins for the final phase of your visit. At home, your garbage is picked up on pick-up days, not later. For an appointment, the other party is most likely waiting for you at the appointed place and time. Within civic order there is an efficient and reliable system for recording and preserving all transactions of importance. They are easily retrievable too and without the need to bribe anyone. Americans take these things for granted.

In many parts of Africa, power supply is sporadic at best; in addition to the blackouts and brownouts, public water supply is on eternal hold. Even days of persistent deluge of rain do not release the hold. In spite of this, there is enough water to be sold by unit at highly inflated prices, and even more interesting, there always seems to be enough water for making beer and other beverages. In some places in Africa, if you should have an emergency and call for police help, the police might ask you to send a car to pick them up.

Even in revenue-earning enterprises, as in the hospitality sector, workers are often not particularly trained to be hospitable. Whiles Africans have resigned themselves to such less- than-satisfactory ways and means of living, such ways and means still present challenges to most Americans, especially when it involves the exercise of patience.

In some places in Africa, traffic jams are the norm. I was in Accra on December 27, 2006. It took me about four hours to get to the bank, a distance that ordinarily should take less than twenty minutes. When I dared ask why the constant traffic jams, the answer I got was "It is worse in Lagos." I was left wondering the logical connection between traffic jams in Lagos and traffic jams in Accra. I knew better than to dare ask any more questions. Low capacity is a major, major problem in Africa.

Against this backdrop, it is not uncommon when in contract with an African to find that suddenly the African contractor does not respond to calls. He or she might be gone, perhaps for weeks.

Gone for the funeral for his or her grandfather's half-sister's husband. This is a more compelling obligation.

The American might query and complain that the contract performance is dragging woefully. The African is quite likely oblivious to the fact that Americans have virtually no superstitious beliefs and no folkways or social conventions that compels such or similar priority of obligations. Thus, the African has profound difficulty understanding why the American simply does not understand that the funeral is important and unlike the business transactions, cannot be deferred.

The existing chasm is profound. What it demands, especially of an American who wishes to do anything meaningful in Africa, is simple. (1) Define the goal(s). (2) Research by Google, call the embassy or consulate. (3) "Go to the spot." Ask lots of questions, see how others have handled the same or similar situations, and find out who to contact first and who not to talk to and perhaps why. (4) Above all, be able to be patient. Dealing in Africa, it is more than virtue. Even the geographic/time difference alone demands patience. Whatever your plans, remember, do not sit on it; go for it with due diligence and with the necessary cautions and prudence. I believe a football and or basketball classic, sponsored by Coke or any other, will at least add symbolic significance to the launching of the Joseph Project. There is still time to make it happen, so go for it! Don't forget to invite me.

American sports agents, scouts, managers, vendors of sportswear, and fans will be shuttling back and forth constantly across the Sargasso Sea. Africans much prefer the option of greater access to Northern markets than offers of loans, which have so far tended to stifle African initiatives and create suspicions and ill-will in the long run. Future loans to Africa, if any, must be limited to productive African ventures that are necessarily tied to liberal import regimen into Northern markets.

The time is almost at hand when, those who must, will see the light. America will begin in earnest to establish new relations with Africa. My daughter asked me when will these new relations be introduced, and will there be a durbar or some sort of fanfare. I replied, "perhaps not, you will know a new day has dawned in American/African relations when you see Tyra Banks or Oprah Winfrey or Susan Rice or Whoopi Goldberg or Jesse Jackson or Michael Jordan or Reverend Al Sharpton or first lady Michelle Obama on the front cover of *O Magazine* or *Vanity Fair*, *Newsweek*, *Jet*, or *Ebony* dressed African. If you should see such features three times in two years or less, my friend, call the station for the A train and book a seat—first class, second class, middle class, no class; round trip or one way. It is headed across the Sargasso Bridge and in a hurry. You want to be on it."

The spotlight will shine on Africa, and the bandwagon will start rolling. It will continue to gather steam from then on, back and forth. . Africa and Africans will be increasingly featured prominently in all areas of life. Even as we speak, in the Atlanta cable television market, there is a channel (182 on Comcast) for African programs. It features Africa, as it really is. It is a great start.

By the year 2020, there will be significantly more African names in college and professional spots, including ice hockey. I strongly believe by the year 2048, there will be professional leagues in baseball, football, and basketball in Africa, and the terms World Series and Super Bowl will reflect greater truth.

Up until the soccer World Cup of 2002, the powerhouses in the sport were in Europe and South America. The World Cup of 2010, staged in South Africa, marked a turning point in the domination of the sport. North America and Africa will probably take over the leadership and domination of the game. You notice in the 2006 games that all the teams that reached the quarter finals (except

Italy) had at least an African or two or more on their squad. It was much the same in 2002. That shift in the domination of the game of soccer, as well as the introduction of traditionally American sports in Africa, will also help increase air travel between Africa and America. It will make it convenient for the advertisement of consumer products in both markets—a bonanza to Madison Avenue and to emerging African advertising companies.

Don't worry about all this; you need not imagine waking up in the mornings to strange languages and dialects that might make you think you were dreaming, trapped somewhere in the kingdom of Sambezy or the ancient African city of Timbuktu. The common language for all, on both sides of the bridge, will be one you are most familiar with - English. And not just any variety of English; it will likely not be the Queen's or any other accent spoken in Britain; it will be neither the Brooklyn nor the Boston accents, certainly not the special hyperbolic English spoken only by the famous boxing promoter Mr. Don King. I also assure you it will not be any one of the two English accents that challenges you the most—the Southern drawl of the American South or the equatorial twang spoken across the bridge in Africa. The later you are probably also already familiar with. You probably hear it often on the Democratic and independent lines of the C-Span morning call-in show - *Washington Journal*.

Standard English—as spoken by individuals like General Colin Powell, Soledad O'Brien of CNN, Bob Costas of HBO sports, Martha Stewart, Michael (Air) Jordan, Barack Obama, Montel Williams, Larry King and Oprah—is the type of English that will be spoken back and forth across and on both sides of the bridge.

Throughout this discussion, I have talked about both material and spiritual linkages between Africa and America and about the higher sciences that were originally organized in Africa and became the basis for the development of Western technology and

Western society. I talked about General Baden-Powell and how he organized the Boy Scout movement based on principles and techniques he acquired largely in Africa. Redemption for both Africa and America hinges on new mind-sets, a new beginning that might foster new relationships mostly between the people: new relationships that will help lift Africa to its economic and social renaissance and will help America regain its glory and respect around the world as a once-again producer nation. It will happen, I have no doubt.

A new relationship would encourage fairer policies with considerate action well reciprocated to reflect and manifest the expression: Africa's growth = America's opportunities. The Coke ad in the first half of the February 2007 Super Bowl that announced the first win by a football coach of African descent expressed it even better, "Give a little love, and it will come right back to you." If it does not come back directly to you, it will certainly come back to your community at large, to your grandchildren and on down, to your nieces and nephews. It is the law of karma in its simplest form.

There are already many positive and encouraging signs for those who can see. The Rev. Jesse Jackson made a strong showing when he run for the Democratic presidential candidacy in 1984 and 1988. Dr. Maya Angelou read her poem at the inauguration of President Bill Clinton in 1993. In 1996 Mr. Kofi Annan was elected secretary-general of the United Nations. In the 2004 American presidential elections, an African-born woman nearly became the First Lady. The following year, the Wimbledon tennis championship matches were only a few days before the tragic bombings in the London transit system. Venus Williams, an American of African descent, won the women's championship. Her male counterpart, winner of the men's championship, was Roger Federer, son of an African. In the summer of 2007, Venus

Williams and Roger Federer won again at Wimbledon, and, on top of that, Donald Young won the Wimbledon Junior boys championship.

And then, in 2007 Tony Dungy became the first African American head coach to win a super-bowl, ever. These are significantly bold steps in the right direction. Whether it is a manifestation of providence, of luck or the sheer logical outcome of good efforts, the trend is encouraging and profoundly prophetic. It got everybody looking up to the next logical step.

To really show that forces are certainly in favor of Africa and Africans, remember President Bush's nifty display of the Westernized Watusi at the White House in the spring of 2007. A couple of months after that spectacular display, the First Lady Mrs. Laura Bush went on a five-day visit to Africa. The Bush administration pledged about one and half billion dollars to help fight malaria, most of it in Africa. In early 2008 the president himself went on a goodwill tour to Africa. What a difference a few years make.

The question still linger, if an American of African descent is elected president of the United States would it necessarily mean the woes, the seemingly endless tribulations of Africans in America, is suddenly over?

On the other side of the Sargasso Sea, conditions necessary to support positive change continue to improve. I have spoken of the peer review conducted by the African Union to check corruption and other important factors. The South African government plans to set up a permanent court of arbitration to help resolve intra-African disputes. Talk of plans for constructive developments seem to be under earnest consideration throughout Africa. Land, the cause of most conflicts, is undergoing wide-range reforms in many areas. Delta Airlines and other carriers have started direct flights between Africa and North America. Indeed, the evidence is unmistakable. Yes, there is no force greater than an idea which time has come.

All that remains and what Africans need to do is to continue to broaden and refine the plans—plans to absorb all the good coming across the Sargasso Bridge and from elsewhere. Good that can help Africans harness the continent's enormous internal energies for the benefit of its peoples, those at home and those abroad, and for all of mankind.

President Bush's five African states visit, in mid-February 2008, also provided emergency aid plan for AIDS Relief (PEPFAR). Indeed, it was a second chance to carve a political legacy that will be remembered for decades if not for centuries. According to a Stanford University research finding, Mr. Bush's PEPFAR initiative has saved some 1.2 million people in Africa. As noble and gracious as this second overture was, it still struck many Africans as largely symbolic. Perhaps understandably so since Africa is massive and malaria is just about everywhere so a few thousand mosquito-nets to young girls in a small area of Africa is not likely to be hailed as anything but symbolic. Perhaps because of its apparent selectivity, even the pledge of material support under the (PEPFAR) program is seen by some Africans as a well finessed strategic aid regimen to favorite African governments on one side and favorite pharmaceutical companies on the other side of the bridge.

The bridge across the Sargasso Sea, once established and opened fully, will be busy; it will be humming 24/7 with fun seekers, journeymen, sojourners, business men and women to and fro whistling many, many, many different and happy tunes—not excluding "Dixie."

Postscript

To describe the election of President Barak Obama as a milestone in the half a millennia long, struggles of the global African community for acceptance is nothing more than the understatement of the millennium. Indeed, it has been a steep uphill climb into Western society.

For Africans and descendants of Africa, the election of Mr. Obama extends a long list of comforting messages that include acceptance and therefore of hope. Hope that someday soon, while America still leads the world, there will come a president who will have the requisite degree of affection and the will to offer greater opportunities that might substantively and positively impact the lives of African-Americans with residual and ripple benefits to the African motherland.

The euphoria and jubilations over his election were intense but not long lived. Even before inauguration, many Africans I talked to expressed reservations and perhaps some misgivings that the same style and approach to African problems will continue and may perhaps even become more difficult to understand. For example, there have already been semiofficial references to a second trouble spot in the Sudan, but not much if anything has been said or written about the ongoing war in the Congo DR or the drill for oil in Nigeria that has so devastated the fishing grounds of many Nigerian communities and spurned bands of rebels in the region.

African fears and reservations do not stem from the announcement of Mr. Obama's cabinet. Frankly, these fears have lingered for some time but have only morphed and intensified with recent official Washington responses, pronouncements and approaches. The suspicion that America plans to take over the entire continent of Africa for all its goods has developed over decades. It is heightened only recently by suggestions such as those in *The Pentagon's New Map* and by the mindset and policies that established Africom and the construction of new, highly fortified embassy complexes that indeed look like modern-day versions of medieval fortresses.

Even American benevolent offers like the introduction of high-yield genetically modified crops that include corn, tomatoes, and sweet yams are accepted with a great deal of caution. The suspicion is that the introduction of these genetically modified crops is the first stages of a long range effort to wipe out the self-perpetuating indigenous strains on the continent, thereby setting the stage to hostage and mortgage Africa's agriculture and along with it Africa's economies and politics further on in the century.

How valid these fears are is difficult for me to fathom out at this point. What bothers me personally is what I talked about a short while ago (i.e., the same old counterproductive, often seemingly insensitive approaches to African issues that sometimes appear to be errors of projection and sometimes appear to be outright charades). For example recent act of piracy off the east coast of the continent have caught the attention of curious-minded Westerners. When you read or listen to accounts in the mainstream Western press, you are almost made to imagine these pirates suddenly germinated from the middle of the Indian Ocean. Hardly any effort to, at least, chronicle the historical developments that now manifests as a threat to international shipping. I expected some in-depth report pointing to - the supply of arms with tie-loans from Western institutions and suppliers in the 1970s that fostered a protracted war between Somalia and its neighbor Ethiopia. Such tie-loan packages that had to be paid for with meager resources, plus a protracted war that left Somalia a failed state from which it never recovered. Such burden was made even more unbearable by

America's failed military intervention purportedly to root-out a war-lord. Noble though the intentions may have been, it is these military offers and approaches that rendered Somalia an even more convenient haven for thugs and terror, domestic as well as foreign. To boot, the encroachment on their fishing grounds by foreign vessels, especially French, Italian and Chinese Fishing vessels which sweeps through Africa fishing grounds with double nets, with utter impunity. Such blazon maritime practice has forced many of the displaced fishermen into all forms of illicit and mischievous occupations.

What is even more remarkable is the rather-typical Western approach and response. Instead of assessing the threat including its social and historic underpinnings and considering more civic-oriented solutions, we impulsively and sentimentally throw the military at the problem—UN Secretary General Ban Ki-Moon suggested military intervention, and even televangelist Reverend Pat Robertson suggested the same. Secretary of State, Hillary Clinton simply dismissed the pirates as common criminals.

My worry is that sentimentality makes it a bit hard for us to learn and we might wake up one morning to find the entire continent surrounded by bands of pirates, threatening all shipping lanes that run through African waters. The main gripe of the rebel groups in the oil-rich regions of Nigeria is that their fishing grounds have been decimated by oil spills, destroying their only source of livelihood. Other West African fishermen are now complaining that those same large fishing trawlers from Europe; especially France and Italy, constantly ply their fishing grounds with double nets leaving behind nothing for even local subsistence.

It has become a big headache for the fishermen, and they feel totally frustrated, because they feel no one, not even their elected politicians are listening to their cries. These are largely subsistent fishermen who know no other source of livelihood but offers of the sea. If, in typical fashion, nothing preemptive is done and soon, many of these displaced, disgruntled, and frustrated African fishermen might begin to band together to seek other maritime occupations, formal or illicit. That might include piracy or worse.

I began to write this book with intent to advocate American and Western aid for Africa. Aid, sufficient for what is critically needed to launch Africa's much expected political and socio-economic renaissance. Much has happened since this book was first published in 2007, to support my suggestions. For one, the economic down turn that started in America, in 2008, speaks to the fact that as rewarding as the services industry may be for some, it cannot sustain itself for long without a the support of a strong productive economy – agriculture as well as manufacturing. Indeed, America needs wider and more vibrant consumer markets, domestic as well as foreign.

To me, this crisis also offers second chance opportunity for America and its Northern allies to respond to the needs of Africa with greater degree of seriousness. A chance to begin to realize and respect the fact that in this, increasingly intertwined, at least half globalized economy, no linkage is stronger than its weakest point. Africa needs to become a more significant participant in the global economy, as a producer and a consumer. The first step in any revised approach to Africa is to begin to take the governments and peoples of the continent more seriously.

I do not see why Africa is not granted, at least, de facto participation at the G-20. The African Union can, quite effectively represent the whole. Africa represents about 16 percent of the world's population and the fact that it only contributes about 3 percent to world trade is an indication of its potentials and a compelling reason to engage the continent at higher levels and to invest more in its future. After all, there are no formal criteria for membership in the G-20. Moreover this nascent global organization is likely to soon broaden its base to include other concerns in addition to finance and economics.

Secondly, the current global economic down turn have hit Africa hard – decreased demands for African commodities, lower prices, shrinking foreign investments and charitable donations. If this is not addressed fully and fast, Africa's growth rate which has been estimated at about 6 percent (2006 -2008 by the World Bank) will drop so far down it will be impossible for the continent's economies to attain middle class status any time soon. The Asian Tigers will certainly jump in, to their long term advantage. Now is just the time to consider extension of a bail-out regimen to African economies with debt cancellation, investment in the infrastructure and more sincere trade-relations that include increased access of African goods into Northern market. Oh, by the way, and less "dumping" of European throwaways onto Africa.

I am confident that the Obama administration, out to restore America's image and stature around the world will recognize this call and respond adequately to it. For the most part however, I am banking my trust, at least my hopes in the extension of popular American charity to Africa, with cash or in-kind offers. This, of course is aid beyond the more formal and controlled regimes that include direct foreign investments. It does not need to be anything fancy really. Simple offers such as digging a well to provide much-needed potable water for a community, building a school or a clinic, and helping a cooperative market its products, would be beneficial and greatly appreciated. Indeed, since I first published this book in 2007, such offers have been flowing. Americans in the thousands are spending their vacations and personal resources on trips to Africa with material offers of help. There is nothing to suggest the tide will end anytime soon. In August 2008, I was on a plane with a group of Presbyterians going to help dig wells to provide potable water for communities near Accra.

On the ground, I visited Korle-Bu Teaching Hospital where I learned a group of Canadians based in Vancouver (The Korle-Bu Neuroscience Project) were working on a proposal to build and equip a modern neuroscience center for the teaching hospital. Africans on the other side of the Sargasso Sea are getting some needed help too. Oprah donated $365,000 to a school for underprivileged kids in Atlanta.

The benefits from such gracious offers can and must be maximized. To that end, I would like to propose to Washington to explore ways and means to reorganize and restructure aid organizations and aid offers, much like how several organizations were placed under the control of one directorate to form the U.S. Department of Homeland Security and how the various intelligence bureaus and agencies have been reorganized under the Office of National Intelligence all in effort to effectively and efficiently achieve objectives. Washington might be well served if it institutes such administrative reorganization to oversee and to coordinate donations from governmental and nongovernmental organizations, church groups, and private individuals like you and me. This will help better organize the war on poverty by more efficient channeling, facilitation, and with checks and balances against redundancies, fraud wastes, and abuse. Organizations such as CARE, the Peace Corp, Africare, the ONE campaign, O Ambassadors, Habitat for Humanity, The Carter Center and the hundreds if not thousands of other registered charitable organizations pledged to the fight against poverty, disease and famine.

Similarly, agencies in Africa that license and regulate non-governmental organizations and their activities may be restructured and organized to help African communities maximize benefits of donations from the global community. Bureaus of NGO affairs in Africa may set up more efficient and considerate systems that will better match offers with need and in ways that will help overall national development efforts.

I have also suggested a shift in expenditure from military to more civil options of handling security issues. Institutions and organizations like the Martin Luther King Center in Atlanta; the Fletcher School of Law and Diplomacy at Tufts University in Massachusetts; London School of Economics etcetera may offer seminars and certification programs to train ordinary citizens in the arts and sciences of negotiations, conflict prevention and resolution, peace management and similar programs that may help make this world a better place.

Indeed, Africans only need a helping hand up. Among other indications, recent conduct of democratic exercises suggest Africans are ready and perhaps eager to step onto the world stage; this is not only in politics but also in trade, cultural enrichment, and all that civil societies around the world aspire for.

In this discussion, I have asked for help from all levels of American society to all levels of African governments and civil society – urban and rural. If you even remotely think I have tried to enshrined Africa as an eternal object of global charity, then you certainly missed the whole point of the discussion. Yes, Africa needs all sorts of help for its myriad of problems, much of which can be alleviated with offers of material help from the outside.

However, I expect neither the need nor the offers to continue for very long. The average African is quite resourceful and is driven by high aspirations and guided by pride. The average African can do much for self with basic opportunities. Alas! African leaders, it seems, do not yet feel compelled to provide such basic opportunities. They seem much too busy raking it all in, for themselves.

When you visit Accra, for example, just as you come out of the airport complex, the signs and trappings of the basic problems are there to greet you. Men and women of all ages—some as young as twelve—paraplegics, and the legally blind all dashing and weaving through dense traffic; from car to bus to truck and back, pitching and dealing, peddling edibles and hardware. Many have left their farming and fishing communities to seek basic opportunities that might help them better themselves and help support their families back in the villages.

African development and economic planners must be compelled by such evidence to favor and focus on plans that might help redistribute opportunities to rural communities.

Establish enterprises in rural communities that may provide basic material needs to the locals. The rural post offices may offer more services - issue passports, help expedite visa acquisition, help facilitate some nonbanking financial and even some basic banking transactions, and so forth. Why must all the major productive and service enterprises be based in the capital? Is only for the convenience of the powerful and affluent? Government may further upgrade, expand, and modernize some existing specialty institutions and broaden their charter to absorb more qualified candidates. In some countries, government may even consider moving the capital as an additional means of redistributing opportunity. The cost / benefit ration of such move may be favorable to the system as a whole in the long run.

In fact, after a point, these issues become fiscal; for failing to spend what is necessary in an area of demand might force higher and perhaps more counterproductive expenditure, even losses, in other areas. For example, the influx from rural areas to the capital creates layers of problems with accommodation, food distribution, utility supply, sanitation, and traffic snarls and jams. I can't wait to read the published report on the amount of petrol (gasoline) subsidized by government, that dissipates into thin air each fiscal year, just from traffic congestions in the capital alone. I imagine it is a whopper, in cedis and dollars.

Issues like these, in fact, must be the responsibility of the African masses. In electing political leaders the African electorate must determine two things; first, which candidate offers the best workable plan for considerate distribution of opportunities. Secondly, which candidate shows greater fortitude, sensitivity and sincerity to fend off untoward foreign influences. If the African masses can do this for the next two decades or more they would certainly have contributed a lot to their own betterment.

All told, Africa is in good standing, just a few trimming and adjustment here and there. Africa will develop, and it is on the right tract and headed in the right direction. Indeed,

Aspirations of the peoples of Africa, to catch up with the developed world, are indeed a challenge at this point. That is why your help counts so much. Indeed, Africa has a lot more to offer the world beyond the supply of raw materials. As America's population ages, Africa's population gets younger. By year 2012, more than 40 percent of Africa's population will be under the age of 20. While America's population growth rate is less than 1 percent, that of Africa's is about 3 percent and its population count is expected to double to nearly two billion by the middle of this century; (according to the Population Reference Bureau's 2007 World Population Data Sheet – www.prb.org).

In a recent PBA News Hour with Jim Lehrer, an in-depth segment reported the case of Jack Stanley, a high ranking official of KBR, a subsidiary of Halliburton. Mr. Stanley had travelled to Nigeria, years earlier, to bribe government officials in order to win concessions in that country, for the company. In the process he also stashed part of the $180 million given to him for the bribery, in his private bank account in Switzerland. It was revealed further that as a result of the favorable outcome of Mr. Stanley's bribery mission to Africa he was tapped for promotion by Dick Chaney, then his boss at Halliburton. Of course we all know Mr. Chaney later became vice president of the United States. Indeed it takes two to Tango, Africans do not hold a monopoly on corruption, often used as a reason for holding back development aid.

Conflict is another excuse that can easily be averted. Earlier I cited the ongoing situation in Ghana where individuals in or close to government use the power and privilege of state to take and to sell GaAdangbe prime lands to themselves and their cronies. Recent reports (online - *GhanaWeb* – 4/24/2009) suggests the problem continues and is getting worse. A group of individuals, all members of or closely affiliated to the former government of President John Kufour are said to have bought large plots of land in an extraordinary and rationalized scheme that purportedly transferred such lands from government. These are GaAdangbe stool lands taken by government for imminent use. What GaAdangbe demand, as they had in similar cases is that since the land is no longer being used for the expressed purpose it must revert to stool ownership. No mention was even made as to whether the rightful indigenous owners of the land were rightfully represented and adequately compensated in the deal. Such sly, blazon scheme with obvious utter contempt only reminds one of the methods and style of America's seventh president, Andrew Jackson. We also remember all too well what it led to decades later. Even in diabolical practices there are ways of doing things and then there are correct and proper ways of doing the same things.

Such reckless and inconsiderate abuse of power, position and privilege is likely to create conflict sooner or later. To the extent that Ghana has so many citizens and residents capable of managing the affairs of the world, it is indeed lamentable that no one is bold and cares enough to step in and make sure such deals are structured to satisfy all concerned, including especially the very week and helpless stakeholders. Such instances I simply cannot blame Northern societies for. I think the African Union with perhaps the help of the regional groups will have to develop protocols and mechanisms that include an office of ombudsman to intervene in such abusive use of position, power and privilege or the inevitable consequences of such abuses will likely befall our grand children's children. We need not wait for its ugly manifestations. It is preventable.

As for you and I, we only need to contribute what we can to help Africa up to the point where, at least, half its people are able to consume appreciably, what you and I and our children and grandchildren produce and sell. You and I will certainly be the better for it. Muse over this for a moment, and see how much good that will do for your community, for your household. It will, at least, help raise your earnings, and therefore your capacity to buy the things and live the way you want if, in fact, Africa with its vast consumer population becomes America's vibrant trading partner. Someone will certainly do it if America doesn't. Yes, you are only one person but you can do at least one thing— whatever you can offer and however you can give it, directly or indirectly.

The cup of Africa is only half full. Help make it full; be like Oprah; be like Ryan; be like Schmidt. Thank you and God bless.

Movies to Entertain You

A Good Man in Africa. 1994. Directed by Bruce Beresford and Starring Colin Friels, Joanne Whalley-Kilmer, Sean Connery, John Lithgow, Louis Gossett Jr., and Diane Rigg.

About Schmidt. 2002. Directed by Alexander Payne and Starring Jack Nicholson.

Amistad. 1997. Directed by Stephen Spielberg and Starring Morgan Freeman, Anthony Hopkins, Djimon Hounsou, and Matthew McConaughey.

Birth of a Nation. 1915. Directed by D.W. Griffith and starring Lillian Gish, Mae Marsh and Henry B. Walthall.

Blood Diamonds. 2006. Directed by Edward Zwick and Starring Leonardo DiCaprio.

Coming to America. 1988. Directed by John Landis and Starring Eddie Murphy.

Critical Assignment. 2004. Directed by Jason Xenopoulos.

Dark of the Sun. 1968. Directed by Jack Cardiff and Starring Jim Brown, Rod Taylor, and Yvette Mimmieux.

Diamonds of War: Africa's Blood Diamonds. 2003. National Geographic documentary.

Forts and Castles of Ghana. 2003. Documentary narrated by Danny Glover

Hotel Rwanda. 2004. Directed by Harry George and Starring Don Cheadle, Nick Nolte, Joaquin Phoenix, Desmond Dube, and Hakeem Kae-Kazim.

Khartoum. 1966. Directed by Basil Dearden and Starring Charlton Heston and Laurence Olivier.

Lumumba. 2001. Directed by Raoul Peck and Starring Alex Descas, Theophile Moussa Sowie, Maka Kotto, and Mariam Kaba.

Nations of the World. 2003. (Documentary) Directed by Bryan Lewis. *Red Dawn.* 1984. Directed by John Milius and Starring Patrick Swayze. *Ryan's Well.* 2006. Directed by Latita Krishna and Starring Nancy Prest.

Sometimes in April. 2005. Directed by Raoul Peck and Starring Debra Winger.

The Air Up There. 1994. Paul Michael Glaser and Starring Kevin Bacon.

The Constant Gardener. 2005. Directed by Fernando Meirelles and Starring Ralph Fiennes, Rachel Weisz, Hubert Kounde, Danny Huston, and Bill Nighy.

The Day After Tomorrow. 2004. Directed by Roland Emmerich and Starring Dennis Quaid.

The Gods Must Be Crazy. 1980. Directed by Jamie Uys and Starring Marius Weyers.

The Good Shepherd. 2006. Directed by Robert De Niro and Starring Matt Damon and Angelina Jolie.

The Last King of Scotland. 2006. Directed by Kevin Macdonald and Starring James McAvoy.

The Nun's Story. 1959. Directed by Fred Zinnemann and Starring Audrey Hepburn.

The Wild Geese. 1978. Directed by Andrew V. McLaglen and Starring: Richard Burton and Roger Moore.

Wonders of the African World. 1999. (PBS documentary) Narrated by Professor Henry L. Gates.

Selected Contacts to Get You Started Across the Sargasso Bridge (*phone, fax, e-mail addresses, and Web site addresses*)
1. Africa Action: (phone) 202-546-7961, (fax) 202-546-1545, (Web site) www.africapolicy.org
2. Africa Recovery: (phone) 212-963-6857, (fax) 212-963-4556,(Web site) www.africarecovery.org
3. National Summit on Africa: (phone) 202-939-2252, (Web site) www.africasummit.org
4. Africa On Line: (Web site) www.africaonline.com
5. Trans Africa: (phone) 202-797-2301, (fax) 202-797-2382, (Web site) www.transafrica.org
6. All Africa: (Web site) www.allafrica.com
7. Spotlight on Africa: (phone) 301-379-3443, (Web site) www.spotlightonafrica.tv
8. African Studies Center Michigan State University: (phone) 517-353-1700, (fax) 517-432-1209, (e-mail) Africa@msu.edu.
9. OIC International: (phone) 215-842-0220, (Web site) www.oicinternational.org
10. SA-USA Chamber of Commerce: (phone) 954-333-7770, (Web site) www.southafricachamber.com
11. Africa-America Institute: (phone) 212-949-5666, (fax) 212-683-6174, (Web site) www.aaionline.org
12. News from Africa: (Web site) www.newsfromafrica.org
13. BBC Focus on Africa: (Web site) www.feedzilla.com
14. Ghana: (Web site) www.ghanaweb.com

References

Armstrong, Herbert W. 1987. *The United States and Britain in Prophecy*. New York, New York: Everest House Publishers.

Diop, Anta Cheikh. 1974. The African Origin of Civilization: Myth or Reality. Chicago, Illinois: Lawrence Hill Books.

Davidson, Basil. 1965. The growth of African Civilization: A History of West Africa 1000- 1800. London, England: Longmans.

Diop, Anta Cheikh. 1978. Black Africa. Trenton, New Jersey: Africa World Press. Ayitey, Dr. George B.N. 1992. Africa Betrayed. New York, New York: St. Martin Press.
Edgerton, Robert B. 2002. Africa's Armies: From Honor to Infamy. Boulder, Colorado: Westview Press.

Rodney, Walter. 1974. How Europe Underdeveloped Africa. Washington D.C.: Howard University Press

Adamo, David Tuesday. Africa and the Africans in the Old Testament. San Francisco, California: Christian Universities Press.

Walz, Terence. 1978. The Trade Between Egypt and Bilad as Sudan, 1700 – 1820. Cairo, Egypt: Institut Francais d'Archeologie Orientale.

Wikipedia. 2009. CIA activities in Ghana, en.wikipedia.org/wiki/CIA-activities-in-Ghana.

Mazrui, Ali. "Kenyan Political Scientist quotes Nyrere" viewed January, 27, 2009, www.nathanielturner.com/juliuskanbabagenyrere.htm

"Hopeless Africa" The Economist, July 2000
"It's Bono, on line one" Vanity Fair magazine, July, 2007

Dagne, Ted. July 1, 2006. Congressional Research Services: Nigeria in Political Transition. Washington D.C.: Thomson Gale.

Uhakheme, Smart. 2008. Nigeria – United States Relations. Lanham: University Press of America.

American Human Development Project. 2008. The Measure of America: American Human Development Report. New York, New York: Columbia University Press.

Wikipedia Encyclopedia. Viewed January 2009. African American Economic Status.

McGourty, Steve. June, 2006. United States national Debt: An Analysis of the presidents who are responsible for the Borrowing: Conservapedia Encyclopedia

Isadore, Chris. June 6, 2005. Rates: Soft and Flat? Danger! CNN/Money

Bernanke, Ben S. October 2, 2003. Banking and Finance. Chester, Pennsylvania, www.nytimes.com

www.tradewatch.org

www.agoa.gov

www.mbita.org/africa/conference.html

www.jessejacksonjr.org/issues/1020499454.html

Public Citizen. July, 1999. Global Trade Watch – Africa trade Bill: A point by point analysis of USTR's Resource book on HR 772(HOPE) and HR 434(AGOA)

www.citizen.org/trade/africa/house-fight/U-S-state

www.webring.com/t/The African-store

Sanger, David E. Reversing Course: Bush signs Bill Raising Farm Subsidies. New York Times, May 14, 2002

National Summit on Africa. National Policy plan of Action For U.S. – Africa Relations In the 21 century. Washington D.C., Frbruary, 2000

Monroe, Susan. G-* Summit in Kananaskis: G-8 Summit in Canada has African Development on the Agenda. June 20, 2002, canadaonline.about.com/od/trade

www.dfa.gove.za/docs/2002/

Department of Foreign Affairs, Republic of South Africa. President Mbeki to Attend G-8 Summit in Sea Island, Georgia, USA on June 10, 2004, www.dfa.za/docs/2004/g8summit0607.htm

Naggaga, Monica. Marchers Provide hope for Africa. BBC News. July 8, 2005. News.bbc.co.uk/1/hi/Scotland.

Federal Ministry of Economic Coorperation and Development. Joint Progress Report on the G-8 Africa Partnership. 2007. www.bmz.de/en/EU_G8/Blickpunkte/g8_africabeauftragte/index.html

www.g-8.de/content/EN/Artike/_g8-summit/

The Financial Express. EU Farm Subsidies help only rich farmers, firms. August, 2005. www.financialexpress.com/news/

Robinson, Randall. 2001. The Debt: What America Owes To Blacks. New York, New York, Penguin Group (USA)

The Times. The Farmers ruined by Subsidy. April 9, 2007. www.timesonline.co.uk/tol/news/africa/

USAID Fact Sheet. USAID supports Coffee Growers Around the Globe. Washington D.C.
September 15, 2004. Wwwusaid.gov/press/factsheet/2004 www.africasource.com
Oxfam International. Press Release: Ethiopia Coffee Farmers Fight Starbucks for more bucks. October 26, 2006. www.oxfam.org

Voice Of America. State Department: US, Ghana sign $547 million Aid Pact. August 1, 2006. www.voanews.com

Westside Gazette. African American unemployment soars to almost 11 percent and job growth drastically below forecast. August 19, 2004. www.highbeam.com

The Community Economic Development Handbook, Chapter 6. Develop your Community Workforce. www.doleta.gov www.usworkforce.org

www.aneca.org/aisi

www.bread.org/about-us/anual_reports/anual_report_2003.pdf

Bureau of Labor Statistics. Economic News Release: Employment Status of the Civilian population by race, sex and age; Table A-2. www.bls.gov/news.release
Mattern, Joanne. 2003. The Cost of Freedom: Crispus Attucks and the Boston Massacre. New York, New York: Rosen Publishing Group. www.americanrevolution.com/crispusAttucks.htm

Rhoden, William C. 2007. Third and a Mile: The Trials and Triumphs of the Black Quarterback. ESPN

www.unwire.org/unwire/20000907

Africa Action, Africa Policy E-Journal. Africa: Human Development Report. July 2003. www.africaaction.org

The Journal of Real Estate Finance and Economics, 6: 103 – 128.
www.nytimes.com/2005/12/25/business/yourmoney/25japan.htm

www.cbc.ca/ideas/features/italy

www.economywatch.com/world_economy?italy

Associated Press. China's Piracy hurting its own industries. MSNBC World business. July 7, 2006. www.msnbc.msn.com/id/13617619/

Associated Press. Police attack on auditor not tied to Los Alamos. MSNBC. Junes 9, 2005. www.msnbc.msn.com/id/8122885

Rafiq, Fauzia. Pakistan Improves ranking to become 46th most corrupt country Love Life. September 24, 2008. Lifethelove.worldpress.com

Boustany, Nora and O'Hara Terence. After Riggs, Embassy Accounts Can't find Home. Washington Post – pgE01. June 10, 2004. www.moneylaundering.com en.wikipedia.org/wiki/Riggs_Bank

Johns, Michael. The Heritage Foundation: Zaire's Mobutu visits America. June 29, 1989 www.heritage.org/research/Africa/em239.cfm

Akande, Tunji. 2002. An Overview of The Nigerian Rice Economy. www.allafrica.com/stories/200812040473.html www.warda.org/workshop/RicePolicy/

www.chinadaily.com.cn

Leonard, Andrew. No more treasury bonds, Thank you, I am full. January 6, 2006. www.salon.com

www.ers.usda.gov/briefing/india/Trade.htm

Webb, Alysha. The Chines Entrepreneur Charges Ahead. ACCA. September, 2003. www.accaglobal.com

Brookes, Peter and Shin, Ji Hye. China's influence in Africa: Implications for the United States. The Heritage Foundation. February 22, 2006. www.heritage.org www.silobreaker.com/view360

Zagaroli, Lisa. McClatchy Newspapers: When Textile quotas end this week, will U.S. jobs go too? 12/29/2008. www.mcclatchydc.com/2005/worldbusiness

www.nti.org/e_research/profile/china/missile

www.bilaterals.org

Robinson, Randall. 1998. Defending The Spirit: A Black Life in America. Los Angeles, California. Dutton Books.

Cerami, Charles. 2002. Benjamin Banneker: Astronomer, Publisher, Patriot. New York, New York. John Wiley and Sons

Hardesty, Von. 2008. Black Wings: Courageous Stories of African Americans in Aviation and Space History. New York, New York. Harper Collins.

Tyson, Neil deGrasse. 2000. The Sky is not the Limit: Adventures of an Urban Astrophysicist. New York, New York. Bantam, Doubleday Dell Books for Young Readers.

Schraff, Anne E. 2003. Dr. Charles Drew: Blood bank Innovator. Berkeley Heights, New Jersey. Enslow Publishers, Inc.

Wheeler, Jill C. 2003. George Washington Carver. Edina, Minnesota. ABDO and Daughters Jackson, John G. 1981. The African Origin of Christianity. Chicago, Illinois. L & P. www.globalmountainsummit.org/statue_of_liberty.html
www.touregypt.net/portsaid.htm

Jeal, Jim. 2007. The Boy-Man: Then Life of Lord Baden-Powell. New York, New York. William Morrow.

www.marketbrowser.com/mbzzzvp.asp

www.law.northwestern.edu/journal/jihr/v4/n1/14/shinsato.pdf
money.cnn.com/2007/02/01news/companies/Exxon/index.htm

www.globalpolicy.org/security/natres/oil/2003/0816blind.htm

www.wsws.org/articles/2007/feb2007/oil-fo3.shtml

www.sourcewatch.org/index.php?title=Riggs_Bank_N.A.

www.independent.co.uk/new/world/africa/toxic_shock=how-westen_rubbish-is-destroying- africa-416828.html

www.nitwitnation.com

Knowledge at Emory. Can U.S. base Companies Overcome Anti-American Sentiments? July 18, 2007. Knowledge@emory.edu

www.globalissues.org/article/26/poverty-facts-and-stats

apf.org.az/article.php3?id_article-271
www.worldbank.org/wolfowitz
Becker, Elizabeth. Global Fund to fight aids, tuberculosis and malaria. International Herald Tribune. 1/31/2004. www.highbeam.com/doc/1P1-90315964.html

www.opic.gov/pdf/04_annualreport.pdf

www.moneybiz.co.za/africa_business_and_technology

en.wikipedia.org/wiki/import_substitution-industrialization
www.liberty1.org/gwvision.htm
www.interaction.org/newswire/detail.php?id-5413
Lewis, C.S. 1980. Mere Christianity. New York, New York. Collins Harper

Joffrey, Grant R. 2007. The New Temple and the Second Coming. New York, New York. Random House, Inc.

Hancock Graham. 1992. The Sign and The Seal: A Quest For The Lost Ark Of The Covenant. Oxford, England. Heinemann Ltd.

World Bank. Land Policies for Growth and Poverty Reduction. May, 2003. Publications.worldbank.org

Address of Vice President Richard Nixon to the Governor's Conference – Lake George, New York. July 12, 1954. www.fhwa.dot.gov/infrastructure/rw96m.cfm

www.truthout.org/article/senate-gives-final-approval-sweepinghousing-bill

www.africa-ata.org/gh9.htm

Airline Industry Information. Delta Air Lines and South Africa Airways extend code-share agreement. May 24, 2002

www.internationalworkshops.com/ghana/index.html

Beehner, Lionel. 2005. Africa: Debt Relief Proposals. Annual Report, Council on Foreign Relations.

Dunn, Elwood et. Al. 2001. Historical Dictionary of Liberia 2nd. Edition. Lanham, Maryland. The Scarecrow Press.

Onishi, Norimitsu. Man in the New, Nigerian Question Mark: Olusegun Obasanjo. March 2, 1999.

En.wikipedia.org/wiki/Foreign_relations_of_Nigeria
www.uneca.org/adfill/riefforts/ref/other2.htm
http://kenyasocialist.org/kswsfiles/2005/The-titanium-mining_scandal.htm

James, Martin W. 2004. Historical Dictionary of Angola. Lanham, Maryland. The Scarecrow Press.

Davis, J.E. 2007. Constructive Engagement?: Chester Crocker and American Policy in South Africa, Namibia and Angola; 1981 – 1988. Athens, Ohio. Ohio University Press.
www.historynet.com/congo-crisis-operation-dragon-rouge.htm

www.pbs.org/frontlineworld/stories/bribe/

Carew, Jan. 1988. African Presence in the Americas: Fulcrums of Change. Trenton, New Jersey. Africa World Press, Inc.

Iliffe, John. 1987. The African Poor: A history. Cambridge, England. Cambridge University Press.

Attoh, E.O. 2002. In Search of Gold. Accra, Ghana. Assemblies of God Literature Center, Ltd.

Giddens, Anthony. 1998. The Third way. Cambridge, England. Polity Press.

Carter, Gwendolen M. and O'Meara, Patrick (Editors). 1986. African Independence: The First Twenty-Five Years. Bloomington, Indiana. Indiana University Press.

Rodney, Walter. 1974. How Europe Underdeveloped Africa. Washington, D.C. Howard University Press.

Press, Robert M. 1999. The New Africa: Dispatches from a Changing Continent. Gainesville, Florida. Florida University Press.

French, Howard W. 2004. A Continent for the Taking: The Tragedy and Hope of Africa. New York, New York. Alfred A. Knopf

Mahajan, Vijay. 2008. Africa Rising: How 900 Million African Consumers Offer More Than You Think. Upper Saddle River, New Jersey. Wharton School Publishing.

Robinson, Randall. 2008. An Unbroken Agony: Haiti, from Revolution to the Kidnapping of a President. New York, New York. Perseus Book Group.

www.ingramcontent.com/pod-product-compliance
Lightning Source LLC
Chambersburg PA
CBHW071612220526
45469CB00002B/327